TrafficKing

TrafficKing

By:

Conchita Sarnoff

The illustration on the cover is a 'Rape Tree." Rape Trees or Rape Bushes mark the spot where sexual assaults and gang rapes occur along the United States and Mexico borders. The child's undergarments are thrown on the branches as markers to intimidate the victims and convey to Border Patrol and Immigration and Customs Enforcement (ICE) officials that traffickers have successfully committed a sexual crime within the U.S. border. Rape Trees instill fear in the victims and deter potential witnesses from coming forward to the police.

ATTENTION CORPORATIONS AND ORGANIZATIONS

Book is available at quantity discount with bulk purchase for educational, business, or sales promotional use. For information, please call or write: info@zumbaba.com or 480-666-9022.

Printed in the USA by Zumbaba.com

Table of Contents

Acknowledgments

Many people made this book possible. This book is dedicated to each and every one of you. Thank you. If your name is not mentioned you know why.

To my publisher, Victor Ostrovsky, the only man who had the courage to publish this manuscript. Thank you for your encouragement, guidance, patience and generosity of spirit. To my wonderful editors who shall remain nameless, thank you for the many hours you invested in this project. Your remarkable patience and encouragement allowed me to move forward in the darkness. To my friends who read the manuscript in its various incarnations, thank you for your time and guidance.

I wish to express my deepest gratitude to the many lawyers, law enforcement officials, journalists, friends and colleagues who in the course of six years stood by me every step of the way. Three insightful and extraordinary agents worked diligently to see this project to fruition although they were held back. Andrew Stuart, principal at the Andrew Stuart agency in NY who represented me in 2010 and 2011. Four years later, Alex Hoyt and Alfred Regnery literary agents and partners who represented me in 2015 and January 2016. Thank you for your time, guidance, trust, and the many generous hours invested in this project.

To Renee and Carlos Morrison their friendship, grace, generosity and energy will forever have a place in my heart. Sally Fitz Morrison, thank you for believing in me, your friendship and providing shelter during the cold days. You are a real friend. To Lisa and Rick Moreno, true friends are hard to find and impossible to forget. Fausto Sanchez, my earth Angel. Thank you for your loving-kindness. Jorge Castaneda, Mexico's former Foreign Minister, thank you for your friendship and taking care of me in Mexico during the investigation. Larry Leibowitz, an extraordinary friend and man. I am blessed to have you as my friend. Thank you for your support. Three extraordinary and steadfast friends guided me to the finish line: Sergio Balsinde, Richard Kramer, and William von Raab, thank you for your nuggets of wisdom, trust and support. Vivien Weisman, thank you for providing shelter and guidance when it was most needed. William Stadiem, an extraordinary author, loving friend and dedicated son, thank you for your pearls of wisdom. Two extraordinary men taught me the reality of modern day politics: my late father, Pedro Suarez, former Minister of Public Works, Havana, Cuba (1948) and Jose Maria Aznar, former Prime Minister of Spain (1996-2004). Thank you Jose Maria for taking me on an exhilarating journey into your world and showing me what political power can achieve when the goal is to improve our human condition.

My everlasting gratitude and respect goes to the survivors and the thousands of unsung heroes, abolitionists, police officers, district attorneys, law enforcement agents, NGOs and opinion leaders fighting at the frontlines. Your courage, faith, tenacity, hard work and generosity have laid the groundwork for my book and provided the strength to carry on. To the countless others who shall remain nameless, thank you for your incredible behind the scenes work, tenacity and faith. The time will come when the truth shall be revealed.

Disclaimer

This book reflects my opinion about the challenges facing the U.S. government and the Department of Justice while prosecuting high profile human trafficking cases. In 2006, when I began investigating the issue of modern day slavery, specifically child sex trafficking, the business was fast becoming a global industry.

Several reasons why this sudden surge explain the increasing figures: greater demand; greater accessibility to child pornography online; increased distribution routes; risk/reward ratio of child prostitution pays; and the limited enforcement of Trafficking Victims Protection Act (TVPA) in some states.

The Trafficking Victims Protection Act is a federal law that helps to protect victims and prosecute human traffickers. TVPA was passed, in 2000, under President Bill Clinton, reauthorized under President George W. Bush, and reauthorized once again under President Obama.

Anti-child pornography laws and the challenges facing law enforcement while prosecuting pedophiles remain in the early stages of enforcement. In 2009, as a result of my extensive fieldwork and research, I began to write this book. Most of the information included in this book was discovered between 2008 and 2016. After my first Epstein report was published in The Daily Beast in 2010, the story went viral.

Given the global figures of trafficked children this book aims to help support the abolitionist movement and promote the message: Human trafficking must stop now. Federal laws that prosecute traffickers must be enforced in every state. The Trafficking Victims Protection Act is an important federal law that needs enforcement in every state.

There was no doubt when I started this journey that the most effective way to help rescue survivors was to provide long term "safe houses" for victims. That remains true today. With this goal in mind, I established a foundation with a group of talented and like-minded community leaders. It took approximately two years to identify the board members.

By mid October 2013, we joined forces and created the Alliance to Rescue Victims of Trafficking, (www.atrvt.org), a bipartisan organization in Washington D.C. Our mission is to help stop child sex trafficking. Hopefully, ATRVT will live on long after we are gone.

The information contained in this book was partly derived from my own observations and conversations taken from official records, court documents, testimonies, written communication, interviews, e-mails, and media reports. The facts and certain anecdotes are taken directly from court files, depositions, police records and hundreds of hours of interviews and conversations conducted over a considerable period of time with countless collaborators, Wall Street insiders, government officials, law enforcement agents, prosecutors, private investigators, lawyers, numerous victims, a victim's mother, accountants, journalists, banking officials, NGOs, Jeffrey Epstein, Ghislaine Maxwell, Alan Dershowitz, a number of their attorneys and hundreds of media reports.

TrafficKing, describes my experience while investigating modern day slavery between 2006-2016. The views and opinions reflect my attitudes relating to those incidents. Some names, identifying details and events have been changed to protect the innocent and survivors.

For fear of retribution, including death, most underage survivors prefer to remain anonymous. Victims also fear going to the police and other law enforcement officials because they fear they will be homeless and possibly alone until their case is tried in Court, if it ever reaches Court. This is particularly true in cases involving foreign-born underage victims who are forced into prostitution and trafficked across borders. Many cases involve children forced to have sex with men in positions of power and influence. If the survivors manage to escape and tell their story their primary concern remains homelessness and retribution.

Jeffrey E. Epstein, a Wall Street hedge fund manager is a convicted pedophile and level 3-registered sex offender. He served 13 months out of an 18 months sentence in a Palm Beach county jail. As part of the sentence he served an additional 18 months under community control or 'house arrest' in his Palm Beach estate. As of 2016, there are three related civil cases pending, two in Florida and one in New York.

Since the first police report was filed, in 2005, fragments of the Epstein case have been widely publicized in a variety of media outlets in the United States: Financial Times, Wall Street Journal, New York Times, Washington Post, Washington Times, Boston Globe, Chicago Tribune, Palm Beach Daily News, Palm Beach Post, Reuters, Associated Press, The Miami Herald, Newsweek, Reuters, AP, The Daily Beast, Politico.com, Drudge Report, The Daily Caller, Mail on Sunday, Mother Jones, Huffington Post, New York Magazine, and others. The Television networks and radio stations reporting the story included: ABC, CBS, CNN, FOX, NBC, MSNBC, Telemundo and Univision have also aired snippets concerning his case.

Since my story was first published in The Daily Beast, in 2010, the foreign press has been following it, including the largest circulating journals and magazines such as: *ABC España (Spain)*, *El Pais (Spain)*, *Corriere della Serra (Italy)*, la Repubblica (Italy), Paris Match (France), *Le Figaro (France)*, *Tribune de Geneve (Switzerland)*, *Suddeutsche Zeitung Germany)*, *Die Welt* (Germany), *Bild* (Germany), The Guardian (England), The Telegraph (England), The Observer (England), The London Times, Tatler (England), and others in Asia, Australia, Canada and India.

In 2010, I published the first of five reports in The Daily Beast. The stories were published between July 20, 2010 and March 25, 2011, after a handful of publishers rejected the original English language manuscript for fear of libel. In England, the reason this story was rejected was because of the relationship between HRH Prince Andrew, Duke of York Fifth in Line to the Throne and Jeffrey Epstein.

It is no secret that publishing houses with interests in businesses regulated by the Federal government tend to be gun shy. Some of the responses conveyed to my agents including, Andrew Stuart, principal at the Stuart Agency in New York, who represented me for a brief period, in 2011, and years later, Alex Hoyt and Alfred Regnery, a former Justice Department official and head of the Office of Juvenile Justice and Delinquency Prevention, who together represented me in 2015 and 2016, revealed that publishers were afraid to print my book for fear of:

1. A Clinton Presidency

2. Libel

3. Legal action by Jeffrey Epstein

4. Legal action by Alan Dershowitz

5. Legal action by Epstein's lawyers

6. Legal action by Epstein's associates implicated in the case

7. Legal action by the investors funding the publishing house

In January 2014, after fve years of withholding publication, Random House Mexico killed the book deal signed in 2009. I was not very surprised. A former CEO of Random House U.S. and a former in-law mentioned that might happen.

On November 5, 2014, Richard Johnson published a story about my book on page six of The New York Post: "Author Faces Off Clinton." Basically, it announced how Random House Mexico killed the book deal in 2014.

Ironically, on December 1, 2015, Richard Johnson published a follow up story in the New York Post on page 25, which read, "Epstein book clears Clinton." The headline was odd, "Clinton clears Epstein book." It implied that someone, in this case America's number one author, James Patterson and his co author John Connelly perhaps approached the former president about the Epstein story and received the former president's blessings to publish their book. What happened to our First Amendment Rights and freedom of expression?

Johnson's article also revealed that a former NYPD police officer, John Connelly, who had approached me while I was writing the report for The Daily Beast, would co-author the book with James Patterson, an Epstein neighbor in Palm Beach.

Little Brown & Co. will publish their book in the fall of 2016 right before the presidential elections. For readers who are wondering why I'm promoting Connelly and Patterson's upcoming book, there are two reasons. First, I believe the more people expose the alleged sexual abuse crimes committed by this seeming gang of traffickers the better; Secondly, Tina Brown's Tweet deserves a mention:

> *"Conchita Sarnoff broke and owned the Epstein story on the Beast in 2010. No one knows more on this story."*

Unexpectedly, in December 2015, two months after Dershowitz was deposed, my former agents, Alex Hoyt and Al Regnery, returned with a proposition. The pitch process in New York began for a third and final time.

Six publishers expressed an interest in my book. This time their focus was different. Most of them wanted a manuscript about the Epstein-Clinton relationship. Given the political climate and the upcoming 2016 elections their request should not have surprised me. After several conversations my manuscript was rejected a third time.

My interest has never been to write a political book about anyone much less the Clinton's. There are plenty of books written about the political couple, both pro and con. Most importantly, the reason for investigating this case was never to discredit former President Clinton, his wife, Secretary of State Hillary Clinton or the Clinton administration. In fact it was under President Clinton's administration that the Trafficking Victims Protection Act was passed in 2000.

On the contrary, the investigation was based on the need to expose the truth, the whole truth and nothing but the truth about the Jeffrey E. Epstein case and why the predator was not charged under the Trafficking Victims Protection Act.

In the fight to stop human trafficking it is important to reveal the egregious sex crimes committed by a handful of alleged procurers who have not been charged with any crimes; and to understand why a rich predator, with a high level of influence, who implicated a number of politicians, British Royalty and opinion leaders, thanks to his wealth and generous donations, is not serving the minimum mandatory.

It is an important story because it exposes a predator who manipulates the system thanks to his political relationships. It is a story about the power of money and influence and how both can undermine justice. It is a story about a billionaire sex offender who knows how to leverage his assets in order to corrupt a system that should be incorruptible.

Party politics and campaign donations should have never played a role in the prosecution of a man who allegedly molested dozens if not hundreds of underage girls over a period of several years.

The mere association of a powerful leader entangled in such a sordid story and his relationship to Jeffrey Epstein and Ghislaine Maxwell should have sent him running to the nearest police department. As a symbol of authority and leadership, men in positions of power have added responsibilities and duties to those they lead.

As one publisher pointed out, Clinton is tangential to this case. My goal was never to prevent the Clinton's from reaching The White House; stir up sex scandals for political purposes; or focus on the Clinton-Epstein-Dershowitz relationship.

On the contrary, the motivation behind this story has been to understand the reasons why the system failed the victims; why the Department of Justice chose not to prosecute Epstein under the federal law, Trafficking Victims Protection Act (TVPA) enacted in Florida, in 2000; and why DOJ chose to identify the underage victims as "prostitutes" in the Non Prosecution Agreement rather than what they really were: child victims of sex trafficking.

The inspiration for this book came from a different source. The need to shed light on the issue of human trafficking and point out what needs to be done to stop sex trafficking. Human trafficking destroys millions of young lives every day all over world over. Unlike some predators, it is not biased in its pursuit. In the United States alone, according to a 2012 Congressional Report, there are over 300,000 children trafficked every year. Yet, only a handful of officials and prosecutors at the Department of Justice are aware of the urgency to enforce the Trafficking Victims Protection Act (TVPA) in human trafficking cases of this magnitude.

* * *

Proceeds

Five percent of the proceeds from the sale of this book will go to Innocents At Risk, a Washington D.C. foundation that helps to raise awareness of human trafficking.

http://www.innocentsatrisk.org

Five percent of the proceeds from the sale of this book will go to Alliance To Rescue Victims of Trafficking, a Washington D.C. foundation that raises awareness of human trafficking and expects to open a safe house to rescue and rehabilitate trafficked survivors.

http://www.atrvt.org

Dedication

I dedicate this book to the countless children who died as victims of sex trafficking and to the million more that survived but remain silent in the darkness.

To the memory of my father whose love and generosity inspire me still and to my inimitable mother who teaches me everyday how to persevere and find strength in pain.

To Deborah Sigmund who changed the direction of my life and became a good friend in this journey; and to my esteemed colleague and friend, Andres Oppenheimer, for generously paving the way forward so that I could write this book. Thank you.

To Cristina and Nicholas, thank you for your love and unyielding loyalty.

Facts

- 2.2 million children (a person under the age of 18) are sold into the sex trade every year. That means over 4 children per minute.

- Average age of entry into the sex trade in America is 12–14 years old. Shared Hope International, May 2009.

- 63% of survivors included in the 2013 report, wearethorn.org, revealed they were sold via the Internet at some point during their trafficking situation.

- The United States has a federal law that can be enforced in every state: Trafficking Victims Protection Reauthorization Act (TVPRA) 22 U.S. Code 7101.

- There are almost 21 million victims of human trafficking world-wide

- 75% of underage sex trafficking victims said they had been advertised or sold online. Report on the Use of Technology to Recruit, Groom and Sell Domestic Minor Sex Trafficking Victims, Thorn, 2015.

Facts

- I am a mother, first and foremost. I am also a victim's advocate. This story is about survivors and the need to enforce the Trafficking Victims Protection Act (TVPA) in every state.

- Like the survivors portrayed in this story, I too feel victimized by a system that filters the truth when it deems expedient.

- Living this experience has been gut wrenching and at times agonizing.

Cast of Characters

Attorneys

R. Alex Acosta, former U.S. Attorney for the Southern District of Florida, Department of Justice and prosecutor in the Epstein case. Currently Dean of Florida international University school of law since 2009.

Roy Black, civil and criminal trial attorney known for high profile civil litigation and criminal defense cases. Represented Jeffrey Epstein during criminal investigation. Partner, Black, Srebnick, Kornspan & Stumpf, Miami, Florida

David Boies, litigator N.Y. firm Boies, Schiller & Flexner. Represents Virginia Louise Roberts Giuffre in defamation case against Ghislaine Maxwell. Represented Vice President Al Gore in *Gore vs. Bush* case, 2000.

Paul Cassell, former Federal District Judge from 2002-2007. Appointed by president George W. Bush now Special Council with Hatch James & Dodge in Salt Lake City. Professor of Law at University of Utah Law School. Proponent of Victims Rights. Represents several victims in Jeffrey Epstein-related cases.

Robert (Bob) Critton, personal injury lawyer, West Palm Beach, Florida. Partner at Critton, Lutier, & Coleman. Epstein's attorney during criminal investigation.

Alan Dershowitz, former Harvard University law professor Emeritus, jurist, author, political commentator and scholar on U.S. constitutional law. Friend of Jeffrey Epstein's and implicated in Epstein case. Involved in civil litigation, defamation case against attorneys Brad Edwards and former federal Judge Paul Cassell. Retired, Miami Beach, Florida.

Brad Edwards, former Trial Attorney at Broward County State Attorneys Office. Senior partner: Farmer, Jaffe, Weissing, and Edwards, Ft. Lauderdale, Florida. Represented and continues to represent several victims in Epstein related cases.

Alice S. Fisher, Assistant Attorney General for Criminal Division in 2007, during Epstein's Non-Prosecution Agreement (NPA). Partner: Latham & Watkins LLP, Washington D.C.

Jack Goldberg, Criminal Defense Lawyer. Represented several victims. Senior Partner: Atterbury, Goldberger & Weiss, Palm Beach, Florida.

Alberto Gonzalez, Attorney General of the United States February 3, 2005- September 17, 2007.

Robert Josefsberg, Partner Podhurst Orseck PA, Miami, Florida, white collar, criminal defense and commercial litigation attorney. Represented a number of victims in civil cases during Epstein criminal case including Virginia Louise Roberts.

Peter D. Keisler, Partner Sidley Austin, Washington D.C. Former Acting Attorney General September 18, 2007- November 9, 2007.

Spencer Kuvin, Partner Craig Goldenfarb, West Palm Beach, Florida. Trial attorney. Represented several victims during civil litigation in Epstein case.

Gerald Lefcourt, Partner: Gerald B. Lefcourt Firm, New York. Leading trial attorney. Represented Jeffrey Epstein during criminal investigation and negotiated non-prosecution agreement (NPA).

Jay Lefkowitz, Senior Partner Kirkland Ellis, New York. Former General Counsel Office Of Management and Budget (OMB) during President George W. Bush administration. Represented Epstein during NPA negotiations. Together with Kenneth Starr negotiated Non-Prosecution Agreement.

Kenneth A. Marra, Federal Judge. Nominated by President George W. Bush to U.S. District Court for Southern District of Florida January 23, 2002. Presided over Epstein criminal case and continues to oversee several related cases.

Sigrid McCawley, complex litigation attorney at Boies Schiller & Flexner, Fort Lauderdale, Florida. Represents Virginia Louise Roberts in New York defamation case. *Virginia L Robert Giuffre vs. Ghislaine Maxwell.*

Laura Menninger, criminal defense attorney and litigator at Haddon Morgan Foreman, Denver, Colorado. Represents Ghislaine Maxwell in defamation case in New York. *Virginia L Roberts Giuffre vs. Ghislaine Maxwell.*

Jeffrey Pagliuca, Haddon Morgan Foreman, Denver, Colorado. Criminal Defense Attorney. Represents Ghislaine Maxwell in defamation case in New York: *Virginia Louise Roberts Giuffre vs. Ghislaine Maxwell.*

Bruce Reinhart, former assistant U.S. Attorney. Represented government at the beginning of Epstein criminal case. Left government and represented Epstein. In private practice: Bruce E. Reinhart attorney at law. West Palm Beach, Florida.

Jack Scarola, partner: Searcy Denney Scarola, Barnhart & Shipley PA. Represented Brad Edwards in case against Jeffrey Epstein and represented Edwards and former Federal Judge Paul Cassell in defamation case against Alan Dershowitz.

Ken W. Starr, former Federal Court of Appeals Judge, 39th Solicitor General under George H. Bush. Independent Counsel during President Bill Clinton's Impeachment Proceedings. A former President Pepperdine University Law School, Malibu, Ca. Currently President and Chancellor Baylor University. Appointed to negotiate Non Prosecution Agreement together with Jay Lefkowitz and represent Jeffrey Epstein

Thomas Scott, Partner Cole Scott Kissane, PA. Miami, Florida. Former US Attorney for Southern District of Florida. Former Circuit Judge for Eleventh Judicial Circuit for Dade County. Represented Alan Dershowitz in defamation lawsuit filed by attorneys Edwards and Cassell.

Ann Marie Villafaña, Prosecutor. Assistant U.S. Attorney Department of Justice, United States Attorneys Office, Southern District of Florida. Worked with R. Alex Acosta's prosecution team on Epstein's criminal case.

FBI Agents

FBI Special Agent Nesbitt Kuyrkendall

FBI Special Agent Jason Richards

FBI Special Agent Jonathan I. Solomon. Retired. Special Agent in Charge (SAC) 2006-2009, Miami, Florida. Headed Epstein's federal investigation.

Alleged principal procurers paid by Jeffrey Epstein. Never arrested, never charged.
Jean Luc Brunel

Lesley Groff

Sarah Kellen

Nadia Marcinkova

Ghislaine Maxwell

Adriana Ross Muscinska

Haley Robson

Predator and Registered Sex Offender
Jeffrey Epstein

Principal victims
Virginia Louise Roberts Giuffre

Jane Doe #1 a.k.a. Rosemary

Jane Doe #102 a.k.a. Virginia Louise Roberts

Jane Doe #1 & Jane Doe #2 (plaintiffs in CVRA case against Epstein filed in 2008)

Johanna Sjoberg

Jane Doe's, names of multiple victims who sued Epstein in civil court. Their real identities have been withheld for security reasons.

Friends of Epstein mentioned in Epstein case

HRH Prince Andrew Fifth in Line to The British Throne, third son of HRH Queen Elizabeth II and Prince Philip.

Allegedly had sexual relations with underage victim, Virginia Louise Roberts.

Bill Clinton: former President of the United States (1992-2000). Impeached by the House of Representatives on two charges, one of perjury and one of Obstruction of Justice on December 19, 1998.

In a landmark U.S. Supreme Court case the judges ordered that a sitting president of the United States had no immunity from civil law litigation against him or her, for acts done before taking office and unrelated to the office. In 1997, President Clinton was issued 5-year suspension of his law license in the State of Arkansas, *Clinton v. Jones 520, and U.S. 681.*

Close friend of Ghislaine Maxwell and CGI recipient of Maxwell's Terra Mar Project donation.

Recipient of Epstein's generous donations

David Copperfield, magician, entertainer, friend and Epstein houseguest.

Alan Dershowitz, former Harvard Law School professor. Friend of Epstein's and attorney during criminal investigation also implicated in Epstein case.

Governor Bill Richardson, 30th Governor of New Mexico (2003-2011). U.S. Secretary of Energy during Clinton Administration (August 1998-January 2001). Friend of Epstein's and recipient of donations.

Leslie Wexner, CEO and founder L brands formerly The Limited Brands Corporation. Original owner of several assets and properties later gifted or sold to Epstein. Close friend, former business associate and client of Jeffrey Epstein. Wexner foundation. Personal estimated net worth: six billion dollars.

The Prosecutor's Letter

R. Alex Acosta wrote this letter on March 20, 2011. Acosta was the U.S. Attorney for the Southern District of Florida (USAO) and prosecutor during the Epstein criminal investigation. Acosta hand delivered the letter to me at the Biltmore Hotel, Coral Gables, Florida. It was originally published in its entirety in The Daily Beast on March 25, 2011.

March 20, 2011

To Whom It May Concern:

I served as U.S. Attorney for the Southern District of Florida from 2005-2009. Over the past weeks, I have read much regarding Mr. Jeffrey Epstein. Some appears true some appears distorted. I thought it appropriate to provide some background, with two caveats: (I) under Justice Department guidelines, I cannot discuss privileged internal communications among Department attorneys and (ii) I no longer have access to the original documents, and as the matter is now nearly 4 years old, the precision of memory is reduced.

The Epstein matter was originally presented to the Palm Beach County State Attorney. Palm Beach Police alleged that Epstein unlawfully hired underage high-school females to provide him sexually lewd and erotic massages. Police sought felony charges that would have resulted in a term of imprisonment. According to press reports, however, in 2006 the State Attorney, in part due to concerns regarding the quality of the evidence, agreed to charge Epstein only with one count of aggravated assault with no intent to commit a felony. That charge would have resulted in no jail time, no requirement to register as a sexual offender and no restitution for the underage victims.

Local police were dissatisfied with the State Attorney's conclusions, and requested a federal investigation. Federal authorities received the State's evidence and engaged in additional investigation. Prosecutors weighed the quality of the evidence and the likelihood for success at trial. With a federal case, there were two additional considerations. First, a federal criminal prosecution requires that the crime be more than local; it must have an interstate nexus. Second, as the matter was initially charged by the state, the federal responsibility is, to some extent, to backstop state authorities to ensure that there is no miscarriage of justice, and not to also prosecute federally that which has already been charged at the state level.

After considering the quality of the evidence and the additional considerations, prosecutors concluded that the state charge was insufficient. In early summer 2007, the prosecutors and agents in this case met with Epstein's attorney, Roy Black. Mr. Black is perhaps best known for his successful defense of William Kennedy Smith. The prosecutors presented Epstein a choice: plead to a more serious state felony charge (that would result in 2 years' imprisonment, registration as a sexual offender, and restitution for the victims) or else prepare for a federal felony trial.

What followed was a yearlong assault on the prosecution and the prosecutors. I use the word assault intentionally, as the defense in this case was more aggressive than any, which I, or the prosecutors in my office, had previously encountered. Mr. Epstein hired an army of legal superstars: Harvard Professor Alan Dershowitz, former Judge and then Pepperdine Law Dean Kenneth Starr, former Deputy Assistant to the President and then Kirkland Ellis partner Jay Lefkowitz, and several others, including prosecutors who had formally worked in the U.S. Attorney's Office and in the Child Exploitation and Obscenity Section of the Justice Department. Defense attorneys next requested a meeting with me to challenge the prosecution and the terms previously presented by the prosecutors in their meeting with Mr. Black.

The prosecution team and I met with defense counsel in Fall 2007, and I reaffirmed the office's position: two years, registration and restitution, or trial.

Over the next several months, the defense team presented argument after argument claiming that felony criminal proceedings against Epstein were unsupported by the evidence and lacked a basis in law, and that the office's insistence on jail-time was motivated by zeal to overcharge a man merely because he is wealthy. They bolstered their arguments with legal opinions from well-known legal experts. One member of the defense team warned that the office's excess zeal in forcing a good man to serve time in jail might be the subject of a book if we continued to proceed with this matter. My office systematically considered and rejected each argument, and when we did, my office's decisions were appealed to Washington. As to the warning, I ignored it.

The defense strategy was not limited to legal issues. Defense counsel investigated individual prosecutors and their families, looking for personal peccadilloes that may provide a basis for disqualification. Disqualifying a prosecutor is an effective (though rarely used) strategy, as eliminating the individuals most familiar with the facts and thus most qualified to take a case to trial harms likelihood for success. Defense counsel tried to disqualify at least two prosecutors. I carefully reviewed, and then rejected, these arguments.

Despite this army of attorneys, the office held firm to the terms first presented to Mr. Black in the original meeting. On June 30, 2008, after yet another last minute appeal to Washington D.C. was rejected, Epstein pled guilty in state court. He was to serve 18 months imprisonment, register as a sexual offender for life and provide restitution to the victims.

Some may feel that the prosecution should have been tougher. Evidence that has come to light since 2007 may encourage that view. Many victims have since spoken out, filing detailed statements in civil cases seeking damages. Physical evidence has since been discovered. Had these additional statements and evidence been known, the outcome may have been different. But there were not known to us at the time.

A prosecution decision must be based on admissible facts know at the time. In cases of this type, those are unusually difficult because victims are frightened and often decline to testify or if they do speak, they give contradictory statements. Our judgment in this case, based on the evidence known at the time, was that it was better to have a billionaire serve time in jail, register as a sex offender and pay his victims restitution than risk a trial with a reduced likelihood of success. I supported that judgment then, and based on the state of the law as it then stood and the evidence known at that time, I would support that judgment again.

Epstein's treatment, while in state custody, likewise may encourage the view that the office should have been tougher. Epstein appears to have received highly unusual treatment while in jail. Although the terms of confinement in a state prison are a matter appropriately left to the State of Florida, and not federal authorities, without doubt, the treatment that he received while in state custody undermined the purpose of a jail sentence.

Some may also believe that the prosecution should have been tougher in retaliation for the defense's tactics. The defense, arguably, often failed to negotiate in good faith. They would obtain concessions as part of a negotiation and agree to proceed, only to change their minds, and appeal the office's position to Washington. The investigations into the family lives of individual prosecutors were, in my opinion, uncalled for, as were the accusations of bias and / or misconduct against individual prosecutors.

At times, some prosecutors felt that we should just go to trial, and at times I felt that frustration myself. What was right in the first meeting, however, remained right irrespective of defense tactics. Individuals have a constitutional right to a defense. The aggressive exercise of that right should not be punished, nor should a defense counsel's exercise of their right to appeal a U.S. Attorney to Washington D.C. Prosecutors must be careful not to allow frustration and anger with defense counsel to influence their judgment.

After the plea, I recall receiving several phone calls. One was from the FBI Special Agent-In-Charge. He called to offer congratulations. He had been at many of the meetings regarding this case. He was aware of the tactics of the defense, and he called to praise our prosecutors for holding firm against the likes of Messrs. Black, Dershowitz, Lefkowitz and Starr. It was a proud moment. I also received calls or communications from Messrs. Dershowitz, Lefkowitz and Starr. I had known all three individuals previously, from my time in law school and at Kirkland Ellis in the mid 90s. They all sought to make peace. I agreed to talk and meet with each of them after Epstein pled guilty, as I think it important that prosecutors battle defense attorneys in a case and then move on. I have tried, yet I confess that has been difficult to do fully in this case.

The bottom line is this: Mr. Epstein, a billionaire, served time in jail and is now a registered sex offender. He has been required to pay his victims restitution, though restitution clearly cannot compensate for the crime. And we know much more today about his crimes because the victims have come forward to speak out. Some may disagree with the prosecutorial judgments made in this case, but those individuals are not the ones who at the time reviewed the evidence available for trial and assessed the likelihood of success.

Respectfully,

R. Alexander Acosta
Former U.S. Attorney
Southern District of Florida

After graduating from Harvard University Law School, Mr. Acosta worked at Kirkland Ellis in Washington D.C. at the same time Kenneth Starr was working at Kirkland. Their professional association perhaps helps to explains why, in October 2007, Epstein's defense team recruited Starr's services to help negotiate Epstein's Non Prosecution Agreement in Washington, in October 2007. Starr was the 39th Solicitor General beginning May 26, 1989-January 20, 1993. Starr, a Republican, also served as Solicitor General during former President Clinton's Monica Lewinsky investigation.

On December 27, 2015, politico.com posted a story claiming the Government had listed six witnesses who possessed information relevant to the case. Two USAO officials, Mr. Acosta and Ms. Villafaña, and four FBI agents who worked on the Epstein criminal case were served. All six, FBI Special Agent E. Nesbitt Kuyrkendall, FBI Special Agent Jason Richards; (Former) First AUSA Jeff Sloman (currently employed at a Miami law firm); (Former) Chief of the Criminal Division Matt Menchel (currently employed at a Miami law firm); AUSA Marie Villafaña; (Former) U.S. Attorney R. Alexander Acosta (currently employed at Florida International University) are awaiting deposition. "The victims asked the Government to make the witnesses available for deposition. The Government objected and said the victims should file a motion. The Government would oppose the motion."[1]

Footnotes

1   http://www.politico.com/f/?id=00000151-de58-d28c-af7b-dff844220001
http://www.politico.com/blogs/under-the-radar/2015/12/victims-in-underage-sex-case-want-prosecutors-to-testify-2171

Chronology

1976

Jeffrey E. Epstein becomes an Options Trader at Bear Stearns. Ace Greenberg and Jimmy Cayne hire Epstein after resigning from the elite Upper East Side Manhattan Dalton School where he taught mathematics and piano.

1981

Approximately two months after he is made partner, Epstein is fired from Bear Stearns for securities law violations in other words, insider trading.

1982

Epstein opens for business as J. Epstein Trust Co. New York. His clients and sources of funding remain unknown. Epstein allegedly worked for Steven Hoffenberg founder of Towers Financial Corporation.

1984

Wexner establishes The Wexner Foundation to strengthen the field of Jewish leadership.

1986

Leslie Wexner, CEO and founder of The Limited (L Brands) invests $1 billion with Epstein's new Manhattan-based investment company.

J. Epstein Trust Co. According to insiders Wexner develops a close relationship with Epstein.

1989-1993

Kenneth Starr is named Solicitor General under George H.W. Bush.

1989

Leslie Wexner purchases the Birch Wathen School, a 21,000 sq. feet property built for Herbert N. Strauss, an heir to Macy's fortune. Located at 9 East 71 Street New York the house boasts a heated sidewalk. Wexner paid $13.2 million for the property and invests millions of dollars in renovation according to the New York Times. Epstein reports to the Times, "Les never spent more than two months there." Ironically, the house sits across the street from Bill Cosby's New York City house. In 1996, Epstein became its new owner.

1990

Forbes magazine estimates Epstein net worth is unknown, in part because his wealth is concealed in a financial entity in the United States Virgin Islands (USVI), a tax shelter where he owns a private island and his primary residence. The only public source of income is derived from his association with his friend, Leslie Wexner. According to Epstein he receives management fees for advising and investing Wexner's capital. He receives a commission as most financial advisors on Wall Street.

1990's

Epstein creates two foundations both domiciled in the U.S. Virgin Islands. Since he began his business in the early eighties and throughout the nineties, Epstein acquired properties around the world. Some of his properties originally belonged to the estate of Leslie Wexner. Those properties include: the Manhattan triplex on East 71, the Zorro Ranch in Stanley, New Mexico, a USVI island, the Avenue Foch Paris apartment, the London flat, Palm Beach estate, 727 private jet, helicopter, yacht, etc.

1991

July, publishing magnate and former member of Britain's parliament, Robert Maxwell, dies leaving scandal in his wake. The Maxwell family is now bankrupt and two sons, Ian and Brian, are charged with malfeasance.

1992

Maxwell's youngest daughter, Ghislaine Maxwell, moves to New York City and meets Jeffrey Epstein. Epstein and Maxwell begin a relationship. He purchases a townhouse for her on 65th Street off Park Avenue.

1992

Arkansas Governor, William J. Clinton is elected 42nd President of the United States. He is in Office for two terms.

1993

January 23, Leslie Wexner (56) marries Abigail S. Koppel (31), Barnard graduate magna cum laude, associate at Davis Polk & Wardell and good friends with Epstein.

1994

Starr joins Kirkland Ellis law firm. Kirkland Ellis is largest private law firm in US. He is criticized for conflicts of interest stemming from his position as independent counsel and ongoing association with Kirkland Ellis since firm was representing clients in litigation with the government. On one occasion, Starr spoke with lawyers for Paula Jones, who was at the time suing President Clinton over an alleged sexual assault. Starr maintained that a sitting U.S. president was not immune to a civil suit.

1994-1995

R. Alex Acosta, federal prosecutor during the Jeffrey Epstein criminal case, a Harvard University Law graduate, serves as a law clerk to Judge Samuel Alito for the US Court of Appeals for the Third Circuit.

1995

R. Alex Acosta hired by Kirkland Ellis befriends Kenneth Starr. He specializes in employment and labor issues and teaches at George Mason University Law School.

2000

Jeffrey Epstein opens a U.S. Virgin Island office and creates a third foundation, Jeffrey Epstein VI Foundation.

2000

Famed lawyer and Clinton supporter, David Boies, represents former Vice President, Al Gore, in the legal fight over the *Bush versus Gore* 2000 election.

2001

January 20, President Clinton's second term expires. He leaves The Oval Office.

2001-2003

Clinton takes 17 trips on board Epstein's private jet. Clinton is accompanied on Epstein's jet with his secret service details, friends, at times Doug Band, plus unidentified females. The pilot manifesto and pilot logs are incomplete and redacted.

Other passengers identified on the jet include Alan Dershowitz, Larry Summers, Vernon Jordan, Jean Luc Brunel, Kevin Spacy, Ghislaine Maxwell, Virginia Louise Roberts, several unnamed females, unidentified males and others.

2002

Newly licensed pilot Ghislaine Maxwell pilots Epstein's black hawk helicopter and flies Clinton out of the U.S. Virgin Islands during his visit. According to Virginia Louis Roberts, an underage victim, two underage girls are reported to be visiting Epstein's island while Clinton is a guest. Maxwell, Roberts and Epstein are in residence during same visit.

2002-2003

Jeffrey Epstein donates $4 million to start the Clinton Global Initiative, according to a source.

2003

Jay Lefkowitz leaves the Bush White House to join Kirkland Ellis. Lefkowitz is made senior partner.

2005

The Clinton Foundation opens as public charity. By 2013, contributions have grown to $144 million.

2005

March 14, Palm Beach Police begin investigation into sex crimes allegedly carried out by Epstein. Dozens of underage girls come forward individually.

2005

Epstein is charged with sex abuse of minors. Over 100 underage girls testify against him.

2005

Virginia Louise Roberts identified on court documents as Jane Doe #102, identifies Clinton, Prince Andrew, Alan Dershowitz and others amongst Epstein's close friends. Roberts' implicates them as material witnesses. Roberts accuses Maxwell and Epstein of sexual abuse.

2005-2007

Law enforcement investigates Epstein's human trafficking case. The Palm Beach Police investigation led to a Grand Jury and a two-year federal investigation.

2007

Between September and October a Non-Prosecution Agreement is negotiated. The original federal indictment included potential money laundering charges.

2007

October 25-27, Prosecutor's federal order charging Epstein is dismissed. Former Bush Administration Mid East Envoy Jay Lefkowitz and former Solicitor General Kenneth Starr renegotiate the Order and a new deal with the Department of Justice in Washington D.C. is struck effectively side stepping federal prosecutor's R. Alex Acosta's order.

Hillary Clinton receives a $25,000 donation from Epstein after his indictment. She does not return donation.

2008

Jeffrey Epstein begins his 18-month prison sentence.

2008-2009

Underage victims begin to file dozens of civil suits against Epstein.

2009

July, R. Alex Acosta becomes the second Dean at Florida International Law School.

2010

September, Ghislaine Maxwell is subpoenaed at Clinton Global Initiative in reference to Epstein case and her relationship with several public figures including former President Clinton. She leaves country and escapes to London.

2010

July, Alan Dershowitz speaks to Sarnoff on the record for the first and last time. Bill Clinton does not return call.

2010

New York: Epstein registered as a Level 3-sex offender.

2010

Chelsea Clinton marries hedge fund investor, Mark Mezvinsky at fabled Vincent and Brooke Astor estate in Rhinebeck, New York. Ghislaine Maxwell is photographed in the U.S. attending Clinton wedding.

2010

December, HRH Prince Andrew's former wife, the Duchess of York, Sarah Ferguson receives 15,000 pounds sterling ($24,000) from Jeffrey E. Epstein, following his arrest to pay off her debts. Sarah Ferguson admits details of loan to news media.

2012

One of three of Epstein's foundations, allegedly the foundation employed to transfer money to Clinton, becomes inactive.

2014

December 31, New Year's Eve, Josh Gerstein reporter at politico.com, exposes victim's sexual abuse claim against Professor Alan Dershowitz.

2015

January, The Duchess of York, admits she had not repaid Epstein's loan when asked about the status of the loan by the Daily Mail.

2015

January, Brad Edwards and former Federal Judge Paul Cassell sue Alan Dershowitz for defamation.

2015

January, Alan Dershowitz countersues, Edwards & Cassell.

2015

The FBI investigation into Hillary Clinton's use of private email as Secretary of State has expanded to look at whether the possible "intersection" of Clinton Foundation work and State Department business may have violated public corruption laws, according to three unnamed intelligence cited by Fox News.

2015

FBI agents investigate the possible intersection of Clinton Foundation donations, the dispensation of State Department contracts and whether regular processes were followed," one source said. This new investigative track is in addition to the focus on classified material found on Clinton's personal server.

2015

The federal prosecutor, R. Alex Acosta, and other assistant U.S. Attorney's Office officials, plus FBI agents who worked on Epstein's criminal case, are issued subpoenas. They are to be deposed on matters pertaining to the Epstein case. The case is ongoing.

2015

October 15-16, Epstein lawyer and one-time friend, Alan Dershowitz, takes deposition and identifies Bill Clinton's association with Epstein and his presence on the private Caribbean island.

2015

September 21, David Boies agrees to represent a victim, Virginia Louis Roberts, a.k.a. Jane Doe #102 in a New York State defamation case against Ghislaine Maxwell. The case is pending. Maxwell is alleged to be a principal procurer in the Epstein case and pivotal to the triangular relationship between Clinton and Epstein.

2015

Boies Schiller act as a go between Dershowitz and Edwards and Cassell in defamation case. Boies sought an Emergency Order in December 2015 to seal Dershowitz's affidavit, which the court granted.

2015-2016

It remains unclear, which of the two lines of inquiry (the email server or the public corruption), was opened first by the FBI and whether they eventually will be combined and presented before a special grand jury. One intelligence source said the public corruption angle dates back to at least April 2015. The FBI's official website lists "public corruption as the FBI's top criminal priority."

2015-2016

The development follows press reports over the past year about the potential overlap of State Department and Clinton Foundation work, and questions over whether donors benefited from their contacts inside the Obama administration.

2016

January, Fox News is told that about 100 special agents assigned to the investigations were asked to sign non-disclosure agreements, with as many as 50 additional agents on "temporary duty assignment." The request to sign such agreements could reflect that agents are handling highly classified material in the emails, or serve as a reminder not to leak about the case.

2016

January, inside the FBI pressure is growing to pursue the case.

One intelligence source told Fox News that "FBI agents would be "screaming" if a prosecution is not pursued because 'many previous public corruption cases have been made and successfully prosecuted with much less evidence than what is emerging in this investigation.' "

2016

January, ongoing Epstein related cases and possible tie in with Clinton scandals. Two open Epstein cases in Florida and one in New York. One case allegedly implicates former President Clinton given his association with Epstein, Maxwell, and Virginia Louise Roberts.

2016

January 13, Sarnoff speaks with New York Supreme Court County Judge, Ruth Pickholz -- the presiding Judge during Epstein's Sex Offender Registration case in New York. Judge reveals she refused to agree with the prosecutor's recommendation and assigned Epstein highest offender status, level 3. Epstein appeals Judge's decision. Pickholz's ruling affirmed.

2016

January, Epstein remains a level-3 sex-offender in New York. Pickholz mentioned how "surprised" she was that Manhattan DA's Office "requested a downward registration to lowest level, level 1," after requesting the highest level of registration for a United States, 24 year old, soldier who was accused of having consensual sex with a 17 year old girl, in a recent case. In the soldier's case, District Attorney's Office requested the highest sexual offender registration permissible, level 3.

2016

April 8, Alan Dershowitz, Brad Edwards, former Federal Judge Paul Cassell settle defamation lawsuit.

2016

April 10, According to The American Lawyer, Edwards and Cassell agree to waive confidentiality. Dershowitz agrees to waive it too provided Edwards, Cassell and David Boies agree to unseal Virginia Louise Giuffre's deposition and Boies Schiller agrees to release Dershowitz's affidavit regarding David Boies.

2016

April 14, former Epstein victim, Virginia Louise Roberts, continues litigation in New York, *Virginia Roberts Giuffre vs. Ghislaine Maxwell.*

April 14, Jane Doe #1 & Jane Doe #2, former Epstein victims, continue litigation in Florida, *Jane Doe #1 & Jane Doe #2 vs. United States Government.*

April 14, The American Lawyer reported:

In January Boies Schiller also sought sanctions against Dershowitz for violating terms of the order. Sanction Hearing is scheduled for May 2016.

David Boies claims in Motion that Dershowitz repeatedly tried to expose false information from confidential settlement discussions on the record.

Boies refuses to release the documents that are the condition of Dershowitz's waiver. Both sides seem to be withholding something they don't want revealed.

Links

http://pagesix.com/2014/11/05/author-faces-off-against-bill-clinton/

http://pagesix.com/2015/12/01/epstein-sex-scandal-book-clears-bill-clinton/

http://www.thedailybeast.com/articles/2010/07/20/jeffrey-epstein-billionaire-pedophile-goes-free.html …

http://www.dailymail.co.uk/news/article-2897086/Cash-strapped-Fergie-took-15-000-paedophile-billionaire-centre-claims-Prince-Andrew-slept-age-sex-slave.html

http://www.politico.com/blogs/under-the-radar/2014/12/woman-who-sued-convicted-billionaire-over-sex-abuse-levels-claims-at-his-friends-200495

http://www.dailymail.co.uk/news/article-2897086/Cash-strapped-Fergie-took-15-000-paedophile-billionaire-centre-claims-Prince-Andrew-slept-age-sex-slave.html

http://www.americanlawyer.com/the-careerist/id=1202754581393/Dershowitz-Settles-Sex-Case-But-Is-He-Vindicated?mcode=1202616610377&curindex=3

http://www.americanlawyer.com/the-careerist/id=1202754666961/Did-Dershowitz-Pay-Big-Bucks-to-Settle-Sex-Case-?mcode=1202616610377&curindex=2

Links

http://www.americanlawyer.com/the-
careerist/id=1202755043865/Whats-Everyone-Hiding-in-the-
Dershowitz-Case?mcode=1202616610377&curindex=1

http://www.americanlawyer.com/id=1202755043865/Whats-
Everyone-Hiding-in-the-Dershowitz-Case#ixzz46JNvBKaI

https://twitter.com/tinabrownlm/status/551577276333428736

http://www.nyu.edu/clubs/act/EventsPage/SCTNow.pdf

https://www.congress.gov/bill/113th-congress/house-bill/898

http://www.weforum.org/agenda/2015/02/how-data-can-help-
fight-human-trafficking/

Introduction

THIS IS NOT A LEGAL STORY THIS IS A MORAL STORY

What matters is usually invisible.

Has our political elite become so corrupted they can ignore moral boundaries and human rights? Why has some of the media establishment turned a blind eye? These two questions propelled me to write this book.

Between 2001 and 2005, Jeffrey E. Epstein apparently sexually abused more than one hundred underage girls from relatively disadvantaged backgrounds in Palm Beach, Florida. The victims submitted sworn testimony to the Palm Beach Police Department.

Police reports confirm that a number of alleged assaults occurred in Florida while others supposedly occurred on his private island, Little St. James, in the United States Virgin Islands, New York and in London, England. Most cases were precluded from the final indictment.

On October 27, 2007, two years after an extensive criminal investigation began that included the Palm Beach Police, FBI, county, city, state and federal law enforcement agencies, Epstein was handed a Non Prosecution Agreement (NPA) by the U.S. Attorney's Office in the 15th Judicial Circuit in Palm Beach County. Epstein did not sign the NPA until December 7, 2007.

Although Epstein pled guilty (not *nolo contendere*) to the Indictment, which means he agreed not to contest the charges in the future: one (1) count of solicitation of prostitution, and one (1) count to an Information filed by the State's Attorney's Office in the solicitation of minors to engage in prostitution, he was not satisfied with the agreement. Why did the Department of Justice identify underage victims as prostitutes and not as victims?

"Of the two offenses he pled guilty, the second offense required Epstein to register as a sex offender. Both charges were contingent upon a Judge of the 15th Judicial Circuit accepting and executing the sentence agreed upon between the State Attorney's Office and Epstein."[1]

"The recommendation by the US Attorney's Office was to have Epstein sentenced to consecutive terms of twelve (12) months and six (6) months in county jail for all charges, without any opportunity for withholding adjudication i.e. settlement or sentencing, and without probation or community control in lieu of imprisonment, the NPA stated. Epstein was also sentenced to twelve (12) months of community control (house arrest) consecutive to his two terms in county jail.[2]

In the end, Epstein served only 13 months in the Palm Beach county jail and was allowed to leave his private cell on an all day work release program. Following his release from the Palm Beach county jail, he served 18 months of house arrest in his Palm Beach estate. During that time period, he allegedly committed 11 parole violations according to Brad Edwards, a South Florida Victims Rights attorney representing several victims.

After Epstein's release from house arrest, his criminal case was closed although the civil cases continued. Unlike other human trafficker offenders prosecuted for far less egregious crimes, Epstein was not prosecuted under the Trafficking Victims Protection Act (TVPA), enacted in Florida in 2000. TVPA aims to protect victims and prosecute human traffickers by imposing a minimum mandatory sentence of 20 years in a federal prison.

This year, 2016, marks the eleventh year (2005-2016) since several related cases have been arguing their way through the courts. So far, two cases are pending in Florida. One case is at the Florida Supreme Court.

A third case is pending in New York: *Virginia L. Roberts' Giuffre vs. Ghislaine Maxwell*. The victim and plaintiff, Roberts-Giuffre accused Maxwell of defamation. In one of the Florida cases, closely related to the Epstein case, Alan Dershowitz, former Harvard University law professor and renowned jurist, was sued for defamation by attorneys Brad Edwards and Paul Cassell. It was the result of his association with Epstein.

On the eve of New Year's Day, December 31, 2014, politico.com posted a blog that rocked the legal world. It also stunned Dershowitz. I'm assuming his colleagues, Harvard Law School students, friends and detractors.

Professor Dershowitz was accused of "having sexual relations" at six different times with Jane Doe #3 a.k.a. Virginia Louise Roberts, who at the time was underage." The New Year's Eve story revealed that, "One such powerful individual that Epstein forced then minor Jane Doe #3 to have sexual relations with was former Harvard Law Professor, Alan Dershowitz, a close friend of Epstein's and well known criminal defense attorney."[3]

The report also illustrated a legal pleading that said, "Jane Doe #3 had sexual relations with Dershowitz on numerous occasions while she was a minor, not only in Florida but also on private planes, in New York, New Mexico, and the U.S. Virgin Islands."[4]

After the Dershowitz story went viral, in January 2015, given my extensive research and long-standing history with the case, I was invited on dozens of domestic and international media networks. I declined the invitations. Dershowitz however, went on an international media blitz defending his position and legacy. He spoke on almost every television network and news outlet in the U.S. and published multiple editorials in leading mainstream publications.

During his publicity campaign, Dershowitz accused Florida attorney Brad Edwards, and former Federal Judge, Paul Cassell, of "character assassination." The two lawyers then sued Dershowitz for defamation. Dershowitz counter sued. Virginia Louise Roberts Giuffre, one of the alleged victim's was a possible witness in that case.[5]

The dictionary definition for a "defamation lawsuit is as a civil wrong or 'Tort,' not a criminal offense. It is a catchall phrase made by one person that hurts someone's reputation. A spoken defamation is called 'slander,' and a written defamation is termed 'libel.'"

The case was settled on Friday, April 8, 2016. All three lawyers agreed to settle the defamation action and as part of the settlement certain pleadings that were filed by Jack Scarola, (Edwards and Cassell's attorney), as well as Dershowitz's attorneys were withdrawn.

In September 2015, Virginia Louise Roberts, the same victim and potential witness in the *Edwards & Cassell vs. Dershowitz* case, sued Ghislaine Maxwell for defamation. Super star attorney, David Boies, co- founder and partner at Boies, Schiller & Flexner, agreed to represent Roberts Giuffre, *pro bono*. Sigrid McCawley is her representing counselor.

The defamation case *Virginia L. Giuffre vs. Ghislaine Maxwell,* is ongoing in New York. Roberts-Giuffre, now in her thirties, is married with three children. She is the same woman implicated in the Florida criminal case who sued Epstein in 2005. Her most recent case, filed in the Southern District of New York, is related to the 2005 Epstein criminal case.

It is interesting that David Boies, in light of his political associations, lack of financial remuneration from the Roberts case, and his aversion to publicity, would decide to accept the Virginia Roberts Giuffre case.

Sometime after Boies filed the Complaint on behalf of his client, I rang him to confirm the merits of the case. He did not return my calls. His assistant, Linda Carlsen, suggested I e-mail the questions. Boies did not respond to my e-mail. On November 6, 2015, someone who is familiar with the Maxwell case responded on his behalf.

Q: Are you personally representing Virginia Louise Roberts Giuffre or is someone at your Florida firm representing the woman in the Ghislaine Maxwell Defamation suit filed on 9.21.2015?

A: The lawyers of record are listed on the complaint and are involved to one extent or another. But any attorney in the firm who works on the case can be said to represent the client.

Q: Why did your firm agree to take on the VLRG case pro bono?

A: I don't know the financial terms of BSF's representation, and they are not typically disclosed for publication by law firms.

Q: Is the jurisdiction of this defamation case Florida or New York?

A: The case has been filed in the Federal District Court in the Southern District of New York.

Q: What are the merits of the Defamation case against Ghislaine Maxwell?

A: The best way to understand the case is to read the complaint. You'll find that it speaks clearly and forcefully to the merits.

Q. If Roberts Giuffre wins the suit, is she looking for remuneration and/or punitive damages or both?

A: The complaint addresses the relief the plaintiff seeks. As a practical matter, it's too early to try to guess what specific relief might be granted.

A couple of insiders suggested that Boies, a well-known Clinton supporter, might have taken the case to help string it out past the 2016 election. Perhaps this is one reason.

It is public knowledge that Maxwell has long been a suspect in the Epstein case. Her role as an alleged procurer of Epstein's has been established in various court files. In spite of volumes of depositions identifying her in the Epstein case, she remains a close friend of former president Bill Clinton and attended Ms. Clinton's wedding. In 2013, at the Clinton Global Initiative, Maxwell pledged support to CGI through her foundation, The Terra Mar Project.

With stakes this high and former Secretary Clinton practically a shoe-in for the presidential nomination, one could presume that Boies' representation of Roberts-Giuffre might have been a strategic decision. Perhaps to help cloak the 'behind the scene' negotiations that took place during the Non Prosecution Agreement Negotiations now under investigation, until after the new President of the United States is elected?

One thing is certain, David Boies has a longstanding association with the Democratic Party and the Clinton family. Not long ago, Boies was a Gore fundraiser and delivered the famous oral argument, in 2000, for Al Gore in the *Bush vs. Gore* case.

Recently, Boies and his partner, Jonathan Schiller, hired a new partner, the notable Karen Dunn who worked for then Senator Hillary Clinton as communications director and senior advisor. Dunn was also Deputy to Chief Strategist, David Axelrod, on the 2008 President Obama presidential campaign. When he took on the Virginia Roberts Giuffre case, Boies assigned two other luminary female attorneys to the case: Ellen Brockman in New York and Sigrid S. McCawley in Florida. Ms. McCawley represented their client in a hearing as recently as March 2016.

On October 15, 2015, during the taking of Alan Dershowitz's deposition, Jack Scarola, representing Brad Edwards and Paul Cassell, reminded Professor Dershowitz of one of his many theories:

SCAROLA: There's an old saying if you have the law on your side, bang on the law. If you have the facts on your side, bang on the facts. If you have neither bang on the table.

DERSHOWITZ: I have never believed that, but I do believe in a variation of that theme. If you don't have the law or legal facts on your side, argue your case in the Court of public opinion.[6]

I agree with Professor Dershowitz and so as a defender of human rights especially children's rights fighting to help stop child sex trafficking, I have set out to shed light on the Epstein case in the Court of public opinion. In an attempt to reveal all the relevant facts, I have uncovered thousands of documents over the course of the eleven-year long case.

As a witness to certain events and a beneficiary to hundreds of private conversations including many "off the record" conversations with prosecutors, Maxwell, Epstein before, during and after his imprisonment, victims, lawyers, the Palm Beach Chief of Police, private investigators and law enforcement officials, the facts are ready to be exposed. Having invested many years researching the characters and cases, this book strives to be the first comprehensive story about the Epstein case.

Since the Epstein case was first reported, in 2006, consciousness around human trafficking has exploded. A decade later, media reports claim there are over 22 million children trafficked worldwide. It is time to pay attention. As parents, guardians, community and religious leaders we have an obligation to protect our children. They are our future. As guardians of the most vulnerable population it is our duty to work closely with elementary schools, teachers, academia, media, IT companies, government leaders, religious leaders and abolitionists to put an end to human trafficking and child sex slavery.

Human trafficking is a form of slavery. The distinction between the two, if any, is that in the Twenty First Century, modern day slaves include the buying and selling of children. These children are held captive mostly against their will and traded on the open market like cattle. They are sold for a number of reasons primarily: labor, sexual pleasure, pornography and organs.

Beginning in 1998 or perhaps earlier, Jeffrey E. Epstein, allegedly trafficked dozens of underage girls for sex to his Palm Beach, Florida home. Epstein and his procurers apparently coerced, lured and conspired to sexually abuse impressionable and vulnerable victims with promises of cash and modeling jobs if the girls provided him and supposedly in some instances, Ghislaine Maxwell, with sexually-charged "massages." The average age ranged between 12-16 years old according to Complaint #09-80656, filed May 1, 2009 in the United States District Court For The Southern District Of Florida.

The facts and merits speak for themselves. The truth might offend some very influential opinion leaders. I trust that irrespective of their personal feelings, the core message is understood. This is not a political story. It is an undiluted and unfiltered story about the Epstein case and how his money, friendships, and influence corrupted the legal system.

His case is a powerful reminder of the obligations we have as American citizens to raise awareness of the blight of human trafficking, of the rights of children and of human rights in general. Moreover, the United States and the Department of Justice should feel duty bound in cases such as Epstein's to enforce the Trafficking Victims Protection Act (TVPA).

The Epstein case is stranger than fiction and far more contemptible than the Lewinsky case, Watergate scandal, and Profumo affair combined. Given the slow grinding wheels of justice and the politics operating behind the scenes, it is up to the reader to determine the truth. I don't know if the victims who have not come forward will ever achieve some measure of justice. With a bit of luck this book will facilitate that process.

Many decades ago, a former British Prime Minister and one of the greatest Statesmen of the Twentieth Century wrote an inspiring statement in *The Unrelenting Struggle*, "When great causes are on the move in the world…we learn that we are spirits, not animals, and that something is going on in space and time, which, whether we like it or not, spells duty."

Winston S. Churchill

Footnotes

1. http://www.politico.com/blogs/under-the-radar/2014/12/woman-who-sued-convicted-billionaire-over-sex-abuse-levels-claims-at-his-friends-200495#ixzz3v7mNdTTy

2. http://online.wsj.com/public/resources/documents/2015_0105_dershowitz.pdf

3. http://abovethelaw.com/2015/04/the-latest-legal-superstar-to-collide-with-alan-dershowitz-david-boies/

4. Case 1:15-cv-07433 Document 1 Filed 09/21/15

5. http://www.dailymail.co.uk/news/article-2904115/Ghislaine-Maxwell-s-link-sex-scandal-court-papers-involving-Prince-Andrew-Jeffery-Epstein-don-t-stop-having-amazing-social-connections.html

6. Alan Dershowitz deposition files, October 15 & 16, 2015, Miami, Florida.

TRAFFICKING

Chapter One

Gathering of The Vultures

"You cannot change what you do not measure."

New York City, February 2005.

Minutes before the slick, 52 year-old Jeffrey E. Epstein, boarded his private plane in Teterboro, New Jersey, he rang Sarah Kellen, an attractive, blond-haired, 27 year-old woman. Kellen, a college graduate and Epstein's personal assistant was born on May 25, 1979. She worked at his Palm Beach estate on 358 El Brillo Way.

Her boss, a rich Wall Street hedge-fund manager was twenty-six years her senior. Born in Coney Island, New York, on January 20, 1953, Epstein was raised in Brooklyn to a middle class family. He graduated from Lafayette High School and learned to play classical piano early on. He was also gifted at mathematics.

Soon after his high school graduation, Epstein attended Cooper Union from 1969-1971 but did not receive a degree. Later, Epstein enrolled at the Courant Institute at New York University. Again, Epstein left without a degree.

Irrespective of his formal education, Epstein was good with numbers and found work teaching calculus and piano at the Dalton School in Manhattan. Dalton is a private, co-educational day school on the Upper East Side between Park and Madison Avenues at 96th Street. His tenure there was short lived.

Thanks to the tutorial sessions he gave after school, his life took a sharp turn, more about that later. By the late nineteen eighties and throughout the nineties, Epstein turned into a jet setting financial advisor to Leslie H. Wexner. Wexner, founder and CEO of The Limited, recently re-named L Brands, became his longtime client and close friend.

The six-foot tall, salt and pepper-haired Epstein, made so much money during the nineties that to this day he continues, 'Living the Life of Riley.' Splitting his time between several homes while satisfying his predilection for very young girls, he can still, in 2016, be spotted in the company of beautiful young girls by the *paparazzi* that follow him on the streets of New York.

Epstein who owns homes in New York, Palm Beach, London, Paris, Little St. James, a private island in the U.S. Virgin Islands and a 10,000 acre Zorro Ranch near Stanley, New Mexico, purchased some of the properties from his friend, Leslie Wexner.

Back to that fateful day, before Epstein's private jet landed in Palm Beach, he asked Kellen to have "Everyone ready and waiting." "Everyone," according to Epstein's arrest report, referred to underage girls who provided him with "sexually charged massages, three times a day."[1]

Under Kellen's vigilant supervision, *El Brillo,* Epstein's Palm Beach estate, immediately sprang into action in preparation for his arrival. After they hung up the phone, Kellen rang Haley Robson.

Robson, a 17-year-old girl at the time she met Epstein, was his dutiful subordinate. Prior to Robson's "employment" with Epstein, she was presumably a victim, who allegedly turned very quickly into a principal procurer.

During her interrogation, Robson told the police in The Probable Cause Affidavit that whenever, "Epstein told Sarah he was traveling to Palm Beach, Sarah, would contact Robson to arrange girls for Epstein because... Jeff likes to have his fun with the girls."[2]

Robson was introduced to Epstein at his Palm Beach house. She was there to give him a massage and earn a couple hundred dollars. Robson told the police that besides giving him the massage, Epstein attempted to molest her. When she rejected his sexual advances, Epstein artfully changed course and convinced the teenager to procure for him "young girls."

Epstein paid Robson two hundred dollars that day and promised to pay her two hundred more for every underage female she recruited to "work" for him. In the affidavit filed by Palm Beach Police, "work" was a euphemism for "giving Epstein (sexually explicit) massages."[3]

Oddly enough, Robson was the daughter of a retired Florida policeman. Born April 9, 1986 in rural Loxahatchee, Florida, the teenager had finished high school and enrolled at the Palm Beach Community College before she met Epstein, in or around 2004.

The two met through a mutual friend, Molly, a young woman who was approximately her age. Based on Robson's testimony, filed with the Palm Beach Police Department, Molly, her family name was unidentified, might also have been one of Epstein's victim's.

When Robson was brought in for questioning at the Palm Beach Police Department, she identified Molly as the first person who approached her to work for Epstein. Apparently they were lounging around at the Canopy Beach Resort in nearby Riviera Beach when Molly made the proposition. On the "Arrest Report," Robson described her "occupation" as "student."

The Police files stated that Molly, "Asked Robson if she wanted to make money." When Robson asked her what sort of work was involved, Molly told her friend that she would have to "provide a massage to a man and should make about two hundred dollars." Robson agreed.[4]

That same day, Molly, Robson, and a friend named Tony, family name unknown, drove to Epstein's house. Molly introduced them in Epstein's kitchen. Robson also met Epstein's assistant, Sarah Kellen. Unbeknownst to Robson at that time, Epstein's kitchen was the usual meeting place for Epstein's first-time victims. There, the girls would meet Kellen, Epstein, some of his staff and at times other procurers.

After Epstein approved, Kellen led Robson upstairs to his master bedroom. She laid out the massage table and organized the oils. Before leaving the room, Kellen told Robson, "Jeff will be here in a minute."[5]

Robson and several other victims described their first meeting with Epstein in much the same way and in great detail. A procurer always drove the girls to his house, probably because they were not old enough to drive a car or have a valid driver's license.

After Epstein approved, the girls were escorted upstairs. Either Kellen or Robson would bring the girl to his bedroom or bathroom suite. They would prepare the massage table for Epstein. The procurers or his house staff including the houseman would always pay the girls in cash. Hundreds of pages of testimony illustrated almost identical testimonies.

Almost all the victims described the grand staircase wall that led to the second floor. In one deposition Robson confirmed the walls, "Were lined with black and white poster-sized framed photographs of naked young girls and boys." Some photos, according to a victim first identified as Jane Doe #102 and later known as Virginia Louise Roberts, were images of girls he had sexually abused.[6]

"Epstein entered the bedroom wearing only a towel," as he always did during the sessions. "He removed the towel and lay nude on the massage table" then he "laid on his stomach and chose a massage-oil for her to rub on him."[7]

During the massage, Robson said, "He tried to touch me and I stopped him." The police asked Robson to describe how he tried to touch her. Robson claimed that Epstein grabbed her buttocks. That made her feel very uncomfortable, so she told Epstein, "I'll massage you but I don't want to be touched." While she performed the massage, she was naked. At the end of the massage, "Epstein paid Robson two hundred dollars."[8]

That was the first and last "massage" Robson gave Epstein according to her police statement. Robson had immediately decided this type of arrangement was not good for her.

Robson said that Epstein tried to make light of the situation and told her he understood that she felt uncomfortable, but promised to continue to pay her if she brought him other girls. "The younger the better," he said. On one occasion, Robson revealed, she tried to bring a 23-year-old female and Epstein responded, "She was too old."[9]

Apparently, Epstein's unexpected financial offer pushed Robson in the opposite direction, turning her, perhaps unwittingly, into an accomplice. Over time, she became a key procurer, who according to court files and police reports, identified, sourced and transported dozens of underage girls to Epstein's house to perform sexual favors. Robson made two hundred dollars in cash for every girl she procured.

After Robson told her story and admitted to participating in a number of likely crimes, "Sergeant Frick of the Palm Beach Police Department entered the room and explained that based on her own statements, she had implicated herself by bringing underage girls to Epstein's house. Robson then provided the cellular telephone numbers and addresses for the girls she had mentioned previously..."[10]

Robson explained that, "Once her parents discovered she had been visiting Epstein, she stopped." In a 2006 report, Robson said that, "Sara still tried to call the house and leaves messages."[11]

During her confession, Robson described how she lured another victim, a.k.a. Rosemary, to Epstein's house. On that fateful day, Robson called several underage girls from a list she had created over time. Epstein had apparently approved the list. None of the girls on her list who were all teenagers seemed to be available that day. All the girls lived on the other side of the bridge, in West Palm Beach, in the less privileged neighborhoods.

In order to make money, Robson felt obliged to find girls outside her list. Thanks to her 'boss,' Ghislaine Maxwell, an alleged procurer and Epstein's former girlfriend, cum-Girl-Friday, Robson had developed a somewhat fail-proof system of identifying the perfect candidates for their boss.

Maxwell, now in her fifties, is the daughter of the late, Elisabeth "Betty" Maxwell (*nee* Meynard) and Robert Maxwell. In 1991, father Maxwell, a former British Member of Parliament (MP) and media tycoon, was either killed or committed suicide. The circumstances of his death remain a mystery. Media reports maintain that he disappeared while sailing in the Canary Islands on his yacht, *The Lady Ghislaine*, christened in honor of his youngest daughter, Ghislaine.

A few media reports attributed the elder Maxwell's death to the Mossad while others maintained he was besieged by debt and consequently ended his life. During my investigation, a former Mossad agent, who wishes to remain anonymous, suggested the Mossad killed Maxwell. Whatever the truth is, Maxwell died a tragic death given the many blessings bestowed upon him throughout his colorful life.

Unlike her father, Ghislaine was known as a "fixer." She has to this day an impressive list of friends from around the globe including presidents, heads of state and a bouquet of British aristocrats. For years, she was known as the go between former President Clinton and Epstein.

On July 31, 2010 Maxwell was among the few guests to attend Chelsea Clinton's wedding at the former Astor estate in Rhinebeck, New York. This auspicious event followed an embarrassing incident for Maxwell, only a few months earlier, while attending the Clinton Global Initiative. At the end of an Indian summer, in September 2009, a process server walked through the packed lobby of the Sheraton Hotel on Eighth Avenue in New York City and served Ghislaine Maxwell.

Maxwell was huddled in a small group talking to other guests as the server approached her. He called out her name. With so many people surrounding her, Maxwell was unsuspecting. Maxwell confirmed her identity and he served her notice. The deposition was in relation to Epstein's sexual abuse case. The server left at once.

Ironically, a photograph of Maxwell taken by a private investigator who accompanied the process server showed Maxwell receiving notice while standing beneath a human trafficking banner. Human trafficking was the Conference's theme at the 2009 Clinton Global Initiative.

Maxwell never appeared at the deposition claiming, the day prior to her testimony, she had to immediately return to England to care for her dying mother. At the time of that trip, the elder Mrs. Maxwell was not gravely ill. Not long after the deposition was scheduled, Maxwell was spotted in New York again. Because Maxwell was a British subject, there was nothing the attorneys could do to force her to take the deposition.

It was Maxwell, according to Haley Robson, who apparently instructed her and several victims, including Virginia Louise Roberts (also known as Jane Doe #102), how to procure young girls for Epstein.

Court files indicate that Maxwell familiarized most of 'Epstein's girls' with his likes, dislikes, and the type of adolescent victims he desired. Britain's *Daily Mail* published several stories about a number of survivors who came forward and exposed how Maxwell instructed them on the ways to best to service Epstein.

Among the many recruits Maxwell introduced to Epstein and hired to "work" at the Palm Beach house, was a young Johanna Sjoberg. The attorney, Brad Edwards, an arduous former lead trial attorney from Broward County, said that unlike most other girls, Sjoberg was twenty and a college student when they met.

The "all-American brunette," who according to her story grew up in "a church going family," entered Epstein's household, in 2001, as an occasional 'housekeeper.' Sjoberg candidly described her meeting with Maxwell and the "strange proposition" that followed.[12]

The young woman was studying psychology at Atlantic College in Palm Beach wanting to become a family therapist when Maxwell approached her. Apparently, sometime around midday Maxwell spotted Sjoberg sitting on a campus bench near one of the parking areas.

Maxwell walked toward the girl and introduced herself and began a conversation. Not long into their talk she offered Sjoberg part-time work, "Twenty an hour to answer the phones and serve occasional drinks at Epstein's Palm Beach home." Sjoberg admitted she, "thought it was a great opportunity! It seemed pretty easy. I felt as if I had fallen into a pot of gold. All my friends were jealous of me for getting such a great job."[13]

On January 27, 2010 Brad Edwards said that according to Sjoberg's testimony, "Epstein paid for her college and living expenses, etc." Soon thereafter, Maxwell made her another type of proposition: "Do you want to make $100 rubbing feet?" Sjoberg replied, "I would love to do that."[14]

It was then Epstein befriended Sjoberg. In no time, he invited her to his New York triplex to meet HRH Prince Andrew. According to Sjoberg's affidavit, "It was Easter 2001, when I first met Prince Andrew." Maxwell and another victim, Virginia Louise Roberts were there, in addition to a couple of other underage girls unnamed in the deposition."[15]

Sjoberg described how, "Ghislaine came down from the second floor with a present for Prince Andrew—a latex puppet of him from Spitting Image." They all had their picture taken together Sjoberg said. "Virginia and another girl sat on a chair," according to the woman and, "Virginia had the puppet on her lap. Andrew sat on another chair, while I sat on his lap..."[16]

"He put his hand on my breast. Ghislaine put the puppet's hand on Virginia's breast, and then, Andrew put his hand on mine... Ghislaine made a lot of sexual jokes...She had a very dirty sense of humor." Eventually, Sjoberg was lured to perform sexual services for Epstein. She claims she refused. Sjoberg also kept quiet for many years.[17]

Unlike Roberts, Sjoberg was an adult. She could not have accused Epstein of sexual abuse with a minor although she might have been able to bring charges of sexual harassment since she claimed, "I felt preyed upon all the same."[18]

The other victim staying at his house, Virginia Louise Roberts, was in New York as part of Epstein's entourage. She was fifteen years old at the time. In 2005, Roberts' spoke to the FBI during the investigation. Years later, in 2011, Roberts spoke again only this time she went public and sold her story to a popular London tabloid, Mail On Sunday. Roberts' alleged that for many years after she "escaped," from his "clutches," she lived in Australia for fear of Epstein's wrath.

One of dozens of depositions taken during the civil investigation stated that Epstein disliked African-American girls, whatever their age and beauty. In the Statement of Facts, Case # 09-80656, filed May 1, 2009 in the Southern District Court of Florida, the representing attorney wrote, "To the Plaintiff's knowledge, the only females specifically excluded from Defendant's sexual escapades were African Americans."[19]

Apparently, Epstein wanted 'his girls' to be very young, pretty and fair skinned. I suspect he also preferred underage girls who came from disadvantaged families in case they decided to go public and report him to the police.

In one of the depositions, Brad Edwards identified the initials of a number of victims he represented who had agreed to come forward. They are: "S.G.; A.D.; V.A.; N.R.; J.S.; V.Z.; J.A.; F.E.; M.L.; M.D.; D.D., and D.N. These girls were between the ages of 13 and 17 when Epstein allegedly abused them." Every girl testified independently. Edwards, has invested more than ten years defending Epstein's victims and in the process has argued forcefully on behalf of Childs Right's.[20]

* * *

Footnotes

1. Arrest Notice To Appear. Palm Beach Police Department Incident Report. Case #05-368 (2). Probable Cause Affidavit. Filed May 1, 2006. Arresting Officer Det. Joe Recarey.

2. Arrest Notice to Appear. Palm Beach Police Department Incident Report Case #05-368. (3) May 1, 2006.

3. http://www.reuters.com/article/dershowitz-lawsuit-boies-idUSL1N0XK1VL20150423#pRtAhxiOIhyv6gxi.97

4. Case 1:15-cv-07433 Document 1 Filed 09/21/15

5. http://abovethelaw.com/2015/04/the-latest-legal-superstar-to-collide-with-alan-dershowitz-david-boies/

6. http://www.dailymail.co.uk/news/article-3245036/Virginia-Roberts-claimed-sex-Prince-Andrew-sues-British-socialite-Ghislaine-Maxwell-denying-claims-recruited-sex-slave.html

7. Arrest Notice to Appear. Jeffrey Epstein Probable Cause Affidavit. Police Case #05-368. Palm Beach Police Department. March 15, 2005. (1)

8. Probable Cause Affidavit, Palm Beach Police Department Agency ORI # FLO 500600. Police Case # 05-368 (3). Defendant Haley Robson. May 1, 2006.

9. Probable Cause Affidavit, Palm Beach Police Department Agency ORI # FLO 500600. Police Case # 05-368 (3). Defendant Haley Robson. May 1, 2006.

10. Probable Cause Affidavit, Palm Beach Police Department Agency ORI # FLO 500600. Police Case # 05-368 (2). Defendant Haley Robson. May 1, 2006

11. Arrest Notice to Appear. Palm Beach Police Department Police Case #05-368 (2) Defendant Haley Robson. May 1, 2006.

12. http://docplayer.net/4070674-Exhibit-c-epstein-vs-edwards-undisputed-statement-of-facts.html

13. http://docplayer.net/4070674-Exhibit-c-epstein-vs-edwards-undisputed-statement-of-facts.html

14. http://docplayer.net/4070674-Exhibit-c-epstein-vs-edwards-undisputed-statement-of-facts.html

15. http://docplayer.net/4070674-Exhibit-c-epstein-vs-edwards-undisputed-statement-of-facts.html

16. http://docplayer.net/4070674-Exhibit-c-epstein-vs-edwards-undisputed-statement-of-facts.html

17. http://docplayer.net/4070674-Exhibit-c-epstein-vs-edwards-undisputed-statement-of-facts.html

18. Civil Action Case #09-80656: Clerk U.S. District Court Southern District of Fla. Miami, Florida.

19. Statement of Facts, Case # 09-80656, filed May 1, 2009 in the Southern District Court of Florida

20. http://cases.bms11.com/Documents/FL76/09-34791/ECF_DOC_1603_10567451.pdf

Chapter Two

Sodom and Gomorrah

The criminal investigation formally began March 15, 2005. It ended February 2006. During that period, the Palm Beach Police Department conducted a sexual battery investigation of Jeffrey Epstein, Sarah Kellen, Haley Robson and Ghislaine Maxwell.

After a one-year police investigation that concluded in February 2006, the Palm Beach Police Department decided that the defendants should be charged with sexual battery felonies. Epstein was charged with "unlawful Sexual Activity with a Minor (4) counts and Lewd and Lascivious Molestation. Robson was charged with Lewd and Lascivious Act on a child under 16 years of age (1) count and Kellen was charged with Principal in the 1st Unlawful Sexual Activity with a Minor (4) counts and Principal in the 1st Lewd and Lascivious Molestation (1) count." Maxwell was not charged. Why?[1]

Dozens of sworn statements were taken from five victims and seventeen witnesses. All the witnesses gave testimonies relating to criminal sexual activities that occurred at Epstein's Palm Beach residence.

Epstein's pilots, Larry Visoski and David Rogers, the former house managers, Juan Alessi and Alfredo Rodriguez, and the entire Palm Beach staff were interrogated. Several more victims beside those identified in the police reports were brought in for questioning. The sworn statements revealed that Epstein usually paid the victims directly or via his staff, to provide him with special 'massages.'

At the beginning of the investigation, in order to determine the range of crimes perpetrated and the number of adolescents recruited, the Palm Beach Police together with the Sanitation Bureau of the Town of Palm Beach hid trash pulls outside Epstein's house. This was done to retrieve the trash.

Telephone messages and other information discarded inside the bins helped the police learn a great deal more about Epstein and his staff. Important messages were found from one particular victim, Jane Doe #102 whose deposition was filed on May 1, 2009. Her case, *Jane Doe #102 v. Jeffrey Epstein,* best illustrates the scope of crimes committed by Epstein and his entourage of procurers.

On February 6, 2005, Haley Robson made the fatal mistake of calling "Rosemary," known as "Jane Doe 1" in the original criminal investigation because she was the first victim to come forward. Rosemary was also Robson's neighbor and a family friend. According to the Police Report, on the day Rosemary and Epstein first met, her academic life was fragile at best.[2]

The fourteen-year old American girl of Cuban extraction was very pretty. She was fair-skinned, soft-spoken and demure. Rosemary had large brown eyes and long brown silky hair. She wore reading glasses. She was attending a school for kids with special needs when she met Epstein. Although her parents were divorced, her family lived in Royal Palm Beach about twenty minutes north of Palm Beach. Rosemary had a twin sister who did not meet Epstein. Rosemary lived mostly at school during the week and would spend most weekends with her father and stepmother. Her twin lived with their mother.

Early during her childhood, Jane's father had gone through a series of jobs including several construction projects that never worked out. By exposing his family to financial hardship, the father's lack of steady employment threatened the marriage and his ability to meet his parental responsibilities, according to Jane's mother. Her parents eventually divorced. Both parents later remarried. Living in this family environment was very difficult for Rosemary and created a breeding ground for trouble- the kind of trouble- adolescents find difficult to get out of.

During the investigation, her father testified to the police that the first time his daughter met Epstein was on Sunday, February 6, 2005. According to the deposition, her father was unaware of his daughter's whereabouts that day and thought she was being driven to a nearby shopping mall by Haley Robson. Instead, Rosemary--"was driven to Epstein's house by Robson and a Hispanic female in a pick up truck in order to provide a massage for him." It turned out the Hispanic looking female was in fact Adriana Ross who was Eastern European.[3]

When they arrived at Epstein's gate, Epstein's houseman, Alfredo Rodriguez, according to the police report, let them through. Rodriguez worked for Epstein from November 2004 until May 2005. During the interrogation, Rosemary told the Palm Beach Police she had "met the house chef in the kitchen." Minutes later the girl was introduced to Sarah Kellen and Epstein. After a brief introduction, perhaps five minutes or so, Epstein approved and left the kitchen. Kellen led the girl upstairs and into the master bedroom.[4]

Once inside the bedroom, Kellen prepared the massage table located inside his large bathroom suite. Rosemary said the bathroom was so large it contained a couch. Epstein entered the room wearing only a towel. He dropped it exposing himself completely.

Before he lay on the table Epstein told Rosemary to take off her clothes. Nervous and frightened Rosemary did as she was told. "It was hard," she said, "to be believable in his eyes." So she took off her clothes, save for the undergarments, and began to give Epstein a massage. She was so short that she could not stand up tall enough to reach his back.[5]

Although Rosemary never acknowledged this during our taped interview, the police report stated Epstein used a purple vibrator to massage her vagina. According to the Notice to Appear/Arrest Report, there was no penetration as the vibrator was on top of her undergarments.

While driving to Epstein's house, Robson had instructed Rosemary to say she was eighteen if anyone asked. Rosemary said that while she was "massaging" Epstein she pretended to be eighteen; acting and talking like what she thought an eighteen-year-old girl would be. She had to constantly remind herself not to act so fidgety.

At fourteen, like most teenage girls her age, Rosemary was not very mature and did not know how to behave in situations that were inappropriate for her age. Several times during the interview she repeated how strange she felt to be in the company of such an "old man" and know what to do to make him believe she was 18.

The videotaped interview I produced and later posted in The Daily Beast on January 25, 2015, revealed that "Epstein must have known I was younger than 18 because I had no boobs and was little and very skinny, like a shrimp," Rosemary said.[6]

At some point during the "massage, "Epstein grabbed her buttocks and pulled her close to him." Rosemary confessed that Epstein made her feel uncomfortable, but was too nervous to say anything. At the end of the massage, she was paid three hundred dollars rather than the usual two hundred, "because, he said, I watched him masturbate." Rosemary claimed she never returned to Epstein's house.[7]

The girl confirmed that after the investigation began, Epstein's representatives constantly harassed her. A man followed her from school several times. She does not remember his name. A man, she does not remember his name, rang her many times at home almost everyday to ask if she was going to testify. The man on the phone offered her monetary compensation to prevent her from testifying. She said they made her life miserable and almost unbearable.

I believed Rosemary was telling the truth because, in 2009, a similar situation happened to me. One morning a friend rang me. I did not know my friend was also friendly with Epstein so I spoke candidly about my research and the book during our conversation. I had no reason to suspect otherwise. During our conversation our friend made an offer.

Would I continue to write this book if I were given five million dollars? I challenged our friend. My friend repeated the offer and said that five million dollars would be "a life changer." That assumption was correct. Five million dollars would have been a "life changer," only it would have changed my life in the wrong direction.

That same year, 2009, I found Rosemary's mother. A kind, soft-spoken, Southern woman, Mrs. Doe, moved out of Florida shortly after the scandal broke and was living further north. For security reasons and fear of what Epstein might do to her family, she does not wish to be identified.

By the time we met, Mrs. Doe was remarried and working a full time job. She was trying to go about her life and forget the Epstein case ever existed. It was challenging. Over the course of two years, we had many conversations and eventually struck up a friendship.

At one point, she acknowledged how agonizing her life had become during the criminal investigation. She was angry at the system and more upset at her ex husband for forcing their young daughter into a life-altering situation.

Mrs. Doe revealed that her daughter had never wanted to move forward with the investigation. In fact, it was Rosemary's father who insisted their daughter talk to the police. The father had found out about his daughter's meeting Epstein through his then wife, Rosemary's stepmother. The story went like this.

Rosemary was talking on the telephone with a friend sharing her secret about the encounter with Epstein. Perhaps mistakenly, the friend's mother picked up the line. She eavesdropped on their conversation. According to Rosemary, the mother immediately rang Rosemary's stepmother and told her what she had overheard. The following day Rosemary's friend, who apparently was not such a good friend after all, started to spread rumors at school. She revealed Rosemary's secret.

Word spread quickly. There was even a physical altercation between Rosemary and another girl and both were brought into the Principal's office. Two hundred dollars was found in her handbag. Eventually, Rosemary confessed. Her parents were called in. Rosemary admitted she had been paid $200 to give "an old man" who lived in Palm Beach a massage.

At the time of the investigation, her father, a thirty something year old Cuban-American, was not financially secure. For many years he had been unable to provide for his young family. Perhaps he was searching for retribution or conceivably he wanted to right a wrong. Whatever the reason he decided the police should be informed of his daughter's incident.

After their first visit to the police department he hired a lawyer to represent Rosemary. Unhappy with their choice of legal representation they decided to change lawyers. Soon after, they met Brad Edwards. Edwards currently a partner at Farmer, Jaffe, Weissing, & Edwards PL agreed to represent Rosemary.

Under a 1997 Florida State law, it is a felony for an adult to practice massage without a massage therapist license. It is also against the law for anyone under the age of 18 and without a high school diploma or graduate equivalency diploma (GED) to provide massage therapy. A minimum of 500 hours and a board approved massage course must be completed and certified to practice massage therapy.

Throughout the investigation Rosemary was an emotional wreck. The police report revealed that on October 4, 2005, Kellen left Rosemary a voice message asking her to call. Kellen wanted to know about Rosemary's conversations with the police. Kellen left her cell number. It seemed odd that Kellen would know about Rosemary's visit to the police unless someone on the inside was on the take. So far, no one has exposed the informant.

When we first spoke, Rosemary hardly said a word. It was difficult for her to trust me and open up no matter how much I tried. It was difficult to get through to her. I suppose it was tough for the young girl to trust an outsider after what she had gone through during the criminal investigation. I'm sure she did not want to relive her worst nightmare.

In spite of the many sworn testimonies, the Palm Beach Police Department also had a difficult time convincing the federal government to investigate the case. All charges were eventually dropped. Robson's information along with several others alleged procurers and victims were ultimately submitted to the Grand Jury.[13]

In 2009, I reached out to Robson several times. She did not return my calls. Unable to convey Robson's version of the story there are details that will remain a mystery. Epstein's attorneys, who are also not talking for now, are mindful of Robson's long list of secrets and suspected crimes. Perhaps, after publication of this book, victims who have not come forward will find the courage to do so.

Kellen, Robson, Ross, Groff, Marcinkova and Maxwell apparently committed unjustifiable sex crimes against countless underage girls if police reports are accurate. Yet, in spite of the overwhelming evidence, the United States Attorney's Office was unable to convict them for the suspected crimes committed against the underage girls.

A number of criminal attorneys following this case suggested that, "Hardball tactics and 'chits' leveraged by Epstein's attorneys during the negotiations with the Justice Department, insulated the procurers from criminal prosecution."

* * *

Sometimes, she would talk for only five minutes then make up some excuse and quickly hang up. This happened many times over the course of a year before the entire story surfaced.

Thanks to the relationship I developed with Rosemary's mother, the girl finally agreed to meet and give me an on camera interview. She was approximately 20 years old, nervous and timid when we first met in person. It was around mid morning in Palm Beach. We agreed to meet at a well-known open-air boutique mall on Worth Avenue. I wanted her to feel safe and at ease so I brought along a female friend and well known TV anchor who was with us during the interview.

The interview went very well. Rosemary was receptive and informative. Segments of that interview are available on The Daily Beast filed January 25, 2015, "Before Randy Andy's Accuser, A Jane Doe #1."

Rosemary has come a long way since our first telephone conversation. She is tender, sweet and soft-spoken perhaps with a perceptible wariness of men. Now a college graduate she found work that she enjoys. Recently, she became engaged to a wonderful young man. Outwardly, she seems happy although admits she is still ashamed and does not like to talk about the incident. Mrs. Doe explained that her daughter still bristles at the mention of Epstein's name.

The last time we spoke, in 2015, Rosemary told me she wanted to put the entire incident behind and move forward with her life. She is quickly moving in the right direction. Rosemary and her twin sister remain very close and they both have wonderful relationships with their mother who is now a proud grandmother. She prefers not to talk about the relationship with her father. I have no doubt that as she matures she will evolve into an even stronger and more caring woman. She is one of the lucky few to have emotionally survived because she has an extraordinary role model.

As for Rosemary's procurer, Haley Robson, the Complaint and Demand for Jury Trial filed on May 1, 2009 in *Jane Doe #102 vs. Jeffrey Epstein* stated that, "On the day of Epstein's arrest, police found two hidden cameras and photographs of underage girls on a computer in Defendant's home." No charges were filed against Robson and she remains free. According to an online social media app, in 2006, she was living in Orlando, Florida.[8]

Robson came to the police station voluntarily after Sergeant Frick and Officer Recarey drove to her home for questioning. Following the interrogation at the police station she was driven home again. During the drive back a tape recorder inside the police car was turned on to record conversations.

Some time during the drive, Robson made a strange revealing her arrangement with Epstein. 'I'm like a Heidi Robson told the police, "referring to the Hollywood mad television personality who ran an infamous prostitution ring Angeles, California.[9]

The other alleged pimps who worked directly for and were identified in police reports and depositions in Leslie Groff, Nadia Marcinkova, Ghislaine Maxwell, and A Ross Muscinska, a Polish girl living in Miami.[10]

During her deposition, following in her former footsteps, Ross-Muscinska, who Rosemary first identified young Hispanic woman and friend of Haley Robson's, cit Fifth Amendment throughout the entire testimony in or protect herself from self-incrimination. Many times she br responded, "I refuse to answer."[11]

For several years, Robson was at the epicenter of Eps life although she told the police that her relationship with E did not start out that way. As a matter of fact, the first time met Epstein told her, "I was too old for him." Robson was 17 old.[12]

It remains unclear for what length of time Robson pro underage girls for Epstein, although there was a period of at two years during which Epstein paid her for every girl procured for him according to legal filings. As their relatio grew, court documents confirmed, Epstein came to rely or services more than any other procurer with the possible exce of Maxwell and Kellen.

Footnotes

1. Probable Cause Affidavit, Palm Beach Police Department Agency ORI # FLO 500600. Police Case # 05-368 (3). Defendant Haley Robson. May 1, 2006.

2. Probable Cause Affidavit, Palm Beach Police Department Agency ORI # FLO 500600. Police Case # 05-368 (3). Defendant Haley Robson. May 1, 2006.

3. Probable Cause Affidavit, Palm Beach Police Department Agency ORI # FLO 500600. Police Case # 05-368 (3). Defendant Haley Robson. May 1, 2006.

4. Probable Cause Affidavit, Palm Beach Police Department Agency ORI # FLO 500600. Police Case # 05-368 (3). Defendant Haley Robson. May 1, 2006.

5. Probable Cause Affidavit, Palm Beach Police Department Agency ORI # FLO 500600. Police Case # 05-368 (3). Defendant Haley Robson. May 1, 2006.

6. Probable Cause Affidavit, Palm Beach Police Department Agency ORI # FLO 500600. Police Case # 05-368 (3). Defendant Haley Robson. May 1, 2006.

7. http://www.thedailybeast.com/articles/2015/01/25/epstein-s-first-accuser-tells-her-story.htmlhttp://www.thedailybeast.com/articles/2015/01/25/epstein-s-first-accuser-tells-her-story.html

8. Complaint and Demand for Jury Trial filed on May 1, 2009 in *Jane Doe #102 vs. Jeffrey Epstein*

9. http://www.thedailybeast.com/articles/2015/01/25/epstein-s-first-accuser-tells-her-story.html

10. http://www.thedailybeast.com/articles/2015/01/25/epstein-s-first-accuser-tells-her-story.html

11. http://www.thesundaytimes.co.uk/sto/news/uk_news/Peopl e/article576480.ece

12. Probable Cause Affidavit, Palm Beach Police Department Agency ORI # FLO 500600. Police Case # 05-368 (3). Defendant Haley Robson. May 1, 2006, p.5

13. Probable Cause Affidavit, Palm Beach Police Department Agency ORI # FLO 500600. Police Case # 05-368 (3). Defendant Haley Robson. May 1, 2006, p.5

Chapter Three

Principal Procurers

The five foot eight, hazel-eyed, Sarah Lynnelle Kellen soon became a suspect. An attractive brunette, Kellen was also young, calculating, and driven. Kellen and Robson worked closely together.

At first, when Kellen was brought in for questioning she told the police a number of misleading facts including her home address. Kellen resided in South Florida and gave the police Epstein's New York business address as her own. In fact, the address written on the police report, The Villard Mansion at 457 Madison Avenue, New York City is an office building. It was never her home address.

The Villar House is one of the most prestigious and smallest of commercial properties in New York. It adjoins the New York Palace Hotel. The two-story architectural gem constructed in 1884, and designed by McKim, Mead & White sits between 51st and 50th Street in midtown Manhattan. As the former parish house to St. Patrick's Cathedral it remains a popular tourist destination. Back in the late eighties and early nineties, Epstein had leased an office space on the second floor. Epstein's offices have since closed.

Kellen's sworn statement and inaccurate details should have drawn immediate concern with the police and later the Federal Bureau of Investigation. If Kellen could have so easily lied about her home address, other more important facts could just as easily have been fabricated. To this day, nothing about Kellen appears genuine.

In 2010, after the Daily Beast stories posted, Epstein's principal assistant changed her name from Sarah Kellen to Sarah Kensington. She adopted her mother's maiden name in an obvious effort to hide from her past and ongoing friendship with Epstein. In 2009, I rang Kellen several times. She did not return my calls.

Sworn taped statements were taken from five victims and seventeen witnesses regarding massages and unlawful sexual activity that took place at his Palm Beach residence. Some facts were discovered in the police report—primarily, Kellen's principal role as procurer, her close relationship with Epstein and Maxwell, and the multiple introductions of underage girls she provided Epstein.

Exhibit C, document #1603-3 filed on 4/8/11 titled the *Undisputed Statement of Facts in the Epstein vs. Edwards Case pages 1 and 2* stated the, "Defendant, Epstein, has a sexual preference for young girls... He repeatedly assaulted more than 40 young girls on numerous occasions between 2002-2005 in his mansion in Palm Beach, Florida."[1]

Several of the victims were recruited and brought to the residence by Haley Robson to perform massages for Epstein, for which Robson received monetary compensation. During their visits the girls would be introduced to Sarah Kellen in the kitchen, who apparently recorded their telephone numbers and names.

During the visits, the girls were introduced to Kellen and or Robson, and then Epstein. Once he gave his approval, one of the two women would escort the victim to Epstein's bedroom to provide the massage. Most meetings between the underage victims and Epstein first took place in the presence of Sarah Kellen and Haley Robson.[2]

Once inside his bedroom, "Epstein would rub his fingers on their vaginas and on occasion introduce a massager/vibrator or rub the victim's vaginas as they gave him 'the massage.' On three known separate occasions, according to the report, Epstein had intercourse and inserted his penis and fingers in the victim's vaginas."[3]

"At the end of each massage the victims were paid between two hundred and one thousand dollars." Several depositions revealed the assaults included vaginal penetration. Epstein abused dozens if not hundreds of girls over a period of several years.[4]

During a sworn taped interview, recorded in Sarah Kellen's Probable Cause Affidavit, the Arresting Officer, Joe Recarey, said that when he executed the search warrant at Epstein's home he, "Located various phone message books. First names of girls, dates and telephone numbers were on the copy of the messages."

Officer Recarey recognized some of the names and numbers of the girls since they had been interviewed at the station. "The messages included the time of day they called and Kellen's signature at the bottom of the messages.[5]

Several victims confirmed the interior of his bedroom. One victim said that, "Upon entering his room there was a large bathroom to the right and a hot pink and green sofa in the room. There was a door on each side of the sofa. Some girls rememberd a mural of a naked woman in the room, as well as several photographs of naked women on a shelf." Two years later, while taking his deposition, when asked about these allegations, Epstein pled the Fifth Amendment from beginning to end.[6]

In addition to paying a multitude of women and young girls to procure for him, Epstein befriended a different type of procurer. The co founder and eighty-five (85%) stakeholder of a modeling agency, MC2, was a Frenchman known as Jean Luc Brunel. For many years, Brunel apparently provided a dozen or more young and underage models for Epstein. A story posted in the Daily Mail on January 18, 2016, suggested that Brunel continues his association with Epstein and has been providing young models to please his friend for many years.[7]

"Model, Svetlana Pozhidaeva, was spotted leaving the Epstein house, in Manhattan, while eating a whole avocado. The brown-haired, blue eyed beauty-who often goes by 'Lana'—is represented by MC2 Model Management in New York and Elite Model Management in Milan."[8]

It seems strange that the 71 year-old Frenchman who sued his friend, Epstein, in January 2015 for unspecified damages, as the Complaint revealed, would allow his young employee, a model under contract, visit and associate with the defendant only one year after he sued his friend. If Brunel believed that Epstein ruined his business and reputation, as he claimed in the lawsuit, why would he allow 'Lana' to visit Epstein at his home?[9]

'Lana' claims she is not underage and has a college degree. Her social media app also revealed she had obtained a 'politics degree' in Moscow before moving to the U.S. Beside 'Lana,' other young women of unidentified ages have been photographed outside his Manhattan triplex following his registration as a sexual offender.

When asked by the Daily Mail about their relationship with Epstein, none of the young women photographed were willing to talk to the reporters.[10]

On March 8, 2016, Richard Johnson published another story about Epstein and the model, 'Lana,' in The New York Post. According to his source, a woman living inside Epstein's Manhattan triplex confirmed that Epstein still had girls of unidentified ages brought from Russia. The Russian girls, revealed Johnson's source, were living with Epstein in New York and traveling together on his private jet to his island home. When I spoke with Johnson via e-mail, he said that with the exception of Svetlana, the informant did not know if other girls associated with Epstein worked for MC2.

Perhaps for fear of retribution, the girls and the employees for MC2 and Epstein are not talking. Epstein apparently has contacts in Moscow who make the introduction to the girls and, "When the Russian girls arrive in the city, they already have Jeffrey's phone number," the New York Post reported.[11]

Photographs and multiple media reports illustrated that some girls who continue to visit Epstein are American born girls but not all. As this reports showed, several come from Russia too. Given the usually stringent requirements enforced by the probation enforcement guidelines especially registered level 3 sex offenders in the State of New York, it is surprising no one has filed a Complaint and that the District Attorneys Office in Manhattan has investigated Epstein's current relationships with the very young women who frequent his Manhattan home.

Brunel's history with Epstein dates back to the late eighties. Brunel moved to the United States from France supposedly because he and his brother, who jointly owned a modeling agency in Paris, were quarreling over the business. A Brunel insider explained, the agent had unresolved legal issues with his brother and was forced to leave the country. He exiled to New York where he first met Epstein. They soon became close friends.

Maritza Vazquez a former accountant at MC2 and associate of Brunel's revealed in a 2010 interview that Epstein generously agreed to fund Brunel's MC2 agency by providing a generous 'loan' of one million dollars. Not long after she discovered the extent of the Epstein-Brunel association, Vazquez was fired from MC2 and charged with embezzling company funds. Vazquez has a criminal record.[12]

After the Daily Beast published the story, Brunel and Epstein vehemently denied it. All the same, the accountant's information was correct and became part of Brunel's legal filing in his 2015 complaint against investor and friend, Jeffrey Epstein.

With Brunel and MC2 as Epstein's presumed 'partners-in-crime,' Epstein was seemingly able to create a well-structured trafficking network that sourced, transferred and distributed young women from all over the world, some assumingly underage, into the United States without suspicion.

Their business model seems similar to the Russian and Ukrainian trafficking cartels that smuggle children to the United States for the purposes of sex trafficking. The cartels set up modeling, au pair and domestic staffing agencies in their countries as the perfect alibi. They lure the girls under false pretenses and then apply for U.S. visas and all the necessary documents for the girls to work or study in the U.S. By observing stringent U.S. Immigration laws, agencies remain under the radar.

The Epstein-Brunel association apparently found the way to source and transport underage girls legally by employing them under false pretenses as models hired for work at MC2. This model corroborated the testimony given by a number of the victims in their depositions, that Epstein promised some of the underage girls modeling jobs at MC2 and Victoria's Secret. It is also true however that some girls brought into the U.S. by MC2 are in fact working models. The question is: what percentage of those girls brought into the U.S. actually earn a living as MC2 models?

Over the years, it seems Epstein relied heavily on Brunel's friendship and modeling business to source underage girls for sex. Evidently, thanks to his one million dollar capital investment in MC2, the predator was introduced to a slew of underage and pretty young girls. According to Maritza Vazquez and Sergio Cordero, a former Brunel associate and source I had interviewed in Miami, Florida. Cordero also knew Epstein and worked with Brunel and MC2 for more than ten years.

Brunel's lawsuit against Epstein also disclosed that one year after opening his agency, Brunel, "received a letter of credit from Epstein at 5% interest." The case, *Brunel vs. Epstein*, filed as No 14-21348CA- 01, in the Dade County Eleventh Judicial Circuit Court, accused Epstein of accountability for MC2's losses and Brunel's current financial distress.

Brunel explained in paragraph nine of the Complaint that he, "Lost multiple contacts and business in the modeling business as a direct result of Epstein's illegal actions." In paragraph 22, Brunel's attorney claimed that his client, "Lost potentially ten million dollars in profits to his $1 million loan."[13]

Documents filed during the lawsuit exposed that, "MC2 employees told the attorney, Brad Edwards, who at the time was representing several victims, that Epstein's Manhattan condominium at 301 East 66th Street was used to house the young models."

The Complaint also made public that, "MC2 brought underage girls from all over the world, promising them modeling contracts. Epstein and Brunel would obtain a visa for the girls and would charge the underage girls rent."[14]

Brunel admitted he, "Evaded depositions by Brad Edwards on behalf of several of Epstein's victims and that his "Evasion was due to Epstein's instructions." In paragraph 33, Brunel disclosed that Epstein insisted he "leave Palm Beach in anticipation of a deposition linked to Epstein's criminal case."[15]

Other relevant charges in the *Brunel vs. Epstein* case revealed that Brunel, "Was forced to commit illegal acts by traveling away from the sight of the deposition and during the time period of the deposition." Epstein's instructions prevented Brunel from clearing his name and explaining the relationship with Epstein in order to clear his name from any wrongdoing. Brunel claimed, "Epstein attempted to subvert justice and contributed to the destruction of my business, MC2."[16]

Two former underage survivors who don't wish to be identified came forward in 2009 and 2010. The girls corroborated the information revealed in the Brunel Complaint and went a step further. They said that Epstein lured some victims by baiting them with potential modeling contracts if they "massaged" him. They mentioned MC2 and Victoria's Secret. Victoria's Secret is a lingerie chain owned by Epstein's friend, Leslie Wexner.

Jérôme Bonnouvrier, a Brunel acquaintance told the press that, "Jean-Luc is considered a danger." According to Bonnouvrier, Brunel "Knows exactly what girls in trouble are looking for. He's always been on the edge of the system. The late John Casablanca, a renowned model agent, gets with girls the healthy way. Girls would be with him if he were the butcher. They're with Jean-Luc because he's the boss. Jean-Luc likes drugs and silent rape. It excites him."[17]

"I really despise Jean-Luc as a human being for the way he's cheapened the business," said the celebrated Casablanca, who died in 2013. "There is no justice. This is a guy who should be behind bars. There was a little group, Jean-Luc, Patrick Gilles, and Varsano...They were very well known in Paris for roaming the clubs. They would invite girls and put drugs in their drinks. Everybody knew they were creeps."[18]

Vazquez and the two survivors, who asked to remain unidentified, acknowledged that MC2 provided legal passage and all the necessary visa requirements to transport the girls into the United States, including all appropriate documentation that would allow them to earn a salary and work as models independent of their age.

Apparently, Epstein, not one to forfeit a good deal, at times generously provided accommodations as well as transportation to some of the young models coming to work for MC2.

Epstein's building, at East 66th Street in Manhattan, managed by his younger brother, Mark Epstein, is the apartment complex on Second Avenue known to house some of the girls. The building presumably continues to provide a few accommodations for several foreign-born models that allegedly work for MC2. MC2 has offices in Tel Aviv, Miami and a satellite office in New York.

Although sex trafficking is a crime against humanity it is disguised in many forms. The business of luring, coercing, and transporting underage girls for sex can be implemented in many ways and is punishable in the United States by the State and Federal Courts.

The United States government is aggressively prosecuting most trafficking networks- large and small, local operators or international cartels working with local operators who engage in a "Combination of deception, fraud, coercion, rape, threats, physical violence, isolation, intimidation, psychological manipulation, to compel their victims to engage in prostitution," under state and federal laws including the most current re authorized Trafficking Victims Protection Act (TVPA).

* * *

Footnotes

1. Probable Cause Affidavit, Palm Beach Police Department Agency ORI # FLO 500600. Police Case # 05-368 (3). Defendant Haley Robson. May 1, 2006, p.1

2. Probable Cause Affidavit, Palm Beach Police Department Agency ORI # FLO 500600. Police Case # 05-368 (3). Defendant Haley Robson. May 1, 2006, p.1

3. Probable Cause Affidavit, Palm Beach Police Department Agency ORI # FLO 500600. Police Case # 05-368 (3). Defendant Haley Robson. May 1, 2006, p.1

4. Probable Cause Affidavit, Palm Beach Police Department Agency ORI # FLO 500600. Police Case # 05-368 (3). Defendant Haley Robson. May 1, 2006, p.1

5. Probable Cause Affidavit, Palm Beach Police Department Agency ORI # FLO 500600. Police Case # 05-368 (3). Defendant Haley Robson. May 1, 2006, p. 18

6. Probable Cause Affidavit, Palm Beach Police Department Agency ORI # FLO 500600. Police Case # 05-368 (3). Defendant Haley Robson. May 1, 2006, p.

7. http://www.dailymail.co.uk/news/article-3405407/The-busy-life-Jeffrey-Epstein-Group-gorgeous-Manhattan-girls-billionaire-pedophile-s-mansion-flies-private-jet-attractive-brunette.html

8. http://www.reuters.com/article/us-epstein-lawsuit-brunel-idUSKBN0MM2H420150326

9. http://www.thedailybeast.com/articles/2015//03/26/model-king-sues-billionaire-perv-jeffrey-epstein.html

10. http://www.dailymail.co.uk/news/article-3405407/The-busy-life-Jeffrey-Epstein-Group-gorgeous-Manhattan-girls-billionaire-pedophile-s-mansion-flies-private-jet.attractive-brunette.html

11. http://pagesix.com/2016/03/08 jeffrey-epsteins-east-side-mansion-houses-russian-playmates/

12. http://www.thedailybeast.com/articles/2010/07/20/jeffrey-epstein-billionaire-pedophile-goes-free.html

13. http://www.thedailybeast.com/articles/2010/07/20/jeffrey-epstein-billionaire-pedophile-goes-free.html

14. http://www.thedailybeast.com/articles/2015/03/26/model-king-sues-billionaire-perv-jeffrey-epstein.html

15. http://www.palmbeachdailynews.com/news/news/lawsuit-documents-link-jeffrey-epstein-to-modeling/nMGzH/

16. http://www.palmbeachdailynews.com/news/news/lawsuit-documents-link-jeffrey-epstein-to-modeling/nMGzH/

17. http://jezebel.com/5603638/meet-the-modeling-agent-who-trafficked-underage-girls-for-sex

18. http://radaronline.com/wp-content/uploads/2015/04/Epstein-Docs-4-7-15.pdf

Chapter Four

So Many Victims

On November 21, 2005, the Palm Beach Police Department interviewed Jose Alessi, Epstein's former houseman. Alessi worked for Epstein between 1993 and 2004. Like the houseman who followed, Alfredo Rodriguez, Alessi was fired in 2004 for allegedly stealing.

Alessi's responsibilities comprised a number of chores including: preparing the house for Epstein's arrival, driving his guests, driving staff, and overseeing the maintenance of the house. Unlike Epstein's cooks, pilots and some of the personal assistants, Alessi never traveled with Epstein on his private plane. During the interrogation, Alessi told the police that his boss usually, "received three massages per day," when he was in residence.[1]

"Each masseuse that visited the house," Alessi said, "was different." Toward the end of his employment he revealed Epstein's, "masseuses were getting younger and younger. Some appeared to be sixteen or seventeen years of age at most." The massages were given in Epstein's bedroom and bathroom and many times. Alessi at times set up the table.[2]

Following Alessi's dismissal, Officer Recarey interviewed his successor, Alfredo Rodriguez, on January 4, 2006. The new houseman lasted a very short period at his new employ and like his predecessor was let go for apparently the same reason: stealing.

During his sworn video taped statement, Rodriguez stated he worked for Epstein for approximately six months, from November 2004 through May 2005. Rodriguez's responsibilities consisted of running errands, cooking occasionally, chauffer duties and being a full time butler. Rodriguez told the police he was, "Expected to make the girls comfortable until either Sarah Kellen or Epstein met them."[3]

One of their duties, Rodriguez and Alessi admitted, were to meet the girls upon their arrival and escort them to the kitchen. The staff would offer the girls something to drink but not alcoholic since Epstein did not allow it and did not drink alcoholic beverages.

Rodriguez acknowledged he, "Knew the girls were still in high school." After every massage, Rodriguez, "Often cleaned Epstein's bedroom. He discovered hand held massagers, vibrators and sex toys scattered on the floor," and later revealed, "the girls always needed rides to and from the house."[4]

The police issued subpoenas for several cell numbers and home lines. Records from several victims and witnesses including Sarah Kellen's telephone numbers were investigated.

Records showed that many telephone calls were made between Kellen and the victims and were "consistent with the dates and times the victims stated they were contacted." The records also, "showed Kellen called Robson during the exact times and dates when the victims advised the incidents occurred." Kellen coordinated the encounters with several victims, nine initials were entered during the same time frame the girls indicated they occurred."[5]

The Probable Cause Affidavit corroborated much of the information conveyed by the victims. For example, "Sarah Kellen coordinated and aided in the recruitment of minors to "work" for Epstein secured their appointments for the purposes of lewd and lascivious acts and arranged the bedroom for the minors to perform sexual activities with Epstein."[6]

Of the two-dozen or more victims allowed to testify, not all their stories were included primarily because most shared similar accounts of abuse. A few cases stood out. The most troubling incidents became the basis for this book. The level of abuse and recurring criminal activity was heinous.

Document #1603-3, referred to as Exhibit C, filed on April 8, 2011, identified dozens of victims. According to the court file, "Epstein repeatedly sexually assaulted more than forty (40) young girls on numerous occasions between 2002 and 2005 in his mansion in West Palm Beach, Florida."[7]

The same document revealed that, "Epstein has a sexual preference for young children." In addition, Jeffrey Epstein's deposition taken March 17, 2010 made known that "Epstein invoked his Fifth Amendment right to remain silent rather than make an incriminating admission, when questioned about his participation in the sexual abuse of minors.[8]

"Epstein abused many of the girls dozens if not hundreds of times," the deposition stated. When asked, "How many times did he engage in oral sex with females under the age of 18," Epstein again, "Invoked the Fifth Amendment."[9]

Another Deposition dated September 24, 2009 and continued on March 11, 2010, identified a minor girl as 'Jane Doe.' Doe "was sexually abused at least 17 times by Epstein." Doe alleged there was, "Vaginal penetration by Epstein with his finger and vaginal penetration by Epstein with a massager."[10]

On the same day, September 24, 2009, L.M. another victim, revealed in her deposition, "The way in which Epstein abused her beginning when she was 13 years old. According to L.M. Epstein touched her vagina with his fingers and vibrator." She "was personally molested by Epstein more than 50 times and was paid $200 per underage girl she brought Epstein. She brought him more than seventy (70) underage girls." L.M. told Epstein, "She did not want to bring him any more girls and he insisted she continue to bring him underage girls."[11]

A victim identified as E.W. was deposed May 6, 2010. E.W. explained that, "Beginning at age 14, Epstein paid me for touching my vagina. He inserted his fingers and used a vibrator. He also paid me $200 for each other underage female I brought him to molest." E.W. claims she brought him between twenty (20) to thirty (30) underage females."[12]

Jane Doe 4, a minor, declared in her deposition she was, "15 years old when she was first taken to meet Epstein." According to Jane Doe #4, Epstein, "Fingered her, used a vibrator, grabbed my nipples, smelled my butt, jerked off in front of me, and licked my clit, several times."[13]

In light of the number of testimonies, Brad Edwards determined that, "Epstein was able to access a large number of underage girls through a pyramid scheme in which he paid underage victims $200-$300 cash for every underage victim brought to him.[14]

The Palm Beach Police Incident Report described Epstein's scheme. "Among other things," the Incident Report outlined some of the abuses performed by Epstein on his victims." For example, when, "S.G. a 14 year old girl at the time of the incident was brought to Epstein's home, she was taken upstairs by a woman she believed to be Epstein's assistant. The woman started to fix up the room, putting covers on the massage table and organizing lotions on the table."[15]

The 'assistant' then left the room and told S.G. that Epstein would be up in a second. "Epstein walked over to S.G. and told her to take her clothes off in a stern voice. S.G. explained she did not know what to do, as she was alone with him so S.G. took off her shirt, leaving her bra on. "[16]

Epstein came in covered only by a towel wrapped around his waist. He told her to take everything off. S.G. removed her pants leaving on her panties. Epstein instructed S.G to give him a massage. As S.G gave Epstein a massage, Epstein turned around and masturbated. S.G. was so disgusted she could not speak. Epstein told her she, "had a really hot body." S.G. admitted she saw Epstein's member and stated she thought Epstein was on steroids..."[17]

Only Epstein knows the exact number of underage girls he sexually molested over the years. However, the attorneys, including Edwards and former federal Judge Paul Cassell, believe there were substantially more than forty, (40) female victims. Given the number of girls who confessed and later testified they had in fact introduced Epstein to other underage girls in order to make their two hundred dollar ($200) commission, the total number of victims identified on the police report could be a conservative estimate.[18]

A Complaint filed on April 14, 2010 stated, "There is overwhelming proof that the number of underage girls molested by Epstein through his scheme was in the hundreds." During his depositions taken to assess the accuracy of the claims, Epstein "Invoked the Fifth Amendment on questions about his daily abuse and molestation of children."[19]

Edwards and most of the attorneys representing the victims believed, "Epstein and his attorneys knew of the seriousness of the criminal investigation against him and corresponded constantly with the United States Attorney's Office in an attempt to avoid the filing of numerous federal felony offenses. In retrospect, it seems their efforts were successful."[20]

In spite of the level of exploitation and abuse, the cases failed to answer a number of important questions. One in particular troubled me: How did this middle class boy from Brooklyn, a true rags to riches 'boy wonder' and savvy Wall Street investor, grow to be such a menacing pedophile and registered sex offender?

Perhaps some day if another victim comes forward and the Courts administer an independent and objective psychological examination, a more accurate evaluation of Epstein's profile will reveal the truth.

* * *

Footnotes

1. http://cases.bms11.com/Documents/FL76/0934791/ECF_D
   OC_1603_10567451.pdf

2. http://cases.bms11.com/Documents/FL76/0934791/ECF_D
   OC_1603_10567451.pdf

3. http://cases.bms11.com/Documents/FL76/0934791/ECF_D
   OC_1603_10567451.pdf

4. http://cases.bms11.com/Documents/FL76/0934791/ECF_D
   OC_1603_10567451.pdf P22

5. http://cases.bms11.com/Documents/FL76/0934791/ECF_D
   OC_1603_10567451.pdf

6. http://cases.bms11.com/Documents/FL76/0934791/ECF_D
   OC_1603_10567451.pdf

7. http://cases.bms11.com/Documents/FL76/0934791/ECF_D
   OC_1603_10567451.pdf

8. http://cases.bms11.com/Documents/FL76/0934791/ECF_D
   OC_1603_10567451.pdf

9. http://cases.bms11.com/Documents/FL76/0934791/ECF_D
   OC_1603_10567451.pdf

10. http://cases.bms11.com/Documents/FL76/0934791/ECF_D
    OC_1603_10567451.pdf

11. http://cases.bms11.com/Documents/FL76/0934791/ECF_D
OC_1603_10567451.pdf

12. http://cases.bms11.com/Documents/FL76/0934791/ECF_D
OC_1603_10567451.pdf

13. http://cases.bms11.com/Documents/FL76/0934791/ECF_D
OC_1603_10567451.pdf

14. http://cases.bms11.com/Documents/FL76/0934791/ECF_D
OC_1603_10567451.pdf

15. http://cases.bms11.com/Documents/FL76/0934791/ECF_D
OC_1603_10567451.pdf

16. http://cases.bms11.com/Documents/FL76/0934791/ECF_D
OC_1603_10567451.pdf

17. http://www.nytimes.com/2008/07/01/business/01epstein.ht
ml?pagewanted=2&_r=2

18. http://cases.bms11.com/Documents/FL76/0934791/ECF_D
OC_1603_10567451.pdf

19. http://cases.bms11.com/Documents/FL76/0934791/ECF_D
OC_1603_10567451.pdf

20. http://cases.bms11.com/Documents/FL76/0934791/ECF_D
OC_1603_10567451.pdf

Chapter Five

Virginia Louise Roberts: The Proposition

On April 7, 2011 South Florida attorneys, Jack Scarola and Brad Edwards, interviewed Virginia Louise Roberts on the telephone. At the time of their conversation, Roberts, now in her thirties, was living with her husband and three children in Australia.

Roberts, one of more than two-dozen victims who testified against Epstein, had been sexually abused before she met Epstein. Her home life, not unlike Rosemary's, the first victim to come forward, was problematic. Known as Jane Doe #102 in the original criminal case filed, in 2005, Roberts' agreed to talk with attorneys Edwards and Scarola, only after she settled with Epstein and sold her story to The Mail on Sunday.

Although her attorney, Robert Josefsberg, spoke with me several times he would not disclose details of the settlement agreement. Several other attorneys working the Epstein case mentioned that Epstein agreed to settle with the victims paying each approximately $150,000. I had no way other than through the attorneys and victims to confirm the amount. When I spoke with Rosemary's mother she mentioned the percentage received by her daughter was a fraction of that.

The Mail on Sunday originally published her story on February 26, 2011. It was later redacted and an edited version was published again on March 5, 2011. This chapter includes a transcription of the telephone conversation filed in the Fifteenth Judicial Circuit in Palm Beach County on behalf of Brad Edwards, a defendant in a separate case against Jeffrey Epstein. In that case, Jeffrey *Epstein vs. Scott Rothstein, Bradley Edwards and LM* (an underage victim), Epstein had filed a civil suit against Edwards for wrongdoing.

The *Epstein vs. Rothstein, Edwards and LM* case, although inconsequential to Epstein's criminal case and the ongoing civil cases, began in 2009. Epstein attempted to derail Edwards' efforts and the legal representation of his clients by falsely accusing Edwards of conspiring with his former boss, Scott Rothstein, to swindle Rothstein clients out of millions of dollars in "settlements" funds.

Epstein falsely claimed that Edwards, notified potential investors of having reached a large settlement with Epstein and that the investors could share in the profits, "For as much as $200 million." When I spoke with Edwards pertaining to this case he confirmed the information.[1]

Edwards was never involved in the Rothstein scheme and left the firm before Rothstein was indicted. The judge who quickly saw through Epstein's charade promptly dismissed the *Epstein vs. Edwards* case since there was no evidence whatsoever that Edwards committed any criminal and unethical activities. Scott Rothstein on the other hand was sentenced and is now serving a 50-year sentence for cheating his clients out of $1.2 billion.

The telephone conversation that follows took place between Virginia Roberts and Jack Scarola. Edwards was present during the entire conversation.

Virginia:

I walked away from it all... it hadn't really ended... Jeffrey sent me to Thailand where I met my husband and escaped to Australia, never to return back to the States. Six months prior to that, he came up with a proposition that I thought was really disgustingly sick. And it really showed me for the first time in four years, I had been with him, that nothing was going to change and that I was always just going to be used by him.

He offered me a mansion and some of his money every month. I forget what he called it, a monthly income, in order to bear his child.

The proposition was to have a child with him but to sign my child over to him. Basically the child would be his and Ghislaine's and I would be looking after it as long as nothing happened between Jeffrey and me. So, I was kind of freaked out by all of that.

I was 19 (by then) and he likes females a lot younger, so I pushed Jeffrey to get me some more training since I was getting older and no longer of much interest to him. He sent me to Thailand in September 2002, where I was supposed to meet a girl and bring her back for him, but I never met up with her. Instead, I got a short course in Thai massage. Sending me there was his way of shutting me up about my training... so I went.

One day one of my friends from school invited me to watch a *Muay* Thai fight, which is a form of kickboxing. I went and saw this guy who was a really good fighter... and looked really hot. I asked my friend, who knew him, to introduce me. We fell in love immediately. Three days later Rob proposed and seven days later I was married in a Buddhist temple.

I called Jeffrey and told him I'm never coming back, I'm married I've fallen in love. I thought he'd wish the best for me. He was rude and said, "Have a good life," and hung up the phone. That was the last time I talked to him- ever- until all this started again.

In the summer of 1998, before her fifteenth birthday, Virginia Louise Roberts was working as a bathroom attendant at Donald Trump's *Mar-A-Lago* Club in Palm Beach, Florida. Trump publically admitted that Epstein's membership to Mar-A-Lago was revoked after his arrest. Born August 9, 1983, Roberts was earning $9 an hour, the day she met Ghislaine Maxwell and Epstein. Her father, Sky William Roberts, a maintenance manager at Trump's property, helped his daughter secure the job.

The fourteen-year old Roberts' was working part time when Maxwell made the proposition. The telephone interview was later filed as a court document to "Supplement the Proffer made in support of Edward's Motion for Leave to Amend to Assert Punitive Damages," in relation to the ongoing Jeffrey *Epstein vs. Bradley Edwards* Palm Beach, Florida case.

While reading a book about anatomy, Ghislaine Maxwell, met me at the spa, not having an education or anything behind me, I thought this was a great opportunity to work for her...to make some extra money and learn about massage. So, I went to Jeffrey's mansion about five or six that afternoon.

My dad drove me there. My dad worked at Mar-A-Lago with me and he met Ghislaine (the same afternoon) and she seemed (to him) like such a nice and proper English lady, and I mean, you know... She just seemed really nice and like someone who would like to help me out. So, my dad dropped me off and I had no problem getting home that night. One of her drivers would take me back after my trial.

She led me upstairs into Jeffrey's bedroom past Jeffrey's massage room that has a steam room, shower and massage table. There is actually an extra room that has- that nobody knows about- a kind of secret room and it's got a whole bunch of pictures of pornographic literature and sex toys and I can just imagine what happened in there.

The room wasn't concealed. It was more like a door that you would normally go into, like some kind of special opening you open and then a little door, so it looks like it's a little closet so-to- speak, but when you walk in, it's obviously a lot bigger than just a closet. It wasn't too big, but it was bigger, you know. It wasn't a gigantic room it was just like a small room, which probably could fit some shoes in there. It had racks of shoes, boxes, some sweatshirts neatly folded and from the ceiling to floor covered in pornographic pictures of the girls that he had met.

By the time Victoria met Epstein, "he was lying naked on top of the massage table. And for a recently turned 15 year old girl seeing a man on the table like that was weird, but having to learn about anatomy and massage, I thought this would be part of the massage program, so I said to myself ok, this is fine."

He instructed me how to touch his body, how to massage him and for the first hour, it was actually a real massage, maybe not an hour, maybe like 40 minutes or something like that; and then he turned over on the other side and exposed himself fully. Ghislaine who had stayed in the room told me to undress and began to take off my shirt and skirt- that is- my white Mar-A-Lago uniform.

Suddenly, she took off her shirt and got undressed.

I was there with just my undies on, and she was completely bare, and she made some kind of flakey remark about my underwear because it wasn't my normal sexy-girl underwear, I think it had red hearts on it or something like that; just your normal, you know, real cute underwear. Anyway, during all of this time I'm kind of like wondering what's going on, how do I act, what do I say? I was so afraid.

Not afraid or fearful for my life but unsure of how all this started and wanting to obtain a profession, I was so afraid about upsetting and disappointing them, I don't know, it was a weird situation... and I was expected to lick his nipples and give him oral sex while he fondled me and then at the end I was told by Ghislaine to get on top and straddle Jeffrey sexually.

When we were done, we all went and had a shower in the bathroom and Jeffrey told me to wash him up and down, you know with a bar of soap and make sure he was all cleaned up. And then he took me downstairs to meet two of his guards and told John to bring me home. John Alessi was the butler at the time.

Virginia admitted during the telephone conversation she had been sexually abused, as a child, by a close family friend.

I was on the streets at 13 years old. I was picked up by a 67 year old man named Ron Eppinger, who did exactly what Jeffrey did to me- abuse and violate my youth- and I was with him for six months.

After Ron, the victim had a boyfriend "who was like a school friend from young days but we just kept in contact with each other and we were on and off constantly, and that was Tony Figueroa. There was another younger guy near my age, Michael, I can't remember his name, but yea, there, I mean, there wasn't like a string of men or anything like that. But there was Ron."

Like I told you, he was the first guy expecting me to do so-called disgusting affairs. Jeffrey actually knows Ron; it was quite weird when I told Jeffrey the Ron story, Jeffrey had actually met him.

From floor to ceiling there must have been one hundred, even more, pornographic photographs, even more in boxes. Some of them were A4 photographs, like the large size, some of naked women posing in positions, sexy positions. Others were of girls with bikinis on. But they were all of women and all had a sexual nature... There were lots of naked photographs... Some photographs had frames, some of them were out of frames, but they were all of women and all sexual in nature.

Ghislaine took several nude photographs of me for Jeffrey... and since he wasn't shy, that wasn't the only place in his house that he kept the photos. He liked photos all over his house. If you looked in his den or on his desk or in the hall table, a giant hall table in his house, there were at least a hundred photos of girls in frames. Not all of them were naked. A lot of the ones that were around his house were pictures of celebrities and politicians he has known.

Sometimes, Jeffrey could have 7 girls in one day, and he would only see those girls once if he got bored. I heard he's gotten a lot sloppier since I left... But, when I knew him, there was just such an influx of girls coming in and out, so I did not recognize a lot of them. They were all definitely beautiful they were all ranging in age, some of them young- but all beautiful.

I knew from my first visit they were pleased with me and after that encounter was finished, the sexual encounter, he went and told me I did well and I have a lot of potential to becoming a massage therapist. He asked me if I could return tomorrow, you know, and do the same thing and get paid two hundred dollars an hour.

Jeffrey insisted that I come after work and over the next few days the relationship grew more, and within a couple of weeks, not even a couple of weeks, maybe one week I had quit Mar-A-Lago and was working for Jeffrey full time.

While her father was still "a maintenance supervisor managing the tennis courts and air conditioners and things like that," Virginia was making two hundred dollars an hour giving Epstein happy ending massages.

"I came out in public," Virginia said, "because after seeing Epstein and Prince Andrew together again in a picture published in December 2010 in the New York Post, I am angry about how they, (Epstein and Prince Andrew), are still up to their old ways together and that they're still hanging out; however I didn't contact the media including the Mail on Sunday and didn't bring the story out.

According to the transcript Virginia said she was out, "To help the bigger picture. You know, I think all of us can make a big difference in a lot of other people's lives and I think that this has gone on long enough and it's a big slap in my face that he can get away with hurting me so bad let alone so many other girls and laugh about it."

I guess I talked to you guys because I want to see the right thing happen, not just to him, but I want people in the world to understand this is not the way of life, you know, it's not acceptable to go out and procure young girls and make them think that, this is the way you should be living.

That's all. Yeah, I guess my reason for doing this is to help the bigger picture, you know, I'm a big believer in karma and I believe that good things will come back to you, so I guess that's why I'm doing this.

During her first conversation with Edwards and Scarola, Virginia said,

Nobody has made me feel like I've been bribed or bought or had to say anything. I've told you everything that I know not things somebody told me. If anything, Brad's been extra careful not to tell me anything and let me do all the talking, so it's quite opposite I think.

You know I was just a locker room attendant and sometimes I did babysitting for the rich and famous so, I wasn't anything big. I worked in a spa. That's why I was studying anatomy, because I was really, really interested in becoming a massage therapist and at the locker room, I didn't do much. I mean I was making tea for a living, I would, you know, make sure the toilet paper had a little triangle in it after everybody went to the toilet or wipe down the water from the basin, you know, it was a very easy-peasy job.

During the entire hour of what I call the legitimate massage, it was a cat and mouse game trying to get information from me in order to find out who I am, if I was a willing participant in these kind of things and how would I react if they were about to take the next step.

They got information off me, they got my age, they got my, a little bit of history so they knew I was, you know, not very stable at home, and they knew that I was actually interested in making my life better by studying so what they were offering me was a chance to become a legitimate masseuse but it was the getting trained...

They would have people show me how to work the body called massage therapists and buy me books on it and you know, keep me interested. Every time I was with Jeffrey, literally it was about massages, I don't mean just going in and having sex with him. I mean giving him a massage. Because it would always start out with a massage and then it would lead into sometimes other things.

By the time the fifteen year old was Epstein's full time employee or masseuse, Virginia began to travel with Epstein.

When he was in Palm Beach, I stayed at my apartment, and he would call me once or twice a day sometimes to do things with him. Sometimes, we'd go out shopping, sometimes, we'd go out and watch a movie. You know, simple things like that, go to an expo or a fair, whatever it was.

But when we were in other cities, I lived with him full time. Even in the middle of the night, I could get a ring on my phone and he would tell me to come in his room, you know, so it was literally full time. After I quit Mar-A-Lago, Jeffrey offered to get me an apartment in Palm Beach, somewhere on Royal Palm Beach Boulevard, and it was a nice apartment. He furnished it for me, it was absolutely beautiful, but yeah, that was the only time I would spend time away from him really.

The FBI asked me the same question about where I lived and I've been trying to rack my brain... to find out... I didn't get to spend as much time there since I was only there about an entire week out of every month probably because the majority of the time I was with Jeffrey.

Because of her age, Virginia could not drive without a license and would be driven to and from her apartment. The apartment Epstein rented for her was close to her family since she "wanted to be close enough to everybody else so that when I was in town, I could just go see them quickly."

There were times we would fly back from some city maybe too late at night for me to really want to go back home, so you know, it's like midnight or one in the morning and I would just stay in the yellow room, or one of the guest rooms in his house in Palm Beach. But the majority of the time, I would definitely want to get back to my own apartment.

There were no set hours. It wasn't like logging, and you know, hitting the shift button, nothing like that. The way I would get paid would be if I was in Palm Beach, I would get $200 an hour to massage Jeffrey or some of his friends and then go home. If I were traveling with him, it would be per massage, so I would be getting paid per day.

So I wouldn't be getting paid on an hourly rate. He wouldn't say ok, today you're going to work for me from seven in the morning until eight at night. It was never like that. I was on call all the time... I was paid from the time the massage started.

Sometimes we'd go there and I would wait for a while or talk with Ghislaine and Jeffrey about something or we'd meet somewhere and talk about something. A lot of times, I'd meet him upstairs in his room when he was ready for me. But then there were a lot of times where it didn't start right away, so he couldn't really pay me from the time I got there. I was paid from the time I massaged him until the time the massage was over."

According to Virginia's testimony she "was asked to do the same things that I did to Jeffrey to a few of his fellow colleagues."

Those were my duties. Jeffrey looked at it this way. I was going to be a professional massage therapist and maybe I needed some clientele, so he had me perform erotic massages on a few people.

The first massage started in Palm Beach County about six to nine months after she first met Jeffrey. He would always pay for her services. "I would get paid the next time I saw Jeffrey, so if I was invited to the Breakers Hotel to give a massage to one of his buddies, I would give the massage, I would go home, and the next day when I saw Jeffrey, he would pay me for what I did. So, it was paid always by him, it was set up by him, so he always knew what to pay me. I did get tips and things like that, if you call it that, you know, like a hundred dollar tip or something from a few of them.

In so many ways, Jeffrey really, really, had to train me, and that was why Ghislaine said that she and Jeffrey enjoyed me so much because they never really had to speak much to tell me what they wanted me to do. You know, I wasn't waiting for their directions.

Jeffrey would tell me to go give an erotic massage to (his) friends, he wouldn't give me many details, but he would say "treat them like you treat me." So I would do what he wanted without having him say anything.

I complied with what he wanted because it was somewhat of a... I mean... I don't know how to say it, it was just very mindboggling how I let him have so much control or power over me basically. The massages would be routine... with my so-called new clients, and in their own words they would ask me to provide them with sexual pleasure after the massage.

I always reported back to Jeffrey about what happened after I provided massages to his friends and I knew that his friends were reporting back to him as well because there were times where he would instigate a conversation by saying, 'You know, so and so had a great time, you did wonderful, and he gave me a call and told me how it went.' Jeffrey would have a laugh with me a few times about some of their different mannerisms, I guess you would say, like some of them, one guy had a foot fetish and that was really weird and I mentioned it to Jeffrey and we had a laugh over it.

There were about eight guys perhaps for whom Virginia provided massages. Jeffrey always paid for those services, according to the telephone transcription. When asked to name the eight men, Virginia grew scared and refused to identify them.

No, not at this stage, I just—some of these people are really influential and powerful and I don't want to start another shit-storm with a few of them. I'll tell you there were some erotic massages given to... I'm just afraid to say it to you. I'm really scared of where this is going to go.

Scarola quickly changed the subject detecting Virginia's distress and asked her about her travels with Epstein.

I started traveling immediately. Not internationally until I think about, gosh, I can't remember, I think it was a year later, that we started doing international travel maybe like 9 months to a year—somewhere in the summer of 1999. But like I said, we started doing domestic traveling immediately, so my first destination with him was New York then Santa Fe, the Caribbean and California.

I would take trips with him occasionally. Sometimes we would travel to St. Louis or New Orleans or Santa Cruz. We were traveling just about everywhere I think in

Jeffrey's private jet. Unless I was being sent somewhere by myself for a client, then I would travel on what do you call a public jet, whatever it is.

"Commercial flight" interrupted Scarola, 'Yes,' Virginia said, 'Just a normal flight, an e-ticket.' "Like the rest of us common folk," Scarola said.

But when I was with Jeffrey, the majority of the time would be on the black jet. If one of his colleagues would be at the Caribbean or Santa Fe or even New York home, or wherever, he would call me up when I was not with him and ask me to get on the next plane to so and so and go meet so and so, and that's when I would use e-tickets. His assistant would organize the trip for me and give me the details and I would just walk up and they'd let me right through.

'And on those occasions how much time would you spend with one of Jeffrey's friends when you were sent to a location that you would have to travel to,' Scarola asked.

Only a couple of days, only two days, that's it. I would be paid in cash upon my return back with Jeffrey. So, whenever I was back with Jeffrey, he would count up how many days I've had, sometimes give me even more than what I deserved, not deserved, but what I earned and give me a little extra. I would do to them the same thing I would do to Jeffrey.

Again, it would start out as a massage, which would start with them being naked, and give him a legitimate massage to begin. I'd start with his feet, go up to his calves, up his legs, buttocks, back, his neck, his head, his arms, yada yada… and then it would be time to flip over, and some of the men would want me to massage the front side of them and they would instigate it so I would have to begin having sex with them or foreplay, whatever you want to call it.

"So routinely," Scarola said, "these massages involved sexual activity. Is that accurate?" "Yes," replied Virginia. According to the pilot manifesto, pilot logs and several depositions, the passengers on the plane when Virginia traveled consisted of "Larry the pilot, a short, small old guy, I don't know his name, but he was the copilot, and then he changed and there was another guy brought in.

Generally, there was always Jeffrey, sometimes Ghislaine, sometimes Emmy Taylor, sometimes a whole bunch of other girls, sometimes famous people, sometimes politicians or just about anybody could fly on his plane. There was never any set routine. It was an influx of people on Jeffrey's airplane. There was Naomi Campbell, Heidi Klum, and Bill Clinton. There was Al Gore, a whole bunch of models. There was also Matt Groening, producer of The Simpsons cartoons, Jack Cousteau's granddaughter a lot of interior designers, architects, and politicians.

What went on the airplane was a lot of the same thing that went down on the ground. A lot of times, it would just be me and Jeffrey, or me and Jeffrey and Ghislaine, or me and Jeffrey and some other girl, sometimes Emmy, Sarah, and Nadia Bjorlin.

Bjorlin, an opera singer is now married, has a son, and is a television actress on 'Days Of Our Lives.'

There would be sexual conduct, there would be foreplay, and there was a bed, so we could basically reenact exactly what was happening in the house. It would start off with massaging or we would start off with foreplay, sometimes it would lead to, you know orgies.

There was a constant influx of girls coming in and going out. And we were all very young. On occasion, there were some older girls, and I don't mean older as in like in there 30s. I mean like 28, 29, just very rarely; the majority of the girls that Jeffrey actually met or had on his plane or in his house were under age.

Jeffrey would send me personally or with other girls to clubs or shops to pick up other girls anywhere, I mean we were constantly on the lookout for other girls that might satisfy, Jeffrey.

Our instructions were clear: young, pretty, a fun personality. They couldn't be black. If the girls were any other race other than white, they had to be exotically beautiful. That was about it.

They both gave us instructions and it wasn't just me, Jeffrey asked most girls to bring a friend to make extra money. They would use us young girls so that way it probably looked a lot safer to a girl that we were procuring younger girls that were already doing it. That was the way Jeffrey did it. Jeffrey and Ghislaine both taught me how to, depending on the circumstances, depending on the girl, how to procure a girl.

You could offer them a job as a massage therapist or you could tell them you have a really rich friend with great contacts in the acting world or modeling world and he loves pretty girls, you should come back and meet him, make some money... We had a whole bunch of ways to be able to procure girls. There could have been a hundred girls, there could be more, honestly. I'm not sure how many girls, really. I wish I did know. Like I said there were so many over the course of 4 years, between 1998-2002, with Jeffrey... I would say definitely more than one hundred.

Epstein's gifts didn't stop at just giving tips to Virginia. He loved to dress her as well.

He wasn't out to dress me like a porn star or anything. He would always dress me very classy, but we'd just go shopping all the time together... It was nice, classy outfits I was wearing like Gucci, Dolce Gabbana, Chanel, and things like that.

He was buying me a lot of very, very nice clothing. It was provocative. I mean I was wearing miniskirts and tight short shorts and little shirts that showed my belly and my cleavage and everything, but they were expensive clothes. There was, also role playing-lots of it.

Jeffrey loved the latex outfits Ghislaine had for us girls. He had bondage outfits, he had all different kind of outfits, but his favorite was the schoolgirl. Ghislaine would dress me up to surprise Jeffrey or Jeffrey would ask me to get dressed up. This would include wearing a tiny little skirt with nothing underneath, a white collared shirt that you would be wearing to school with a tie, tied up in a bow, my hair in pigtails, stockings up to my knees and I would go in there and act like a kid and we'd do role playing sex.

Apparently, Epstein boasted to Virginia all the time and to some friends about the ages of the girls with whom he had sex.

The worst story I heard directly from his own mouth was about these pretty 12 year-old girls he had flown in, transported to Palm Beach by somebody else, for his birthday. It was a surprise birthday gift from one of his friends. They were from France. I did see them. I did meet them. Jeffrey bragged after he met them they were 12 years old and flown over from France because they are really poor over there, and their parents needed the money or whatever. That was the worst. He was constantly bragging about the girls' ages or where he got them from or about their past and how terrible their past was and good he is making it for them.

Scarola circled back and asked Virginia more questions about what took place on Epstein's jet.

The crew was told to knock if they had to come out of the cockpit and told to come out as little as possible. So they were not hanging out watching everything. But it doesn't take an idiot to put two and two together to say well there's a whole bunch of half-dressed teenagers on board with this old man who is constantly being massaged by them and he wants me to keep the door shut for what reason? I mean, only they could figure that out, but yeah, they knew.

He would laugh about it. I never really knew what to take seriously, because he was such a funny character at times. Yeah, lots of people owed him favors from what he told me. He's got everybody in his pocket, and he would laugh about how he helps people for the sole purpose- in the end- to owe him something. That's why I believe he does so many favors in the first place.

CONCHITA SARNOFF

Scarola asked, "Do you have any recollection of Jeffrey Epstein's specifically telling you that Bill Clinton owes me favors?" "Yes, I do," Virginia, said.

I remember asking Jeffrey what's Bill Clinton doing here... he laughed and said, 'Well he owes me a favor.' He never told me what favors they were. I never knew... He told me a long time ago that everyone owes him favors. They're all in each other's pockets...

"Virginia," Scarola asked, when asked Epstein why is Bill Clinton here, where was here?" Virginia replied, "On the island." Besides living in Palm Beach, Epstein owns a private island, Little St. John's in the U.S. Virgin Islands (USVI). "When you were present with Jeffrey Epstein and Bill Clinton on the island, who else was there?" Scarola asked.

"Ghislaine, Emmy (Taylor), and there were two young girls that I could identify. I never really knew them well anyways. It was just 2 girls from New York." Scarola asked, "And were all of you staying at Jeffrey's house on the island including Bill Clinton?"

"That's correct," said Virginia. Jeffrey's house has about 4 or 5 different villas on his island separate from the main house and we all stayed in the villas." Scarola continued, "Were sexual orgies a regular occurrence on the island at Jeffrey's house?" "Yes" responded Virginia.

Not mentioned in Virginia's transcript were the names of Epstein's staff at the island: Crystal and Michael Gillich, the current caretakers of his USVI villa. A 2015 online advertisement posted one of the villas at a daily rental of $2,317 per night. That particular villa has 5 bedrooms and 2 bathrooms. There is a 7 night minimum stay.[2]

Scarola continued, "If we were to take sworn testimony from the people I am going to name, and if those people were to tell the truth about what they knew, do you believe that any of the following people would have relevant information about Jeffrey's taking advantage of underage girls"?

"Yes," confirmed Virginia.

"So, I'll just name a name, and you tell me 'yes' if they told the truth, I think they have relevant information or 'no', I don't think they would, or 'I don't know whether they would or not.' Ok? You understand?"

"Yes," responded Virginia.

Scarola: Ok, Les Wexner?

Roberts: I think he has relevant information, but I don't think he will tell you the truth.

Scarola: What about Alan Dershowitz?

Roberts: Yes.

Scarola: David Copperfield?

Roberts: Don't know.

Scarola: What about Tommy Matola?

Roberts: Don't know.

Scarola: Prince Andrew?

Roberts: Yes, he would know a lot of the truth. Again, I don't know how much he would be able to help you, but seeing he's in a lot of trouble himself these days, I think he might, so I think he may be valuable.

Scarola: Ok Virginia, I think that's all I have for you...

As I told you in the beginning of this conversation, we've been recording it, and hopefully, we've got a clear enough recording so that we've taken down everything accurately and when it's transcribed, it will be clear and accurate, but what I would like to do is transcribe it, sent it to you, have you take a look at it, and if there's anything that we got wrong in the statement, you can write back and you can make changes in the transcript so that it is accurate. Is that fair? Virginia responded, "No worries. That is fair. No problem."

Brad and Scarola said goodbye.

* * *

Footnotes

1. Virginia Louise Roberts Telephone Transcript filed April 7, 2011. Telecom Participants: Jack Scarola, Brad Edwards and Virginia Roberts. Taken via telephone. Privileged Pursuant to FS 766.205(4) and /or Work Product.

2. http://www.vrbo.com/455157

Tagnotes

On January 2, 2015, The Guardian, a British daily, contacted Buckingham Palace for comment. According to the report: "Buckingham Palace declined to comment on the allegations contained in the court document. A palace spokesperson said the royal household would, 'Never comment on an ongoing legal matter.'"

Buckingham Palace issued the following statement: "This relates to the long-running and ongoing civil proceedings in the United States to which the Duke of York is not a party. As such we would not comment in detail. However, for the avoidance of doubt, any suggestion of impropriety with underage minors is categorically untrue."

Virginia's telephone testimony substantiated many of the facts previously included in her earlier testimonies given under the alias Jane Doe No. 102. Her earlier Complaint described in detail how Maxwell apparently recruited underage girls turning the victims of sex trafficking into both procurers.

Chapter Six

In Her Own Words: Virginia Makes a U Turn

On December 23, 2014, Virginia Roberts Giuffre incorporated a non-profit foundation in Florida, "Victims Refuse Silence: From Victim to Survivor." Her mission: "To change the landscape of the war on sexual abuse and human trafficking." Her strategy: "to help survivors break the silence associated with sexual abuse."

Media reports continue to suggest different reasons why Roberts started the foundation. One report claimed that Roberts' attorneys, Edwards and Cassell, funded the organization with an initial seed capital of eighty thousand dollars. In 2016, when I prompted Edwards if this was true, he did not confirm or deny.

Given the many published opinions about the victim and because I have not spoken to Virginia directly I thought it best to include her statements in her own words rather than paraphrase the story. The following statements are taken directly from the website's home page.

> Where do I even begin? My story does not start in the way a typical fairy tale starts. Hoping for a nice life and happy ending was a fallacy. I was forced to endure abuse as a child. After that, I was left to my own demise. I saw the streets as a way to escape, but quickly learned that it was just as bad as before. Nothing changed. I was still being victimized.

In and out of safe-homes and rehabs, they all contained a product of treachery. Survival had to become my first instinct.

It felt as though no matter where I ran, nothing would change. I couldn't see any way around this. The people closest to me rejected me.

Many days followed, bringing more shame than I could have imagined. My life was tumbling down around me. And then I turned 15.

At 15 years old, very wealthy and powerful people promised me a higher education and a better life. I was a vulnerable teenager and the offer was appealing. But before I knew it, I was thrown into a world of sexual servitude and believed that I was indebted to those who used me as a sexual servant.

While traveling the world with some of the most powerful and connected world leaders in politics, science, and business, they made me believe that I was important, yet I was really there to service these individuals sexually.

In order to protect myself, I quickly appreciated that I had no choice but to comply with my master's directives. I was still only a child, and because of the extraordinary power that my abusers had, I believed that I could not report them.

I did not think that anyone would listen to me.

When I turned 19, I was sent to Thailand and finally found the opportunity to break free. I met a man who gave me the courage that I needed to escape. Instead of following orders and returning to the United States and my life of sexual abuse, I went to Australia, where I hid in fear for years.

While there, in Australia, I matured. I gained perspective. I had my beautiful children and began watching them grow.

My family and I came back to the United States with my mind set on making a difference. Not for myself, but for all of the children victims of sexual abuse and sex trafficking.

The family moved to Colorado.

In trying to make a positive difference, certain people continue to take shots at me and put me down, but I am no longer the young and vulnerable girl who could be bullied. I am now a survivor and nobody can ever take that away from me.

While I cannot save every child, I know that with my voice and my story, I can save some. And if I save just one, then my mission is a success. Sexual abuse and sex trafficking is an epidemic that crosses over all socioeconomic boundaries. By spreading awareness, we can decrease the frequency of abuse. By providing support and services, we can heal those who have suffered as victims.

By giving other victims confidence to speak up, and refuse silence, we can empower them to transition from victim into survivor, and to save the lives of others. If every victim refuses silence, we can end this epidemic. I want every victim to know that there is someone who will believe in them and who will help them heal

Today, I am a mother of three. I have a wonderful and supportive husband, and I am just lucky to be alive. We all have choices in life. Close your eyes and just imagine peace for yourself or someone you know who has been through sexual abuse. It is daunting and no one seems to want to talk about it because of the shame associated with sexual abuse. But just know, even if you have no one to turn to, you have us!"

Virginia Louise Roberts Home Page:

http://www.victimsrefusesilence.org.

Chapter Seven

Ghislaine Noelle Maxwell

Ghislaine Noelle Maxwell was born on Christmas Day, 1961, in Headington, Oxford, Great Britain. Her birth came only days after her oldest brother, Michael, died in a coma after six years following a tragic car accident.

Headington Hill Hall in east Oxford was her family home from 1959, when her father leased the estate until it was placed in receivership shortly after his death, in 1991. Prior to the conversion of the Hall as a family residence, Maxwell used the estate to operate his successful publishing business, Pergamon Press.

Like all great family homes, Headington Hill has a storied history where once C.S. Lewis came to stay in 1919 and never left... and decades earlier Oscar Wilde attended an all night, fancy dress May Day Ball in costume as Prince Rupert. The famous Hall, built in 1824, was designed by architect John Thomas for the Morrell family, a family of local brewers who lived there for over one hundred years.

Maxwell was educated nearby at Headington, a private school for girls. After graduation she went off to university to finish her studies at Marlborough and Balliol College, Oxford. On December 10, 1984 after her father made Ghislaine Director of Oxford United, a British football club, she received the Fiat Team of the Year Award.

Maxwell is fluent in several languages. A helicopter pilot and a certified deep-sea diver, she recently started a non-profit, The Terra Mar project, to protect the High Seas.

Ghislaine was the youngest of nine children born to the late French Huguenot, Elizabeth "Betty" Meynard and Robert Maxwell, nee Jan Ludvik Binyamin Hoch. Born in Czechoslovakia he was a British national and former Member of Parliament.

She lived a charmed childhood as her father's doted daughter. In July 1991, somewhere between dusk and dawn, Maxwell disappeared off the Canary Islands. It was a warm summer evening in the Mediterranean when Robert Maxwell capsized off *The Lady Ghislaine*, the yacht he named after his favorite daughter. Perhaps her life congealed upon his untimely death.

Following his disappearance, Ghislaine was "desolate and almost destitute," media reports revealed. Her financial state was not much better. This might help explain her instant attraction to Epstein and the reason she agreed to go along with his unusual lifestyle. They met and apparently fell in love.

During their years together she introduced Epstein to many of her friends including HRH Prince Andrew, even brought him along to attend a birthday celebration for Queen Elizabeth II at Sandringham Hall in Norfolk, England, the Queen's hunting lodge; and introduced him to former President Clinton.

Not too many years into their romance, their relationship took an unusual turn. Maxwell apparently became a sort of 'Madame' for Epstein and as one of the victim's, Virginia Louise Roberts', claimed Maxwell was "the undisputed leader of the girls in Epstein's entourage." According to Roberts, she was also, "Funny and boisterous. I was scared of ever saying no to her. I was always compliant. I knew if I said no to anything, I would be on the street."[1]

Over the course of several sworn testimonies Virginia said, "Ghislaine was a photographer, and took many of the nude pictures that were all over Epstein's houses, including the ones of me in a hammock that Bill Clinton and Prince Andrew and all their visitors had to have seen."[2]

"One year," Roberts claimed, "I couldn't think of what to give Jeffrey for his birthday," so I asked Ghislaine. Maxwell told her, 'Just give him a photograph of you.'

"I had a nice picture, lying against a tree, fully clothed. But when I showed it to her," she said: 'No, you can't give him that,' so she took me and laid me naked across a hammock and put a sheer piece of net across me and I posed with my legs open, a bit provocatively, and that was the picture she had me give Jeffrey."[3]

In 1995, before Maxwell's relationship with Epstein formally began, Alex Witchell, a reporter at The New York Times interviewed her mother, Elizabeth 'Betty' Maxwell. Witchell reported that the Maxwell family, or at least Mrs. Maxwell, was in "spectacular ruin," as a result of her husband's fiscal mismanagement. "Debt, dishonor and the potential destruction of two sons' careers," was the only thing Maxwell bequeathed his family," wrote Witchell, in spite of his "vast holdings, which included The Daily News in New York and Macmillan Publishing."[4]

His story insinuated that Maxwell's father was, "trying to escape the consequences of accumulating a $5 billion debt," a debt that automatically catapulted her two older brothers, Ian and Kevin, into a criminal investigation; and "Liable for the pension funds of thousands of employees he had illegally utilized as security against other businesses." Of all his children, Robert Maxwell employed only Ian and Kevin.[5]

If Kevin and Ian were in financial ruin as reports claimed, then Ghislaine, her mother, and the rest of the family still dependent on their father's generosity, were also insolvent. To make matters worse, less than one month after Maxwell's death, the Serious Fraud Office in England began an investigation into Ian and Kevin Maxwell's participation in Maxwell's companies.

As a result of the investigation, both sons, Kevin and Ian, were arrested and charged with conspiracy to commit fraud; allegedly misusing pension funds; use of pension funds to finance the Maxwell Group of companies; and use of fraud by the Maxwell's to extend bank credits.

In 1996, after an eight months trial, Kevin and Ian Maxwell were acquitted on charges of fraud. Three financial institutions: Lehman Brothers, Goldman Sachs, and Coopers & Lybrand, interceded on their behalf in an effort to rescue them and their partner, the American financial advisor, Larry Trachtenberg.

Trachtenberg, 38 at the time of the indictment, "was a former compliance officer at London & Bishopsgate, the pension fund managing company at the center of the 400 million pound sterling black hole in Maxwell's Mirror Group pension assets."[6]

The Los Angeles Times reported that, "Kevin Maxwell and Trachtenberg were charged with defrauding Swiss Bank Corp of $101 million by selling stock they did not own and stealing $13 million worth of stock belonging to Mirror Group Pension Trustees Ltd., one of Robert Maxwell's company pension funds."[7]

When Ian, Ghislaine's older brother, "was charged with defrauding Swiss Volks Bank of $35.5 million by misrepresenting ownership of stock in Berlitz International after his father's death, according to the fraud office documents," Trachtenberg and Kevin were also charged with same crime."[8]

Ghislaine may not have been privy to her father's business activities, although that was never proven. With the exception of Maxwell, no one will ever know with any certainty the professional relationship that existed between Ghislaine and her father. Except that Maxwell's media empire was considerably overextended by the time he attempted to take over The New York Daily News and MacMillan Publishers where Ghislaine was to begin her apprenticeship.

Had the deal materialized, it was reported that Maxwell would have moved to a position of power. One can assume that if that was going to be her role, then during the negotiations, Ghislaine might have also been privy to some of the financial details of the deal.

What is known is that, "at the time of her father's death, auditors discovered that about $670 million was missing from the Maxwell companies' pension funds. All but some $50 million were recovered, mostly through settlements among the funds and Maxwell companies, their auditors and financial advisers, including Lehman Brothers, Goldman, Sachs, and Coopers & Lybrand, "the very same financial institutions that later came to the brother's rescue.[9]

During that emotionally volatile period a number of stories surfaced about her father's financial misdeeds. A New York Times article stated that Robert Maxwell's "trial attracted intense publicity in Britain, and the Serious Fraud Office, the Government agency that prosecutes white-collar crime, who invested a reported $30 million on its investigation and legal case."[10]

Not unlike Epstein's near miss acquittal, her father's clearing, "Brought immediate criticism of the Serious Fraud Office from politicians who said the agency had a record of failure in high-profile financial fraud cases...Technically, the Serious Fraud Office could bring additional charges against (the Maxwell brothers) and Mr. Trachtenberg... But lawyers said mounting a new case would be so expensive and difficult that the prosecutors were not likely to do so," reported the New York Times.[11]

On January 19, 1996, after an eight-month trial, an English jury acquitted, Kevin and Ian Maxwell along with their partner, Larry Trachtenberg, of fraud and conspiring to defraud the pension plans of Maxwell-owned companies.[12]

In the midst of this Greek tragedy, Ghislaine was alone, probably in need of protection and lacking a trusted companion. By the time Epstein walked into her life she was probably receptive. Perhaps, like her father, Epstein gave Ghislaine the same sense of comfort and security she so urgently needed at that time of her life.

* * *

Footnotes

1. http://www.dailymail.co.uk/news/article-1361039/Prince-Andrew-girl-17-sex-offender-friend-flew-Britain-meet-him.html#ixzz1c0ttCLPi. March 28, 2011: *Mail On Sunday*:

2. http://cases.bms11.com/Documents/FL76/09-34791/ECF_DOC_1603_10567451.pdf

3. http://cases.bms11.com/Documents/FL76/09-34791/ECF_DOC_1603_10567451.pdf

4. http://cases.bms11.com/Documents/FL76/09-34791/ECF_DOC_1603_10567451.pdf

5. http://www.nytimes.com/1995/02/15/garden/at-lunch-with-elisabeth-maxwell-questions-without-answers.html?pagewanted=all

6. http://articles.latimes.com/1992-06-19/business/fi-530_1_kevin-maxwell

7. http://articles.latimes.com/1992-06-19/business/fi-530_1_kevin-maxwell

8. http://articles.latimes.com/1992-06-19/business/fi-530_1_kevin-maxwell

9. http://www.nytimes.com/1996/01/20/business/international-business-british-jury-acquits-robert-maxwell-s-sons.html

10. http://www.nytimes.com/1996/01/20/business/international-business-british-jury-acquits-robert-maxwell-s-sons.html

11. http://www.nytimes.com/1996/01/20/business/international-business-british-jury-acquits-robert-maxwell-s-sons.html

12. http://www.nytimes.com/1996/01/20/business/international-business-british-jury-acquits-robert-maxwell-s-sons.html

Chapter Eight

Conversations with Epstein and Maxwell

Maxwell and I met in London at a dinner party hosted by a mutual friend. That evening Maxwell exuded charm, warmth and self-assurance. Bubbling over with witticisms, I sensed she was quite a character. In the course of the last two decades Maxwell and I saw each other several times. We did not become friends in the traditional sense rather social acquaintances.

Maxwell was always friendly, giggly and curious-particularly about my history. At the time, there was nothing I did not like about her. I never felt uneasy around her and did not suspect anything unusual even though I was familiar with her family history. In the early nineties it was difficult not to be. Since everyone has a history and not everyone can choose his or hers, I chose not to follow the commentaries in spite of her father's tragic ending.

On the rare occasions we met, it was either at a social function or friend's dinner party. A couple of times we met in London. A few times in New York and a couple more times at a mutual friend's home on New Year's Eve in Palm Beach, Florida.

It was in or around 2002 when I first became aware of Maxwell and Epstein's romantic relationship. I stumbled into the couple at the New Year's Eve celebration in Palm Beach, not far from Epstein's house. The host, a close friend, mentioned they were together.

The 'ringing in the year' bash was the family's annual theme party held at their home on Via del Lago, just a few blocks north of El Brillo. It was always a magnificent and generous affair. Like the family who hosted the evening, their home was splendid, inside and out. Built in 1934 by Sims Wyeth, the Colonial Revival style home overlooked the Florida Inter Coastal. It was almost visible from Epstein's lawn. Somewhat reminiscent of a Spanish *hacienda* it had 3 acres of beautiful manicured gardens and lush foliage surrounding the property.

Every year that I attended, Maxwell and Epstein, our host and I, spent time chatting and becoming better acquainted. On several occasions, Epstein and Ghislaine invited us to brunch at their home the following day. It would be just the four of us. On one occasion, my friend could not attend. I felt awkward going alone so I asked Maxwell if I could invite a female friend.

My friend and I had met years before while I was still at university in New York. A lawyer by profession, she was working for a local Miami TV station. Today, she is a Judge in Berks County, Pennsylvania. Punctuated by Maxwell's characteristic wit, we had an interesting afternoon chatting about the latest goings-on and "getting lost in let's remember."

The only time I visited Epstein's house nothing seemed out of place or screamed for attention. In fact, Ghislaine and Epstein gave the impression they were a happy go-lucky couple.

I never noticed nude photographs of young girls in the living room where we spent a few minutes before we were escorted out into the patio for brunch. There were photographs mostly of politicians with Epstein. I did not walk up the grand staircase so I did not see what the girls had described as a wall covered in nude photographs.

When I began the investigation, I rang my friend to confirm I was not forgetting any important details about that day. Her recollection was the same as mine. Nothing at Epstein's house seemed out of place during our brunch on New Year's Day.

A year or two later, I attended my friend's New Year's Eve celebration once more. Epstein and Maxwell were also there. Again they invited us for lunch the following day. We declined the invitation. That was the last time I saw Epstein.

Several years went by before I ran into Maxwell again. It was 2007, while attending the Clinton Global Initiative (CGI) in New York City. CGI, as it is commonly known, is a mammoth quasi-political/ public relations fund-raising conference created by former President Clinton. According to a well-known global events executive who wishes to remain anonymous, the former president modeled CGI after Professor Klaus Schwab's, World Economic Forum.

The World Economic Forum (WEF), which began in 1971, is the foremost global public policy conference in the world. It is held annually in Davos, Switzerland. A perennial high-octane platform for debate, it is committed to improving our world by catering to King's, heads of state, world leaders, and CEO's of multi billion dollar corporations who influence our planet.

The source revealed that the Clinton Global Initiative was originally funded by a generous gift from Epstein for a sum of four million dollars. I have been unable to verify or refute the amount of this claim since the organization's accounting records do not disclose the information and Clinton did not return my call. However, one media report claimed that Epstein's lawyer, Gerald Lefcourt confirmed in a media report that his client was among the founders of CGI.

That same year, while attending CGI, I ran into former President Andres Pastrana of Colombia, an acquaintance and exceedingly charismatic man. During our conversation, Maxwell sneaked up behind me. She physically lifted me off the ground and hugged me from behind. It was very strange.

Perhaps Maxwell was attempting to add a bit of humor or simply wanted the president to know we were friends. I don't know the reason for her behavior. Whatever her intentions, her gesture was peculiar since we had not seen each other in several years, and more importantly, President Pastrana was a former Head of State.

What I didn't realize was that Maxwell and the former president were good friends. I found out later when a source close to Maxwell and Pastrana confirmed their friendship and mentioned that his name was listed on Epstein's pilot logs.

His reaction to that incident took me aback. I will never forget the look in his eyes when my body lifted halfway off the ground. Before I could wriggle myself down to the floor again, still in midair, he asked how I knew Ghislaine? I was very embarrassed.

By the time my feet hit the ground I could barely speak. Suddenly, his tone took on an air of familiarity. It reminded me of my father's—surprised and concerned.

Until that incident and in spite of our narrow relationship, I believed Maxwell was a charming lady. Very engaging. Yet that one gesture gave me a different sense to her. Maybe an insight into part of the character I had never witnessed. I did not see Maxwell again during the conference except to say hello in passing. In all the years I've known Maxwell we never had a discordant word. That was the last time we had a conversation.

In 2010, the day I collected the police reports and after I read the Complaints, I telephoned Maxwell. She answered at once. We said hello and chatted a minute or two about the last time we met at CGI. Maxwell had given me her cell number to confirm a dinner invitation she had extended during CGI. The dinner was held at her New York home on 116 East 65th Street in Manhattan. I could not attend.

For a few minutes our conversation revolved about nothing in particular. As delicately as possible I approached the subject. She was silent. Suddenly she blurted out, "Nonsense. All lies," and dismissed the allegations.

I wanted to give her the benefit of the doubt. Early on I had learned that common values, common interests, mutual alliances and good times spent together, count. It was difficult to believe Maxwell was on the wrong side of the issue. I offered to help and suggested she hire a lawyer. Little did I know what was to come?

We did not continue the conversation. I wished her well and hung up. I returned to the documents and read them for a third time. I wanted to be certain what I was reading. During the third reading, I had a flashback to CGI.

The moment Maxwell was standing behind me and lifted me off the ground. I remembered the president's expression too. With eyes wide open I carried on with the investigation. Maxwell and I have not spoken since.

Sometime in 2012 or 2013, after my Daily Beast reports were published, I ran into Maxwell at a neighborhood café— Amaranth-- on Manhattan's Upper East Side. A friend and I were having dinner when Maxwell walked in accompanied by a couple. We had a center table in the back of the room facing the entrance. We were midway through our dinner when they arrived. There was no escaping as I was in her direct line of vision.

The Maître d' walked directly toward me escorting Maxwell and her friends to their table. For a split second we looked at each other. I looked away and continued my conversation. I was not certain that she would refrain from something unpleasant in front of my friend. She did not. Their table was to the right of ours. Maxwell did not ask to change tables.

As she walked past us, she drew a blank expression sauntered around the table and sat down. Her chair faced mine. Until my friend and I left, we did not exchange a single glance. That was the last time I saw her.

The Media continue to report her whereabouts. Maxwell continues to live an active social life. Photographs show her shuttling between San Francisco, New York, London, Paris and all points in between. In early 2016, a handful of media reports revealed, she is quietly selling her Sixty Fifth Street townhouse for $19 million and has considered leasing the house for $50,000 per month.[1]

Her professional activities are far narrower than her social life. Publicity for her foundation, The Terra Mar Project, started in September 2012. According to one article, The Terra Mar Project was blessed if not partially funded by the Clinton's since according to a Vanity Fair report, Maxwell "is passionate about Bill Clinton, with whom she is close friends."[2]

The Terra Mar Project was created to raise money, "To protect the high seas." I tried to access the foundation's website to find their mission statement but could not open the home page unless I submitted my email information. It seems the public does not have access to the charity's home page without disclosing personal information.[3]

As for Epstein, the last time I had a face-to-face conversation was approximately a year before his arrest on New Year's Day, in January 2004. Six years went by before I heard his name mentioned. It was July 2010. I went to visit a friend recovering from surgery.

My friend and her husband lived in Palm Beach not far from *El Brillo*. They were acquainted with Epstein albeit superficially. Given the size of the community and the close proximity of the residents it is hard not to know what your neighbor is up to.

The island's two popular newspapers, The Palm Beach Daily News and Palm Beach Post like to incite the town's wagging tongues. The daily coverage of the comings and goings of residents prevent most from retaining anonymity and so the islanders like in every small town know what everyone else is up to.

That morning, still somewhat under the influence of anesthesia, my friend causally mentioned the latest stirrings in Palm Beach. The conversation went like this: My friend: "Did you hear about Epstein's imminent release?" Me: "Release?"

I was astonished and reached for the paper lying beside her. As my friend was rambling on, I found it difficult to believe her. Perhaps she was mistaken? I would have more easily believed that Epstein had been arrested for tax evasion or money laundering or any other white-collar financial crime than child sexual abuse. It sounded preposterous.

I asked to use her laptop to read more about the case and began the search. My friend was still a bit groggy so I sat at the edge of her bed and read everything I could find. I was shocked to the core. Three stories, published by The Palm Beach Daily News, were particularly alarming.

Michele Dargan's story, a gifted journalist and staff reporter at the Palm Beach Daily News, caught my attention first. Not only did it announce Epstein's imminent release from house arrest on July 21, 2010, the story revealed most of the alleged crimes he had committed.

The story reported Epstein had served 13 months of an 18 months sentence at the Palm Beach County jail and 18 months of 'community control' in his Palm Beach home. Dargan also wrote that Epstein chafed at his restrictions, which in comparison to other sex offenders who committed the same or similar crimes was ludicrously lax.

"Epstein made several apparent missteps. His probation records shows he has never been arrested for any violations. In fact, all his activities seemed to be a departure from the Florida Department of Corrections guidelines. However, they all received the blessing of the court or his probation officer. A report by a Palm Beach police captain states that, Epstein violated probation in August when he was walking along State Road A1A, but his probation officer deemed him compliant," Dargan wrote.[4]

The story revealed that, "Epstein spent blocks of time in Home Depot and Sports Authority multiple times. On March 31, 2010, Epstein was at Home Depot from 6 to 10 p.m., according to his daily probation logs; and on March 27, Epstein was at both stores from 11:30 a.m. to 5 p.m."[5]

Jane Musgrave an equally talented reporter at The Sun Sentinel wrote another jaw dropping account. Musgrave wrote that Epstein, "Complained about ongoing news coverage," and 'seemed somewhat agitated by all the last-minute press,' according to his probation officer who wrote a memo on May 19, 2010. No longer will the 57 year old 'be forced to get permission to fly his private jet to New York or his home in the Virgin Islands or to climb aboard his helicopter to meet with his lawyers in Miami,' Musgrove added.[6]

"Those who criticize the breaks he has gotten say he has little reason to complain. Since he was placed on house arrest in July 2009, he has taken several trips each month to his home in New York and to his private island in the USVI," Musgrave wrote.[7]

Spencer Kuvin, one of several attorneys who represented three underage victims during the civil cases and Adam Horowitz, who represented seven underage female victims during the civil litigation, agreed. "I thought community control meant you stayed within your community and there was some level of control," Horowitz said. "There was very little information disclosed about where he was going and why. It was shocking to me," Kuvin agreed.[8]

The articles hit home and hard because I had just returned from a harrowing trip to Mexico where my life had been endangered during an investigation. I was followed while walking around Mexico City looking for the whereabouts of a victim. A few days later my life was threatened while interviewing a Mexican agency official in San Miguel de Tenancingo, in the district of Tlaxcala.

While investigating the case, I decided to visit the alleged sex trafficker's house. A 64-year-old woman had been arrested in Mexico, extradited to the United States and was awaiting sentencing in New York. The woman, a mother of two sons and a grandmother, operated one of the most heinous local international rings in Mexico. The family lured, coerced, sourced and transported pretty underage girls from nearby towns, smuggled them into the United States, transported them across the country and then forced them into prostitution.

Child sex trafficking was one of the alleged crimes also perpetrated by Epstein and some of his alleged procurers. I felt sick to my stomach. Flashbacks of that harrowing trip overwhelmed me.

A security guard and driver, 'Victor' had been assigned to my care during the investigation thanks to a Mexican government official. He was to drive us to the town of San Miguel de Tenancingo, located about 80 miles west of Mexico City. The drive lasted approximately two and a-half hours. We left early in the morning to avoid rush hour traffic, which is treacherous in Mexico.

Months earlier, while conducting research in New York, I had spoken to the trafficker's New York attorney and located her home address. The reason for my visit was to find the whereabouts of her daughter-in-law who had seemingly escaped and was looking for her baby and wanted to conduct more research into the network and how they smuggle the children across the border from the Mexican side.

What I found instead shocked me and it was not the trafficker's daughter in law. By the time Victor found the house it turned out to be an office for *Desarrollo Integral de la Familia*, (DIF). DIF is a Mexican organization that provides social services, transportation and assistance to the poorest families in Mexico. There is a DIF chapter in every village and town including Mexico City.

The president of DIF is the First Lady of Mexico. Her tenure lasts six years, the same amount of time the President of Mexico, is in office. It is a similar agency, albeit much smaller in scope, to the U.S. Department of Health and Human Services (HHS). HHS provides essential human services and protects Americans, especially the most vulnerable families.

The convicted trafficker's immediate family was already in jail since they had been arrested in New York for trafficking the girls for sex. They were serving long prison sentences in U.S. federal penitentiaries across the country- from twenty five to fifty years under the TVPA federal guidelines. Some of the crimes perpetrated by the Mexican family were similar to the alleged crimes perpetrated by Epstein and a number of his suspected principal procurers.

It seemed peculiar the Mexican government would take the risk of operating a DIF chapter in the house of a convicted sex trafficker, given the likely association between the family and the Mexican cartels.

After he surveyed the neighborhood and the street he allowed me to leave the van. From that moment on I did not leave Victor's side. Together, we walked upstairs and asked to speak to the Director of DIF. A woman came toward me who I assumed was the director. She told me to sit at her desk but refused to speak. She did not acknowledge her position or any of my questions. Several times I attempted to discuss the case and explain the urgency. I explained we had come to look for the child and daughter in law who had gone missing.

She did not budge and remained silent throughout much of the one sided interview. On her desk I noticed a document. At first, it looked like a directory with names, addresses and telephone numbers. I wondered what the list was for. I asked her. She did not answer. Then I asked her about the convicted trafficker, her family, the girl who ran away from New York and her baby. The woman did not respond.

Then suddenly, midway through my sentence she stopped me and in an almost inaudible but firm voice she told me to stop asking questions. If I asked her another question, she said, she would pick up the bell next to her and ring it. This, she said, would alert the townspeople who would come lynch me. It took her perhaps one or two minutes to say that. It took a great deal longer to register that information. My life had never been threatened, certainly not like this.

For a split second, I thought I misunderstood her until I remembered the first story I read in the morning paper, *El Universal*, a leading Mexican daily. Two journalists, while investigating a child sex trafficking case in a nearby town had been lynched by the townspeople and were found dead.

Lynch me? It was time to go!

'Victor,' shot up from his chair pulled out a number of badges from his pocket and threw them on her desk. They landed squarely in front of her. He grabbed my right shoulder and pulled me out from the chair and close beside him.

The woman seemed unfazed. Calmly, she collected his badges looked intently at Victor and without skipping a beat asked a woman nearby to make copies of the badges. The time it took the woman to make copies seemed interminable. Even standing close to Victor, I was racked with nerves. Within a few minutes the other woman returned his badges. Victor grabbed my hand and together we speed walked downstairs and out the door.

As we stepped onto the sidewalk a young woman, maybe in her late twenties, whistled to us from behind a van. A DIF van was parked right outside the offices. She called out my name and asked us to walk toward her. I wondered how she knew my name?

I was petrified. Victor seemed in total control. He gently pushed me behind him and I literally walked on his heels toward the van. Her name was 'Rita.' She warned us. We were in danger. The woman I had spoken to was in fact the director.

Rita explained the woman could not speak to me since she too was in danger. She had no choice but to corroborate with the cartels or risk death or retribution. There was the possibility that her family and children would be killed if she talked. The walls had ears, she said. The woman lived in fear. She had no choice but to obey and do what they wanted.

Who were 'they?' Who was pulling the strings? The cartels? The local trafficking operators who work with the cartels? She would not say. She handed Victor her telephone number and asked him to call her later that afternoon.

The last thing she told us was that the document on her desk, the one she had seen me eyeing was in fact a list of children who lived in the area. Apparently, the DIF director would hand over the list to the cartels when they came calling. That is how the cartels knew the children's whereabouts and could so easily abduct them.

The rest of the operation was easy. Since most families who register with DIF are indigent, single parents, and or illiterate, few have the courage to speak up and report the missing children to the authorities.

In Mexico, it is widely known that all three branches of the Mexican police force: federal, state and municipal are corrupt. It is endemic. Corruption is rampant because the officers don't earn enough money to resist the power of the Mexican cartels. Too much money is being earned trafficking children, drugs and weapons. Child sex trafficking is a $67 billion dollar industry according to some international human rights reports.

In 2016, child sex trafficking is an epidemic especially in San Miguel de Tenancingo. A friend and former Mexican Foreign Minister corroborated the information and took it one step further. His remarks were cold and brutal nevertheless, they made sense. "Until the child of a rich Mexican family or perhaps the child of a government official is trafficked, chances are, human trafficking will not stop in Mexico. There are simply too many poor children that no one cares about."

Given Tenancingo's geographical size, population was approximately 10,000 in 2012, and per capita income that is well below the minimum wage in the United States, the town has become a principal source for trafficked children. Reports indicate that it is also a pipeline for girls trafficked to New York, Miami, Palm Beach and other affluent cities in the United States.

In 2016, the Mexican family I was investigating for committing child sex trafficking felonies in the United States is still serving lengthy sentences in U.S. federal penitentiaries. While, Epstein, who allegedly committed some but not all of the same offenses, is free as are the alleged procurers who were never charged.

The Mexican family was not given the option of a work release program, private cell, or the possibility of parole or even house arrest for perpetrating similar crimes. As soon as their sentences are served they will be automatically deported back to Mexico. While several of the traffickers implicated in the case were prosecuted under the TVPA guidelines at around the same time 2005-2007, Epstein was prosecuted for one count of solicitation of prostitution with a minor.

Back in Florida and still somewhat in shock, I left early that evening. The next morning I rang my friend and promised to visit her in the afternoon. Luckily, my cell phone still had Epstein's telephone number. I rang him at once. If he agreed I would pay him a visit at home. He did not return my call that day.

I left Key Biscayne early. It was a beautiful summer day. The traffic was light driving northbound on I-95 to Palm Beach. By the time I exited Okeechobee Boulevard I headed straight east, crossed the bridge and drove directly to the Palm Beach Police Department on South County Road. I rang the bell, waited for an Officer to respond and submitted my request. The police officer, a very genial man told me to return in half an hour to pick up the files.

I purchased every document available. The files contained every sordid detail of the case including the heinous sex crimes allegedly committed by Epstein, Kellen, Robson, Maxwell and others. Many names were redacted to protect the victim's identities.

I was impatient to read the report so I stopped at a nearby park and sat on a wooden bench. I pulled out the files. Surrounded by masses of fuchsia-colored bougainvillea I read page after page of the sordid story. It took about two hours to consume hundreds of pages of information. I read every document twice---affidavits, arrest reports, and incident reports. I could not believe my eyes. Suddenly, I shut down. I had no idea who Epstein and Maxwell really where.

For the next few days I thought a great deal about the case. Given the limited information I had, back then, Epstein's case presented a challenge. As ghastly as the Mexican case was, they paled in comparison especially because the alleged perpetrators were educated, were not committing the crime to make money and should have known better. One thing was certain whoever opened up Pandora's Box, was not in an enviable position.

Stumbling into the Epstein case was extremely valuable because it provided a birds eye view of some of the legal issues that continue to dog law enforcement officials, the Department of Justice and the abolitionist community. In one sitting, I had suddenly understood the bigger picture and the many moving parts that can prevent well-intentioned prosecutors such as R. Alex Acosta and Ann Marie Villafana to be, from doing their work effectively.

I returned later that afternoon and drove straight to my friend's. Together we poured through the documents. Two heads are always better than one, especially when it's hers. After reading the case again, we decided to seek guidance and more information from the victim's lawyers. I jotted down their information and made it a point to schedule a meeting with each of them: Brad Edwards, Spencer Kuvin, Adam Horowitz and Robert Josefsberg.

All four attorneys representing the victims in the civil cases against Epstein were South Florida attorneys. With the exception of Robert Josefsberg, who was a close friend of Alan Dershowitz and had been solicited by Epstein's legal team to represent Virginia Louise Roberts (a.k.a. #102), the other attorneys worked independently of Dershowitz and Epstein's legal team.

I rang the lawyers that week and scheduled a meeting. As soon as my friend was discharged, together, we met Brad Edwards at his Fort Lauderdale office and two private investigators working on the case. A few days later, we met Spencer Kuvin at his West Palm Beach law office.

I spoke to Horowitz and Josefsberg only on the phone since they were unable to meet with us. Over the course of the year, I spoke to both attorneys many times. I also spoke to Josefsberg over the phone several times. In spite of Josefsberg's relationship with Dershowitz and Epstein's legal team he was very cooperative.

My girlfriend was an incredible source of support at the beginning of the investigation. Her insights and information into Epstein and his world were dazzling. I shall remain forever grateful. Her friendship and generosity of spirit propelled me forward every step of the way and provided the momentum to continue the research to write this story.

Thanks to my friend, I also met several of Epstein's neighbors and a handful of insiders who knew him well. They spoke openly about their neighbor. I gleaned a great deal of insightful information about his day-to-day social activities while on the island which I shared with several attorneys representing the victims. Everyone I met thought he was a very peculiar man.

As I moved further into the investigation, it was difficult to understand why Maxwell continued her relationship with Epstein. Given her history, it did not make sense, unless of course she needed his money desperately. Maxwell seemed a very capable intelligent woman. I often wondered what happened to the woman I had met in London. Then I would remember my mother's favorite maxim, "Don't judge a book by its cover."

In 2010, Epstein and I resumed conversation. He seemed a very different person. His personality was radically different. His *joie de vivre* had all but vanished. We spoke several times while he was still serving time under house arrest. Based on his statements, I'm almost certain the FBI and perhaps other local law enforcement agencies have tapes of our conversations.

Epstein seemed distant and at times disoriented. He was circumspect, his voice sounded gloomy. Several times he repeated himself and said we were being taped. Once he insinuated during a call that his attorneys might not be giving him the most-sound advice. Inevitably, the issue of money came up. He was spending a fortune on attorney fees, he admitted. He asked if I was taping our conversations. I told him the truth that I was not.

He insinuated the attorneys might not be providing him with the most suitable resolutions concerning the "girls." I was never sure if he was on medication. Perhaps he was taking anti depressants or anti-anxiety pills? I did not ask him. In view of the pending civil litigations and omnipresent attorneys and law enforcement agents occupying his life, I should not have expected differently.

Epstein answered most of my questions with his questions. He is very clever. He seemed interested in my life. I sensed he was not being authentic. He asked several questions I assumed he already knew the answers. The most obvious was why I had taken an interest in his case. I was investigating the issue of human trafficking and had reason to believe that some of the girls being trafficked from Mexico ended up in the United States specifically in West Palm Beach, Florida. Apparently, he did not make the connection.

I asked him if he was familiar with the Mexican trafficking cartels. He said, "No." He had no idea about the Mexican Cartels. Perhaps he did not understand the reason for my question.

Most of Epstein's answers were repetitious, hardly informative and unidirectional. They were not introspective or remotely accurate. He did not explain why he ended up in his predicament, why he preferred underage girls to adult women, or why he was interested in those particular underage girls. I believe he did not answer any question truthfully.

He could not explain why he ended up in a state jail and paid millions of dollars in legal fees if in fact he was innocent. He also did not seem to accept responsibility or the reason why dozens of girls filed civil suits against him. Several times he implied the girls were extorting him for money. He insinuated that some girls had boyfriends who drove them to his house and were partly responsible. It was a scam, he said.

During one conversation, Epstein reminded me of his unshakeable memory. After our first introduction, in the early nineties, he rang a couple of times. I did not see him for many years.

In 2010, by the time we spoke again on the phone he was less than candid. We spoke only a few times. He was not in need of redemption. A few days before my first story posted, on July 20, 2010, I rang him again to let him know I was about to publish the story. He hung up on me. After the story posted, I rang him one more time at the insistence of my editor. Epstein did not return my call. We have not spoken since.

Unlike our previous conversations, my talks with Maxwell highlighted several shades of red. One thing was certain Maxwell and Epstein were the grand masters of profitable and triangular relationships.

To obtain a more objective perspective about the couple, I made it a point to speak with as many people who knew them as possible. I initiated hundreds of conversations with mutual friends, insiders who knew them and socialized with them victims, law enforcement officials, the parent's of one of the victim's and the lawyers who represented the plaintiffs.

One of the more enlightening conversations was held with former Palm Beach Police Chief, Michael Reiter. Chief Reiter and I met twice in Palm Beach at my friend's home followed by several more conversations on the telephone as the case unfolded.

Thanks to Chief Reiter's depositions and his candid explanations, I gained a better understanding of the two complex personalities leading the alleged trafficking ring and the apparent associates who helped them cover up the alleged crimes.

Chief Reiter, like so many other law enforcement officials who spoke openly with me, held the same opinion of Epstein and Maxwell as several lawyers who represented the victims and many others involved in the case.

The more attorneys I spoke with, the more outrage I witnessed at the Government's decision to give Epstein so many passes given the crimes. One such pass allowed him to abstain from submitting to the State psychological evaluation. When I approached the prosecutor about these issues, he was reticent at first. Sensing, I was not going away he wrote a letter. I first posted Mr. Acosta's letter in The Daily Beast. It best describes the prosecution's frustrations:

> "What followed was a yearlong assault on the prosecution and the prosecutors. I use the word assault intentionally, as the defense in this case was more aggressive than any, which I, or the prosecutors in my office, had previously encountered. Mr. Epstein hired an army of legal superstars: Harvard Professor Alan Dershowitz, former Judge and then Pepperdine Law Dean Kenneth Starr, former Deputy Assistant to the President and then Kirkland Ellis partner Jay Lefkowitz, and several others, including prosecutors who had formally worked in the U.S. Attorney's Office and in the Child Exploitation and Obscenity Section of the Justice Department.

Defense attorneys next requested a meeting with me to challenge the prosecution and the terms previously presented by the prosecutors in their meeting with Mr. Black. The prosecution team and I met with defense counsel in Fall 2007, and I reaffirmed the office's position: two years, registration and restitution, or trial.

Over the next several months, the defense team presented argument after argument claiming that felony criminal proceedings against Epstein were unsupported by the evidence and lacked a basis in law, and that the office's insistence on jail-time was motivated by zeal to overcharge a man merely because he is wealthy.

They bolstered their arguments with legal opinions from well-known legal experts. One member of the defense team warned that the office's excess zeal in forcing a good man to serve time in jail might be the subject of a book if we continued to proceed with this matter. My office systematically considered and rejected each argument, and when we did, my office's decisions were appealed to Washington. As to the warning, I ignored it.

What made this case so gripping was to witness up close and personal the dark side of humanity and how money and influence almost never take a back seat to justice.

* * *

Footnotes

1. http://www.nydailynews.com/life-style/real-estate/jeffrey-epstein-alleged-madam-lists-mansion-18m-article-1.2183607

2. http://www.vanityfair.com/online/daily/2011/03/notes-on-new-yorks-oddest-couple-jeffrey-epstein-and-ghislaine-maxwell

3. http://theterramarproject.org/#&panel1-1

4. http://www.palmbeachdailynews.com/news/news/jeffrey-epstein-house-arrest-missteps-not-deemed-u/nMGbT/

5. http://www.palmbeachdailynews.com/news/news/jeffrey-epstein-house-arrest-missteps-not-deemed-u/nMGbT/

6. http://articles.sun-sentinel.com/2010-07-11/news/fl-palm-epstein-free-20100711_1_probation-officer-jeffrey-epstein-virgin-islands

7. http://articles.sun-sentinel.com/2010-07-11/news/fl-palm-epstein-free-20100711_1_probation-officer-jeffrey-epstein-virgin-islands

8. http://articles.sun-sentinel.com/2010-07-11/news/fl-palm-epstein-free-20100711_1_probation-officer-jeffrey-epstein-virgin-islands

Chapter Nine

Money & Secrets Make the World Go Round

"Facts are stubborn things: and whatever may be our wishes, our inclinations. Or the dictates of our passion, they cannot alter the state of facts and evidence." John Adams

"I'm not a sexual predator, I'm an 'Offender,' Epstein told the New York Post on February 25, 2011. "It's the difference between a murderer and a person who steals a bagel."[1]

Epstein grew up in a household of five including his father, a former New York City park ranger, his mother a homemaker and the three children: Epstein, his sister, Paula, and a younger brother, Mark, who oversees his brother's real estate properties.[2]

In the late seventies, while tutoring a young student in mathematics, Ted Greenberg, his life took a meteoric turn. But before the drastic career change and in spite of his lack of academic credentials—or any other meaningful credentials-- Epstein, had managed to eke out a living by teaching and tutoring at one of Manhattan's elite preparatory schools.

One day, Epstein met Ted Greenberg's father during one of his tutorials. Alan Greenberg, better known as "Ace," became chairman of Bear Stearns after he hired Epstein as an "options trader," in 1976. It was Ace who ultimately changed the course of Epstein's life. Given Greenberg's lofty position as chairman, their meeting became a defining moment for the ambitious Epstein.

Greenberg who died on July 25, 2014, never fully revealed why he hired and then suddenly fired Epstein only months after he was named partner. A Daily Beast blog posted on January 6, 2015 claimed Epstein was found guilty by Bear Stearns of a Reg d violation, in other words, for insider trading. It seems, however, the primary reason Greenberg employed Epstein was because his son, Ted, had advanced beyond his expectations thanks to Epstein's tutoring abilities.[3]

Unlike CEOs of other investment houses, Greenberg had a penchant for hiring what he referred to as "PSD" candidates: poor, smart and disadvantaged. He coined the term because the young men he preferred to hire were just that: poor, smart, and hungry. Many did not have M.B.A. degrees. Unlike many brokers during his time who worked in investment banking, Ace, "Had been rejected by a number of 'white shoe' investment firms when… first looking for work in New York."[4]

Another man, beside Greenberg, was instrumental in placing Epstein at Bear Stearns. His name was James (Jimmy) Cayne, Greenberg's boss and CEO. He too liked Epstein. Years later, after Epstein left the investment house, Cayne revealed that, "Epstein's forte was dealing with wealthier clients, helping them with their overall portfolios."[5]

As one of Ace's longtime friends, an employee at the trading desk and later a substantial investor in one of the firm's largest real estate funds, Epstein, had the dirt that's fit to print on most everyone in the firm.

Greenberg's obituary in *The New York Times*, claimed that Greenberg, "played a major role as Bear Stearns experienced one of Wall Street's legendary roller-coaster rides, a climb to dizzying heights as one of the country's biggest brokerages, and a breathtaking free fall to the brink of bankruptcy. Stuck with billions in all-but-worthless mortgage securities as its clients made a run on the bank, Bear Stearns was taken over the JPMorgan Chase in a $270 million fire sale sanctioned by the Federal Reserve." As an insider, Epstein clearly knew when to strike.[6]

Ironically, in 2007, while negotiating his Non Prosecution Agreement plea with the Justice Department and before the investment firm crashed and burned, it was Epstein who allegedly played a role in the demise of two subprime hedge funds known as structured funds.

The arrests came on June 19, 2008, when two Bear Stearns hedge fund directors named Ralph Cioffi and Matthew Tannin were charged with securities fraud. The case brought by the Justice Department sought to prove that Cioffi and Tannin deceived their investors, including Epstein. According to reports the case was weak and hinged on a couple of e-mails that were taken out of context. Nevertheless, Cioffi and Tannin were charged with securities fraud and Bank of America subsequently filed a Complaint against the two men.

After their arrests, The New York Times reported, they "Were among the few executives to face a trial on criminal charges in the aftermath of the financial crisis… The bank accused the two men of lying about the health of their hedge funds, which had invested heavily in subprime mortgage-backed securities that plummeted in value when the housing market collapsed.

Judge Alison J. Nathan of Federal District Court in Manhattan rejected Bank of America's claims of fraud and breach of fiduciary duty, ruling that bank had failed to prove damages tied to the conduct of the two men."[7]

By exposing inside information such as the internal workings of Bear Stearns and the structured funds, Epstein and his attorneys were able to negotiate a plea deal with the Department of Justice in return for lesser criminal charges and less jail time. Perhaps as important as his plea deal, Epstein was able to strike back against the firm at the right time. In the end, in 2009, Cioffi and Tannin's were found not guilty.

I spoke with Ralph Cioffi on a number of occasions about his case. On November 17, 2014, Cioffi said, "I do not [know why Epstein was fired from Bear Stearns] and doubt Matt would. I never knew Epstein at Bear. Never met him while he was an employee or even as an investor in the fund." By early January of the following year, Cioffi warned me, "Epstein is an evil person. Makes the 'root of all evil is money phrase ring true. There were always rumors about what went on, on his jet when flying back and forth from Europe, Cioffi said.[8]

A best selling book that became a popular film, "The Big Short," written by Michael Lewis, illustrated a story about the questionable standards at Bear Stearns. In the book, Charlie and Jamie, two of the main characters said they, "Wanted to move their account, their investment pool was approximately twelve million dollars from Schwab to Bear Stearns and mentioned it to their accountant who supposedly knew Greenberg."

"Without ever meeting Greenberg, once they moved their assets to Bear Stearns, their brokerage statements soon came back with Greenberg's name on top. They found it 'bizarre' 'that Greenberg was suddenly their broker and called him on several occasions to talk.' Greenberg occasionally answered but did not respond. "Hold on," is what he would say and immediately pass the phone to his assistant. When they finally met, 'The encounter was so brief, that they could not honestly say whether they had met Ace Greenberg.' They were ushered in for thirty seconds— literally thirty seconds—and then ceremoniously ushered out," said Jamie. Ace Greenberg was still formally, on paper, their broker although they never spoke to him. The Big Short: Michael Lewis. P. 117, Norton Publishing House 2011[9]

During the meltdown, it was interesting to see who at the firm declined from sipping the "Kool-Aid." Unlike most employees who worked at Lehman Brothers, it was not surprising that "Greenberg did not entirely drink the Kool-Aid." Instead he, "cashed in and sold his stake for $50 million in Bear Stearns shares...In 2008, following the firm's collapse, Ace signed a lucrative contract with JPMorgan to stay on as vice chairman emeritus and take 40 percent of trading commissions he generated." If Ace were alive today, he might even thank Epstein for his role in that deal.[10]

With a financial collapse looming tall in the horizon and a global financial disaster on their hands, DOJ might have felt compelled to negotiate a deal that favored Epstein, especially since the Justice Department had no way of verifying the strength of those relationships. In fact, one of Epstein's better-known friend's, Larry Summers, who traveled with Epstein, according to pilot logs, on his private jet between 1997 and 2005, was a very respected man in the United States.

Summers, former Treasury Secretary and Harvard University President around the same time of Epstein's indictment had been reporting about the impending crisis. On September 23, 2007, just weeks before Epstein finalized the Non Prosecution Agreement, Summers reported to the Financial Times that, "Central to every policy discussion in response to a financial crisis or the prospect of a crisis is the connect of moral hazard."[11]

Given the high level conversations that took place behind closed doors in October 2007, I doubt the financial climate did not play a role during the negotiations that led to Epstein's final sweetheart Non Prosecution Agreement (NPA), signed October 27, 2007.

Possibly for DOJ's long-term purposes, keeping Epstein on the outside a while longer, in the right place at the right time and surrounded by the right friends suited their purposes. Certainly, his connections on 'The Street' and willingness to cooperate to bring forward other Wall Street scoundrels perhaps made it easier for DOJ to collect information they could use in pending or future Wall Street cases. In light of his personal investments and those of his primary client, Leslie Wexner, the predator's "inside information' might have helped DOJ by lessening their load and providing the agency with much needed backroom access.

As an informer, Epstein certainly made for a colorful figure. Given his position at the firm, both as an insider and client, the disgruntled Bear Stearns employee and angry investor could certainly teach DOJ a thing or two about the financial markets, hedge funds and what they needed to know about Wall Street's overreach.

Perhaps by agreeing to reduce Epstein's sentence, the Justice Department avoided hundreds of hours of research and averted hour-long meetings with Wall Street's top executives who perhaps might not have been so forthcoming.

As the world learned only too late, the financial climate in 2007 was bleak. Unlike anything ever experienced on Wall Street since the Great Depression of 1929. In 2007, given the billions being made in the markets, it seemed that only a few honest men were willing to risk their future earnings by sharing accurate information with the general public. By the end of 2007, after Epstein negotiated his plea deal, the plunging markets began their descent.

An alarming report published in *The New York Times* a year prior to the stock market collapse, showed how Bear Stearns averted a meltdown even though "hedge funds and pensions funds"—several of which Epstein was heavily invested in--"could be left holding billions of dollars in bonds and securities backed by loans that were quickly losing their value."[12]

The same report held that a, "Hedge fund and a related fund suffered millions in losses and shocked investors had begun asking for their money back. The firm agreed to buy out several Wall Street banks that had lent the fund money, that managers hoped would avoid a broader sell-off without causing a meltdown in the once-booming market for mortgage securities."[13]

Conceivably, it was not just Epstein's high-level banking and political connections that prevented him from a stiff federal prosecution. Perhaps, his generous donations to several Democratic Party leaders furthered his successful defense. Donations to Democrats included: Bill and Hillary Clinton, even after his indictment, Governor Bill Richardson, former New York Governor Eliot Spitzer, and several others. According to media reports The Clinton Foundation received a $25,000 donation in 2006, after Epstein was charged with solicitation of prostitution with a minor.[14]

A Forbes article reported that, "many people still attribute the financial crisis of 2008 to "greed," a lack of regulatory policies and free market capitalism." While other Wall Street insiders claim the *real cause*—which has yet to be acknowledged, let alone curbed or removed—was *government intervention* in *the markets*. There is no doubt that in this mix, Epstein played a role as an, albeit small, investor and more importantly, as Leslie Wexner's financial advisor.

This lethal combination, Forbes maintained, included the Federal Reserve's disruptive manipulations of interest rates, massive subsidies and regulations in housing, banking, and mortgages." Forbes argued that, "for years government policy promoted reckless financial practices (aka "moral hazard") made things worse by bailing out the worst miscreants."[15]

If this is true, then it could also be true the Federal Government acknowledged and allowed Epstein's recommendations and information concerning Bear Stearns to be part of the investigation. Whatever the truth is, one fact is indisputable: The Department of Justice signed a plea deal that was far less defensible than what the U.S. Attorney's Office in Florida had originally prescribed.

One of the reasons the Bear Stearns financial shortcomings are worth mentioning is because, in early 2007, their stock was trading at $170 per share. By the end of 2008, after Epstein signed the Non Prosecution Agreement, their shares were selling under $2.00 per share, the price offered by JPMorgan Chase to purchase the company. Eventually, the offer was raised to $10 per share to ease stockholder backlash and to ensure a quick closure of the proposed transaction.

Could the loss in share price have been partially a result of Epstein's information? As Greenberg wrote in a book published in 2010, "The bank run that swallowed Bear Stearns in 2008 stemmed from a "groundless rumor" that it had a liquidity problem." Clearly, Greenberg felt that someone had started false rumors.[16] To answer this today requires a much broader investigation to determine Epstein's degree of culpability.

As a result of the purchase, most of Bear Stearns' 14,000 employees lost their jobs and some of them lost their entire life savings. Many reports claimed that 30 percent of the company's equity was held by employees, including many senior executives who were wiped out.

It is interesting to see how the firm's unspoken rules and dubious ethics attracted characters such as Epstein and might have set in motion Greenberg's attraction to Epstein. After all, Bear Stearns was a competitive juggernaut that encouraged a "dog-eat-dog" attitude as part of its corporate culture.

Unlike other more genteel Wall Street investment firms, Bear Stearns was a rough and tumble boxing ring that allowed Epstein's character to flourish even if only for a short while. It was known on 'The Street' that, "Greenberg invested a decade nurturing a culture where sharp-elbowed candidates were cultivated for the benefit of the company."[17]

Although there is a 27-year lapse between Epstein's exiting the firm, in 1981, and the 2008 financial collapse, those in-between years, Epstein, maintained a very close relationship with the leadership, including his friends, Jimmy Cayne and "Ace" Greenberg in particular, and the direction of the investment house.

Beyond his relationships at the firm, Epstein's influence and success was in part due to his access to Wexner's vast wealth and investment portfolio, which over time allowed him to leverage his position, gain financial liquidity, and exploit the investment house's moneymaking mechanisms such as their financial instruments and products. Before the firm's demise, the shrewd manipulator served his revenge cold and by September 2008, when the markets imploded, Epstein had the last laugh.

Perhaps, the impending Wall Street fallout; failure of the world financial markets; and the firm's imminent collapse, all contributed in one way or another to the sweetening of Epstein's deal. Given Epstein's considerable financial losses with Bear Stearns and the government's potential liability, the two became one and part of the formula for a sweetheart deal.

* * *

Footnotes

1. http://nypost.com/2011/02/25/billionaire-jeffrey-epstein-im-a-sex-offender-not-a-predator/

2. http://www.politico.com/blogs/under-the-radar/2015/12/victims-in-underage-sex-case-want-prosecutors-to-testify-217139

3. http://online.wsj.com/public/resources/documents/2015_01 05_epstein2011order.pdf

4. http://www.nytimes.com/2014/07/26/business/alan-c-greenberg-is-dead-at-86-led-bear-stearns-through-its-rise-and-fall.html?_r=0

5. http://online.wsj.com/public/resources/documents/2015_01 05_epstein2011order.pdf

6. http://www.nytimes.com/2014/07/26/business/alan-c-greenberg-is-dead-at-86-led-bear-stearns-through-its-rise-and-fall.html?_r=0

7. http://www.nytimes.com/2014/07/26/business/alan-c-greenberg-is-dead-at-86-led-bear-stearns-through-its-rise-and-fall.html?_r=0

8. Conversation with Ralph Cioffi. November 17, 2014

9. Conversation with Ralph Cioffi. November 17, 2014

10. Michael Lewis, "The Big Short," page 117. Norton Publishing House, 2011

11. http://online.wsj.com/public/resources/documents/2015_01 05_epstein2011order.pdf

12. http://www.ft.com/intl/cms/s/0/5ffd2606-69e8-11dc-a571 0000779fd2ac.html#axzz40ZfqAJer

13. http://dealbook.nytimes.com/2013/09/04/judge-dismisses-bank-of-america-suit-against-2-bear-stearns-executives/?_r=0

14. http://dealbook.nytimes.com/2013/09/04/judge-dismisses-bank-of-america-suit-against-2-bear-stearns-executives/?_r=0

15. http://www.americarisingpac.org/clinton-foundation-accepted-25000-bills-pedophile-party-pal/

16. http://www.forbes.com/sites/richardsalsman/2013/09/19/the-financial-crisis-was-a-failure-of-government-not-free-markets/#6467dc10449e

17. http://www.nytimes.com/2014/07/26/business/alan-c-greenberg-is-dead-at-86-led-bear-stearns-through-its-rise-and-fall.html?_r=0

Chapter Ten

Alfredo Rodriguez: Buried Secrets

Two wrongs do not one right make.

Alfredo Rodriguez, Epstein's house manager cum butler committed a federal crime and was sentenced on June 18, 2010 to eighteen months in a federal prison for obstructing justice during a federal investigation.

In light of Epstein's suspected crimes, the criminal prosecution of Alfredo Rodriguez, Epstein's former house manager between 2004-2005, was a travesty. Born in Chile, the 56 year-old Rodriguez was an American citizen when he was indicted.

Rodriguez's imprudent behavior, withholding a copy of Epstein's 2005 "little black book" containing the names and addresses of Epstein's friends, victims and associates, did not warrant such extreme punishment within the context of the greater picture especially given the evidence already in custody at the Department of Justice.

After Epstein was charged with sex crimes against minor girls, in 2005, most of the evidence against him was in possession of law enforcement officials. It was not until years later, in 2009 that Rodriguez attempted to sell his 2005 version of the "little black book, or Holy Grail," as he referred to it, to an undercover agent for fifty thousand dollars.

According to media reports, the charge was in connection with Rodriguez trying to obtain $50,000 from civil attorneys pursuing several civil sexual assault cases against Epstein as payment for producing the book (also identified as 'The Holy Grail' and 'the black book'), to the attorney's."[1]

"Rodriguez said he needed money because the journal or "little black book" was his "property" and that he was afraid that Jeffrey Epstein would make him "disappear" unless he had an "insurance policy" i.e., the journal."[2]

Rodriguez's story sounds as if perhaps someone was looking to strip him of all credibility or wanted him behind bars for fear of what else he might disclose. As a result of his untimely death, many facts will remain a mystery.

The case began in 2009. At the time, Rodriguez lived in Kendall, a southwestern district in Miami, Florida, with his second wife, Bolivian-born, Patricia Dunn, a real estate agent. Rodriguez had four children from two marriages; Cristina Rodriguez, aged 15, who lived with her mother; and Christopher Dunn, his wife's son, who lived with the couple. His two elder children, Cristina's siblings, Monica and Sergio Rodriguez lived on their own.

Rodriguez's wife, Dunn, never met Epstein's victims although according to Rodriguez's deposition, she knew the stories. Before Rodriguez went to work for Epstein, during a career that spanned eight to ten years as house manager, Rodriguez worked for several families.

A handful of his employees were identified in court documents: "Ms. Hammond who lived in Palm Beach, Florida; Arturo Torres who lived between Fisher Island, Florida and his Texas ranch; and Leona Helmsley from New York," whom Rodriguez remarked, 'Was a very demanding lady.'

For a brief stint prior to Epstein's employment, Rodriguez also worked at the Montauk Lake Club & Marina in Long Island, New York, where, according to his deposition, former President Richard Nixon would occasionally visit.

During the early part of my investigation, whenever I attempted to speak with Rodriguez by phone or in person, his wife would almost always intervene. At the time, Epstein was serving the latter part of his sentence--18 months of house arrest (community control) at this Palm Beach estate. We spoke twice. Rodriguez was undoubtedly terrified to discuss the case with a journalist given his investigation.

As with any person placed in a position of trust, Rodriguez was a pivotal witness. Someone who could provide a unique perspective into Epstein's psyche, character, and the crimes, Epstein allegedly committed. When on the rare occasion I spoke with his wife, our conversation did not prove valuable. She glossed over many facts and was perpetually in a hurry. I can't say I blame her given what she was going through.

Frustrated by Rodriguez's inaccessibility, I made it a point to have additional conversations with law enforcement, lawyers, victims, prosecutors and other insiders working his case. A former law enforcement agent turned private investigator expanded substantially about the house manager's role within the Epstein household. Thanks to him I was also able to secure copies of Rodriguez's video taped deposition.

Rodriguez was an important witness because, unlike the rest of Epstein's Palm Beach house staff, he paid the victims directly, was close to Epstein, and was closer to most of Epstein's staff and alleged procurers. It appears Rodriguez, more than most staff members, understood Epstein, had plenty of inside information and was not afraid to speak with the police.

Like some of the victims, alleged procurers and staff members, he also spoke Spanish, a benefit that added to his attributes. As a male employee, he had more opportunities to become familiar with Epstein in ways that his female employees could not. More importantly, as a disgruntled employee, he had an ax to grind.

In Rodriguez's attempt to arbitrarily seek justice and make some extra money, the man did just the opposite. After he copied the little black book, he hid it for a while until he thought the timing was right.

An interesting detail revealed later in the case, after Rodriguez was sentenced, showed that DOJ had a copy of the same 2005 "little black book" in their possession. This would have made Rodriguez's copy extraneous. If the prosecutors had a copy of the same version, then why the 'obstruction of justice' charge? (2)

In fact Rodriguez was never charged with physical or sexual assault, solicitation of prostitution, abuse or anything related to crimes against children. He was not charged with the intent to coerce, lure or deceive underage girls for sex. He did not harm or permanently destroy the lives of countless adolescent girls. And yet for a crime seemingly much less harmful and possibly unfounded, in light of the evidence that surfaced later, the man served the same amount of time in a federal prison as Epstein.

According to my investigation, Rodriguez's life began to unravel around the same time he lost his job. Epstein's justification for firing his house manager was disingenuous. According to court records, Epstein claimed Rodriguez had stolen from him. In fact, the last person Epstein needed lurking around his house during a criminal investigation was the all-seeing houseman who knew his dirty secrets.

Rodriguez was the one person, alongside the alleged procurers, pilots and victims who knew where all the bones were buried. Given the butler's history and culture, he might have been the only staff member who outwardly showed contempt for Epstein's deviant behavior. No doubt, Rodriguez was far too dangerous a witness for the prosecution.[3]

His access to victims and Epstein's friends also posed a greater threat. According to the recorded deposition, he was asked many times to make the payments to a number of underage girls who came to give Epstein a "massage."

Since most people believe that money usually banks on the side of money, it made it difficult for Rodriguez to look for work as a houseman or butler in Palm Beach. He was scared what Epstein would say about him.

And so, in 2005, with a stain on his record and in fear of what Epstein's power and influence could buy, Rodriguez refused to approach potential employees. At the same time, unknown to Rodriguez, Epstein was at the time under a criminal investigation but had not been sentenced.

By 2009, the man was in a desperate financial state unable to support his wife and family. From a place of mortal fear, he reached out, unwittingly, to an undercover agent. I spoke with the agent right after their phone call.

By the time Rodriguez's deposition was taken on August 7, 2009, several attorneys were involved in the case representing a number of victims. Those present included Brad Edwards, Bob Kritten and Richard Willis. Below are valuable 'on the record' slices of conversation.

The four tapes reinforced Rodriguez's previous allegations given to the police during the 2005 investigation and exposed a handful of potential witnesses, victims, and procurers.

The recorded statements described his duties as house manager, which included but were not limited to "Answering the door, mainly the kitchen door for practical reasons so the girls would not to walk through the main house," and "waiting in the kitchen with the girls until Kellen arrived." He was also, "Required to carry with him $2,000 more or less, every day."[4]

Rodriguez revealed that his pocket money was partially used, "to pay the young girls after the massage was given, and that, Kellen would call him by telephone at the conclusion of each 'massage', but not every massage, in order to pay the girls." He would "pay them in cash either in the kitchen or driveway." The money was always given to them inside an envelope, he said.[5]

His testimony described how "Kellen kept notes and pieces of papers with names of girls who came to give 'massages' and telephone numbers." Rodriguez revealed that, "Everything we did would be recorded in the internal circuit through Citrix so it could be accessed by other employees."

In other words, most of the staff's activities "everything the house staff organized was recorded on house computers that way all staff could access [that] information." He revealed that Kellen worked mostly out of the dining room, had a laptop, but did not send emails to Rodriguez.[6]

The transcript stated that Rodriguez, not Kellen, was the person in charge of communicating with the staff via email and always used the Citrix house system. He would email everyone including "Ms. Maxwell, who Rodriguez claimed kept a list of names and phone numbers and photos of young girls who came to do "massages" on her computer too... Maxwell kept her office under the stairs next to the kitchen], he said."

Rodriguez also communicated via email with Bella Epstein's assistant in N.Y., and Leslie, his secretary in N.Y., and all household managers in Paris, Manhattan and the island." 'The island' was Epstein's home in Little St. James, a secluded and private island in the U.S.V.I.[7]

Rodriguez said that Kellen kept photographs on her laptop of many, ostensibly underage girls who would come to give 'Epstein massages'. Some "pictures," Rodriguez confirmed, "Of the girls were taken out of the country and some in the Palm Beach house. There were several photographic cameras in the house, small compact cameras."[8]

"Kellen used one of those cameras to take pictures of some girls," and some were nude young girls. One nude was "Nadia Marcinkova, alias Nadia Marcinkov, Epstein's underage girlfriend from Yugoslavia at the time, and a Brazilian girl who would stay on occasion at the El Brillo house but I can't remember her name."[9]

During his employment, Rodriguez confessed that he was unaware that Epstein had surveillance video equipment installed throughout the house. It was not until after his termination notice that he found out when he read about the cameras in a court file. He remembers however, "there were always problems with the computers and so a young technician from New Albany, Ohio would come to the Epstein's house to maintain the computers and equipment.

The technician "was the only one allowed to touch the equipment in the house because it was very sophisticated equipment. The man was in charge of computers, videos and phone system. They had about 15 phones in the Palm Beach house," Rodriguez said.[10]

Rodriguez does not remember the technician's name, but said the man "worked for Mr. Epstein in New Albany, Ohio." New Albany was the city Epstein and Leslie Wexner had their offices. Epstein travelled extensively to New Albany, Ohio where his friend, Mr.Wexner, and his family live and maintain their base of operations.

"Sometimes, David," Epstein's chef, "also interacted with the young girls who came to give Epstein 'massages.' Some young girls who came to the house brought other young girls to give 'massages,'" Rodriguez explained. "Sometimes, I would pay the girls who brought other girls to give Epstein 'massage' between $300 and $500 dollars even though they did not give Epstein a massage."

Rodriguez admitted he never had a conversation with Maxwell or Kellen about the photos of the young girls in their computers. Richard Willis, an attorney who was present at the 2009 deposition asked Rodriguez if he had spoken to anyone concerning the Epstein case in the years following his termination. Rodriguez said that he spoke only to his wife about the case.

He kept notes and a journal that where eventually given to Palm Beach Police Detective, Joe Recarey. He claimed to have kept the journal at home for a while and then offered it to the detective. "I had some information and put everything in the file that I gave to Detective Recarey."[11]

Some of Rodriguez's allegations used to ask him questions in the deposition were taken from his first deposition initiated by the Palm Beach Police Department and witnessed by a Florida State Attorney identified as Ms. Weiss.

During the taped deposition, Rodriguez told the attorneys that during several conversations with the Palm Beach Police Department and FBI, the agents took notes, but did not ask him to review the statements, or sign a document relating to their conversation. In fact, according to the 2009 tapes, Rodriguez never had the opportunity to review his statements.

Presumably, on three or four occasions, the houseman spoke to Detective Recarey yet, according to Rodriguez, the Detective wrote only one taped statement of a single conversation.

If his statement is accurate, then Detective Recarey failed to follow police protocol since he should have taken notes of all their conversations and had Rodriguez sign a document each time they met. Perhaps there was a lapse in judgment by the Detective given the pressure on the Police department to perform during this particular investigation.[12]

Rodriguez told Epstein's attorney, Bob Kritten that, "When all these actions were taking place I was under an environment where I was…afraid of reprisal, from Mr. Epstein and Ms. Maxwell against me, because I had signed a confidentiality agreement."[13]

Given his premature death, the public will never know if Rodriguez was truly afraid of Epstein or perhaps felt pressured by the circumstances and those protecting his former boss. At the time of his original statement to the Palm Beach Police Department, he believed the victims were over the age of 18. During the same 2009 deposition, he also admitted to having miscommunicated and misinterpreted some facts.

When answering the questions about Ghislaine Maxwell's involvement, Rodriguez said, "we use to have internal books for pilots, masseuses, and chefs, so Ghislaine had a copy of the black book as well and copies in the computer."[14]

It wasn't until 2009 that Rodriguez revealed he had gone into Maxwell's computer in her office without permission. He "turned it on to send some documents to the New York office since it was the only computer working at the time in the house."[15]

Rodriguez sent a number of files to Epstein's New York office using the Citrix system. His computer, he claimed, "Was slower and always breaking down which is why the guy from New Albany, Ohio was always coming over."[16]

Rodriguez also told Kritten he logged on because "it was the only computer working in the house that day," and he felt he had the right and "could use anything in the house to accomplish my job." When asked if Maxwell also kept names of girls who came to give massages, Rodriguez, answered, "Yes."[17]

Most of the computers, he said, including Ghislaine's, contained a transcript of all incoming calls, message and telephone numbers. In fact, that was not the only time Rodriguez accessed Maxwell's personal computer, he logged on several more times without her permission. Rodriguez also admitted he used Kellen's computer but never Epstein's.

Rodriguez confirmed that, "All incoming calls that came to 358 El Brillo were recorded via a transcript of sorts through several computers," so whenever, Epstein or Maxwell wanted to see the missing calls they could access the appropriate computer and retrieve the information.[18]

"The only computers that could access missed calls and messages were Maxwell's, Kellen's and El Brillo's main computer," he said. He could not remember any of the email addresses given to him or those that belonged to the staff during his employment.[19]

Kritten questioned Rodriguez about Alan Dershowitz and his presence at Epstein's home in Palm Beach. Rodriguez confirmed that, "Dershowitz was there. Epstein and Mr. Dershowitz were friends." Kritten asked if, "Dershowitz was at Epstein's house when the women who gave the massage was present in the home?"

"I don't remember that, Sir," responded Rodriguez.[20]

He was asked to clarify the potential allegations swirling around Dershowitz and the "massages" with underage girls. Rodriguez said he did not know. Kritten asked several more times in several different ways. "Is it your testimony that Mr. Dershowitz was there when any of the women came to Mr. Epstein's home to give a massage?"

"Yes," Rodriguez said.[21]

Kritten asked him, "Were any of those women ever associated with Mr. Dershowitz? Would it be a correct statement you have absolutely no knowledge?" Rodriguez answered, "I don't know, Sir. " Kritten asked again, "You don't know?"

"Where you in any way attempting in your response to imply that Mr. Dershowitz had a massage by one of these young ladies. "I don't know, Sir," Rodriguez responded.

"You have no knowledge?" Kristen said. "No, Sir," Rodriguez responded. Not satisfied with his answer, Kritten asked the same question once again. Rodriguez responded, "No, Sir."

Kritten: "You certainly weren't implying that that occurred, you just have no knowledge?" "I don't know. I don't know," Rodriguez repeated.[22]

Later on in the deposition Rodriguez said, he saw pictures of Nadia, nee Marcinkova, now Marcinko and "Epstein's girlfriend at the time," in Ghislaine's computer. She appeared, he said, to be in her twenties.

In fact, Nadia Marcinkova was allegedly 14 years old, in 2005, when Epstein brought her to the U.S. from Eastern Europe to live with him in Palm Beach. It is still a mystery how Epstein met the 14 year old and convinced her parents to allow their daughter to move with him to the United States.

Rodriguez made many statements that day. He confirmed that Kellen started to work for Epstein, in 2002 or 2003, two years prior to Rodriguez's arrival. During a conversation with Rodriguez, Luella, Epstein's housekeeper in Palm Beach, shared her uneasiness with Rodriguez about the sex toys Epstein kept in his bedroom. Rodriguez was receptive to her concerns and said he had placed them inside an armoire at the end of his bed.

A man named Balson became his mentor and "a good friend" in the process. Balson was Epstein's Brazilian house manager in Paris. Apparently, Epstein sent Balson to train Rodriguez in Palm Beach since the Brazilian man had been in his service awhile and knew his taste and style.

Rodriguez explained that besides owning the largest triplex in Manhattan, Epstein also had a home in Paris, in one of the finest streets at 22 Avenue Foch, in the 16th *Arrondisement,* an exclusive district in the city where the road is lined from top to end with chestnut trees. Avenue Foch runs from the *Arc de Triumph* to the *Port Dauphine* at the edge of *the Bois de Boulogne,* one of Paris's most coveted parks.

Rodriguez said that Balson had confessed to him that Epstein, "had a lot 'massages' over there too," meaning, at his Paris home. Brad Edwards asked him, "How did it come up whether or not Epstein had massages at the Paris home?"[23]

Balson "came to Palm Beach on two occasions," Rodriguez explained, "and stayed with me for a week." Epstein required his new houseman, "to get into Balson's style of running the house. He was good enough to give me some inside information about what he liked and didn't like."[24]

In 2005, and again, in 2009, Rodriguez admitted that whenever Epstein was in Palm Beach, he usually had two "massages" per day. Based on the earlier deposition, Edwards asked him if: "Balson had described the Paris massages and girls in a similar fashion to the ones given him in Palm Beach? "Yes, Sir," replied Rodriguez. Their conversation picked up speed.[25]

EDWARDS: "Did he indicate how old these girls were," Edwards asked.

RODRIGUEZ: "No, Sir."

Beside Balson, Rodriguez did not befriend or speak to other house managers about the girls and alleged "massages," even though he was friendly with "JoJo" and his wife, Epstein's house manager at the New York property.[26]

EDWARDS: For the time period you have been familiar with Epstein is it fair to say that he would have roughly 2 girls a day in that same age group wherever he was?

RODRIGUEZ: Yes

EDWARDS: Do you know any of the girls who have been over to his island?

RODRIGUEZ: Yes, Nadia and the girls who use to stay at the home in El Brillo use to go over to the island too.

EDWARDS: How many girls?

RODRIGUEZ: There were so many names girls, I can't remember, Sir.

EDWARDS: Were the girls staying at the island house also the same as the girls staying at the Palm Beach house?

RODRIGUEZ: Yes. Kellen and Nadia Marcinkova would also come over to the island house.

EDWARDS: Was Epstein intimate with Sarah?

RODRIGUEZ: Yes.

EDWARDS: With Nadia as well?

RODRIGUEZ: Yes.

One evening, Rodriguez said, he rang 911 because he was terrified. He was walking alone in the dark carrying a lot of cash in his pockets when he saw a 'clunker,' a dilapidated old car, sitting inside Epstein's driveway. Fearing he might be robbed, he rang the police.

"The police responded immediately and pulled in the driveway," Rodriguez said. One of Epstein's victims identified as AH in court files was sitting in the car. "What did you tell the police?" asked Edwards, "That I was paying AH," Rodriguez said. They asked who are these people?" I told them, "They are masseuses."[27]

In the car, there was a man sitting beside AH. "That was the only man I ever saw accompanying a masseuse at the Epstein house." Rodriguez did not know his name.

Edwards asked if the man was Tony Figueroa. Rodriguez said he did not know.[28]

When Epstein saw I called the police he was upset. I explained to him that "I saw a clunker" parked in front of the house. Since I was coming from Publix and carrying a lot of cash, I was concerned for my safety," Rodriguez told the attorneys.[29]

EDWARDS: Why would you call AH a masseuse? Is this the name you were supposed to call them?

RODRIGUEZ: Yes, Sir.

EDWARDS: And for the massages, given to Epstein, you were paying the girls $300 to $500 per hour, each time, and that was usually for an hour, up in the bedroom with Mr. Epstein?

RODRIGUEZ: More or less yes Sir.

EDWARDS: Did you tell your 15-year-old daughter that she could come over Mr. Epstein's for $500 an hour?

RODRIGUEZ: No, Sir.

EDWARDS: Why is it that you never asked your daughter that she could come over if it was just a massage?

RODRIGUEZ: My daughters are too clean for that, Sir

EDWARDS: Too clean to give a massage?

RODRIGUEZ: Yes. They are good students they are in another type of environment, Sir. We are poor, but you know, they are good students, Sir.

EDWARDS: Is it because you knew there was more than just a massage going on in the bedroom?

RODRIGUEZ: Yes, Sir

EDWARDS: Did you ever ask what he did in terms of making money?

RODRIGUEZ: No, Sir, I didn't inquire as to what he did. I learned that through Google.

EDWARDS: During the day when Epstein was in the cabana (pool house)...

RODRIGUEZ: I would put his coffee there and that was it. It was very private there.

A few minutes later, Edwards realized Rodriguez did not know or would not say much about his business life with the exception of Epstein's ownership of price.com, a local Palm Beach telephone company. A company, Rodriguez said, was later sold.

RODRIGUEZ: There were other offshore companies that I cannot recall. There are too many companies, Sir.

EDWARDS: What about Sarah Kellen's work?

Rodriguez: Kellen would set up appointments for the Comedy Shop, massages, make pilot arrangements and keep track of all the girls in all the houses including Paris, etc.

EDWARDS: What about the black book?

RODRIGUEZ: We had a book in every house, plane, boat, classifying all the people, masseuses, chefs, and important people in the life of Mr. Epstein. So there were many 'black books.' There were tons... in the house. They were organized and once in a while updated and we would discard the old ones.

While working for Epstein, Rodriguez maintained he never heard of or met Virginia Louise Roberts. He recalled seeing a number of photographs of young girls in Maxwell's computer and a naked girl stretched out on a hammock, apparently Virginia, inside a book made for Nadia. Rodriguez said her face was printed on the cover.

He remembered Adriana Ross, another alleged procurer, "She was like Nadia. In the totem pole of responsibilities, she was somewhere between Sarah and me…there to help Sarah in her duties," Rodriguez said.[30]

At some point the attorneys read him a portion of the police report filed November 28, 2005. Suddenly, Rodriguez had an "aha moment." He finally understood the reason he was fired and the gravity of the situation.

The police report revealed that Rodriguez had overheard a conversation between the victim AH and Officer Munyon of the Palm Beach Police Department (PBPD).

RODRIGUEZ: Mr. Epstein use to give lots of gifts to the police department so we had certain latitude when it came to speeding and other things… We were asked to place a PBPD baseball cap on the dashboard of our car to help police identify the Epstein household. The PBPD cap was evidently some kind of password that offered 'generous' Palm Beach residents certain 'perks.'

On the subject of secrecy, Epstein's black book' referred to as Exhibit "F" in the deposition and several court documents, was known as 'The Journal' or 'Holy Grail.' Among the many names it identified, were names of females Rodriguez confirmed were underage. The girls' names were classified under 'massages.'

Most of the girls who 'massaged' Epstein, had met Rodriguez at *El Brillo* before or shortly after their 'sessions.' Rodriguez revealed he was aware that sex toys and vibrators were also found in Epstein's bedroom after the massages.

Rodriguez said, "the message pads located in the first floor of the house" proved that Epstein's staff was frequently working to schedule multiple young girls between the ages of 12 and 16, literally every day, often two or three times per day."[31]

Rodriguez was terrified of Epstein's power. He needed money and believed the journal was his rightful "property." He was afraid that Epstein would make him "disappear" unless he had an "insurance policy," such as the journal, to keep him alive.

The information contained in the journal was important to both the criminal and civil cases for obvious reasons. This might be the reason Rodriguez christened the book 'The Holy Grail.'

While Epstein served 13 months in a private cell, in a private building, on an all day work release program for 'solicitation of prostitution with a minor,' after allegedly committing multiple sex crimes against underage girls, Rodriguez served 18 months in a federal prison without any of the perks Epstein was given, for a single obstruction of justice charge.

On April 6, 2010, Rodriguez was charged a second time with a different criminal offense: "Being a felon in possession of a firearm." Three other men, all friends, were charged in the same case. He was arraigned before U.S. Magistrate Judge Stephen Brown on April 6, 2010.

According to the complaint, "The three other defendants bought hundreds of firearms at gun shops in South Florida for resale to Bolivia. Some of the arms were shipped by a common carrier to Bolivia without making known the real contents and falsely claiming the boxes contained automobile parts. None of the men or Bolivian recipient was licensed to deal in firearms."[32]

Soon after his release, Rodriguez was diagnosed with mesothelioma. He died on December 28, 2014.

* * *

Footnotes

1. U.S. v. Rodriguez, No. 9:10-CR-80015-KAM (S.D. Fla. 2010) (Exhibit "G"

2. http://www.palmbeachdailynews.com/news/news/former-epstein-house-manager-alfredo-rodriguez-sen/nMGXk/

3. http://www.palmbeachdailynews.com/news/news/former-epstein-house-manager-alfredo-rodriguez-sen/nMGXk/

4. http://www.nydailynews.com/entertainment/gossip/billiona ire-jeffrey-epstein-shells-money-latest-sex-abuse-lawsuit-article-1.436147

5. http://www.thedailybeast.com/articles/2010/07/22/jeffrey-epstein-pedophile-billionaire-and-his-sex-den.html

6. http://www.thedailybeast.com/articles/2010/07/20/jeffrey-epstein-billionaire-pedophile-goes-free.html

7. https://ecf.flsd.uscourts.gov/cgibin/show_multidocs.pl?case id=317867&arr_de_seq_nums=931&magic_num=&pdf_he ader=2&hdr=&pdf_toggle_possible=&

8. Deposition DVD #3: 15:57-16:45

9. Deposition DVD #3: 15:25-16:37

10. Deposition DVD #3: 52:07

11. Deposition DVD #3: 52:30

12. Deposition DVD #4: 4:15-4:47

13. http://www.dailymail.co.uk/news/article-2896591/Silence-Epstein-women-Former-model-female-employees-billionaire-refuse-answer-questions-Prince-Andrew-sex-slave-allegations.html

14. Case 09-34791-RBR Doc 1603-3 Filed 04/08/11 Page 9 of 39

15. http://www.dailymail.co.uk/news/article-2897939/Houseman-cleaned-pedophile-Jeffrey-Epstein-s-sex-toys-feared-billionaire-make-disappear-takes-secrets-grav

16. Deposition DVD #4:

17. Deposition DVD #4:

18. Deposition DVD #4:

19. Deposition DVD #4:

20. Deposition DVD #4:

21. Deposition DVD #4:

22. Deposition DVD #4:

23. Deposition DVD #4:

24. Deposition DVD #4:

25. Deposition DVD #4:

26. Deposition DVD #4:

27. Deposition DVD #4:

28. Deposition DVD #4:

29. Deposition DVD #4:

30. Deposition DVD #4:

31. Deposition DVD #4:

32. http://online.wsj.com/public/resources/documents/2015_01 09_rodriguez_sentencing.pdf

Chapter Eleven

"Absence of Evidence Is Evidence of Absence"

New Year's Day 2015 began badly for Professor Alan M. Dershowitz. A renowned American lawyer, Harvard University law professor Emeritus, jurist and author, Dershowitz is also a leading scholar on U.S. constitutional law.

A December 2014 Complaint submitted by Victims Rights attorney, Brad Edwards and former federal Judge Paul Cassell and University of Utah law professor revealed that, "Epstein forced Virginia Louise Roberts to have sex with former Harvard law professor, Alan Dershowitz, 'on numerous occasions while she was a minor, not only in Florida but on private planes, in New York, New Mexico and the U.S. Virgin Islands," The sworn statement accused Professor Dershowitz of having sexual intercourse with Roberts-Giuffre at least six times, in various places, including Epstein's Palm Beach residence.[1]

These humiliating and disgraceful accusations given Professor Dershowitz' accomplishments made for an anticlimactic ending to an otherwise illustrious career. Outraged, Dershowitz filed a sworn affidavit in Florida refuting the allegations and challenging Edwards and Cassell to file affidavits.

Dershowitz disputed Roberts' claims and publically dared Roberts to file a criminal complaint with the Palm Beach State Attorney and the U. S. Attorney regarding her sexual abuse allegation. He also threatened Edwards and Cassell with disbarment.

Shortly after the complaint was filed, Dershowitz organized his own defense on air, online and with his counselors. More than two-dozen television interviews and numerous online reports followed where Dershowitz passionately rejected Roberts' allegations.

Sometime in April 2015, Dershowitz claimed that he and David Boies, another superstar attorney who was representing Virginia Louis Roberts in a separate case, a defamation claim against Ghislaine Maxwell, in New York, held a private conversation.

Dershowitz alleged that during their conversation Boies apparently, "Told him he believed Dershowitz was innocent and his accuser (i.e. his client Virginia Roberts) was mistaken or confused."[2]

Dershowitz then filed an Affidavit claiming, "Boies told him he could not ethically continue to represent the woman if she did not withdraw her claim."[3] Dershowitz' affidavit included notes written by him of his conversations with Boies. The notes said that, "Over the course of several conversations in person, over the phone, and on Skype, Mr. Boies repeatedly stated that he did not believe the allegations that [his client] had made against me were factually true."[4]

Boies, who had been Chief Counsel and Staff Director of the United States Senate Antitrust Subcommittee, in 1978, and served as Chief Counsel and Staff Director of the United States Senate Judiciary Committee, in 1979, denied making those comments. "I never said to him that I concluded that my client's assertions were incorrect," Boies told the New York Times, " I didn't say anything like that."[5]

Dershowitz responded to Boies' denial in a statement he gave to the American Bar Association (ABA) Journal, "I doubt that my friend David Boies will be willing to state under oath that he did not make the statements that I quote in my affidavit. It's one thing to deny making them to the media. It's quite another thing to deny them under pains and penalties of perjury." I rang Boies in New York to confirm the allegations. He did not return my calls or emails.[6]

As a result of Virginia's claims, Dershowitz agreed to take a deposition. The deposition was set for October 15 and 16, 2015. Dershowitz was deposed in Fort Lauderdale, Florida at the law offices of Cole Scott & Kissane, the principal attorney representing Dershowitz in the case. More media drama ensued. On December 12, 2015, The New York Times published, "Dershowitz on the Defense-His Own," where snippets of the private conversation held between Dershowitz and Boies appeared.

Apparently, Dershowitz divulged their private conversation in public, a big "No, No" for any lawyer especially while litigating a case. Another media volcano erupted and on December 28, 2015, The Palm Beach Daily News disclosed Dershowitz's statements concerning his conversation with Boies.

To the surprise of many the, "Judge ruled against Dershowitz, in filing an affidavit regarding conversations he had with David Boies." The supposed 'settlement discussions' were private and confidential and should not have been made public," the Judge claimed.[7]

Boies who amongst his many clients represented Vice President Al Gore, in 2000, following the U.S. presidential election in *Bush vs. Gore* is a loyal Clinton supporter. Oddly enough given the players implicated in the case, he agreed, in 2015, to represent Virginia Louise Roberts Giuffre, *pro bono and* filed a motion to protect the privacy of those conversations.

Judge Gerard E. Lynch who had been appointed to hear the case agreed with Boies' request. He ruled, "The conversations between the two attorneys were protected under settlement discussions and should not have been filed," by Dershowitz.[8]

Judge Lynch, a United States Federal Judge on the United States Court of Appeals for the Second Circuit was confirmed on September 2009 after having been selected by President Bill Clinton, in 2000, to serve on the U.S. District Court for the Southern District of New York. Lynch was also the first appeals court judge nominated by President Barack Obama to win confirmation from the United States Senate.

Dershowitz' close relationship with Epstein, the bevy of influential players implicated in the case, and the scope of sexual abuse claims possibly committed by the procurers, are perhaps some of the reasons Dershowitz agreed to represent Epstein. In fact, in December 2015, The New York Times published a story defending Dershowitz position when asked the question. Dershowitz said that at first he, "Hesitated when Mr. Epstein called [me] in 2006 to ask for help because he was being investigated in connection with sex crimes.... You know Jeffrey, we're acquaintances, maybe that's not such a great idea." Epstein did not take no for an answer. Dershowitz revealed that Epstein responded, "No, no, no I really need you to do this." But after careful consideration, the case "was right in my wheelhouse. "[9]

Information unearthed so far has sparked further investigation into Epstein and Dershowitz's long-standing history and Dershowitz's possible role as a *consigliore*. The very nature of a consigliore is a man who can contend with 'the boss.' A real-life consigliore is usually the number three-person in the pyramid, after the boss and underboss. Arguably, Dershowitz's role provided a shocking glimpse into the power and influence that a rich predator and politically well-connected client can exert over a potentially compromised system. Given the latest revelations and how long it took for the media to print what was known as far back as 2010 then should come as no surprise.

Like with many other high profile criminal cases involving rich and influential defendants such as: Bill Cosby, the American actor accused of allegedly sexually assaulting women; or OJ Simpson, the American football player accused of murdering his wife and her friend; or the infamous Claus von Bulow accused of attempting to murder his wife; money, influence, and political alliances, can at times determine the outcome without necessarily attaining justice or truth.

In the Epstein case, the truth might never be revealed until the documents disclosing the communications and negotiations between Epstein's attorneys and the Department of Justice are unsealed. Documents currently unavailable to the media because they might implicate a number of his high-level leaders and reveal the extent of the Epstein, Maxwell, Clinton, and Dershowitz relationship. The same documents were released to the attorneys, Edwards and Cassell after the Judge ruled in their favor in the *Jane Doe #1 and Jane #2 vs. United States Government* case.

It might not be a coincidence that, after years of extreme silence, a sudden shift in interest came about again around the time of the 2016 presidential elections. I suppose that as party politics go and political treason plays out, reports exposing, "Clinton's acceptance of a $25,000 contribution from Epstein after Epstein's conviction," monies that Clintons have so far not returned, became of unique interest to some in the opposing camp and mainstream media.[10]

As a result of the negotiations that took place during the Non Prosecution Agreement and the cover up that followed, it is no surprise Edwards and Cassell filed *Jane Doe #1 and Jane Doe #2 vs. United States Government*. This case still pending will no doubt continue to attract the media's attention and become another sought after, grotesque, and colossal media circus. I would not doubt if the Epstein case and all its related cases have become the most public and humiliating human trafficking ever brought before the United States Department of Justice.

Against these strong current I struggled to unearth the truth about the Epstein investigation. Thanks to many unnamed sources that guided me, I was able to find information that exposed layers upon layers of deceit, manipulation and human rights abuses.

By the time the Daily Beast report published my first report, I understood the reasons why I had to write the first comprehensive book about this case. There is no doubt, the victim's plight and their cases kept me afloat since the truth was revealed very early on in the investigation. And in spite of the challenges that lay ahead, I understood I had to carry on for the sake of the victims and all future victims.

Given my work in the field of human trafficking, I saw Epstein's case from a number of perspectives. This was not simply a case about an inconsequential misdemeanor or justice not served at the state level. Rather, the Epstein case was and continues to be possibly the greatest cover up ever created in a human trafficking case to protect a rich, influential and politically connected sex offender who purposefully seduced politicians and other opinion leaders into his lair to protect him.

The cover up created to protect Epstein and the Non Prosecution Agreement far outshines the corrupted elements in The Watergate Scandal, Lewinsky Scandal and Profumo Affair. A cover up so vast that it extended from the halls of Harvard University all the way to The White House.

Epstein's alleged criminal sexual activities illustrated how a highly structured human trafficking network with an important international cast of characters with far-reaching tentacles can allegedly exploit and abuse defenseless minor girls and get away with it.

The procurers, pedophiles and pimps were caught in a web that only the predator could ostensibly manipulate, "who owed him favors," as Virginia Louise Roberts' told Scarola and Edwards during the telephone deposition; and who could theoretically shield him from a long-term prison sentence. By implicating high-powered friends and inviting them into his 'den', Epstein not only secured their participation, directly and indirectly, he was able to absolve himself.

The current Child Victims Right Act case, *Jane Doe #1 and Jane Doe #2 vs. United States Government,* is currently evaluating Epstein's negotiated Non Prosecution Agreement and the reasons why the government protected the alleged billionaire trafficker and apparent retinue of pimps and predators from criminal prosecution from federal charges, perhaps this time justice will be served.

Given the thousands of court documents filed in relation to his case, it seems that Maxwell, Robson, Kellen, Ross, Marcinkova, Jean Luc Brunel and several other procurers, were equally as responsible as Epstein for their contribution in forging a successful human trafficking operation employing underage girls.

It might well be that Epstein and Maxwell created a criminal enterprise that thwarted an ongoing investigation by brokering influence at the highest levels of government to protect each other and other predators and traffickers implicated in the case? Perhaps Epstein's legal shield came as a consequence of his generous political donations? As the popular liberal blogger Mother Jones pointed out, "Epstein has given tens of millions of dollars to political and philanthropic causes."[11]

Like the latest high stakes financial scandal making headlines in 2016, The Panama Papers reveal, how money, power and greed can tear open the curtains behind the secretive world of high finance and the commingled relationship that exists between money and power.

In Latin, the term is *ancilla politicae.* It roughly translates to "the maid political," a term that denotes the whims of those who wield money. In the case of The Panama Papers, like perhaps in the Epstein case, reality reduced itself to the political and financial whims of those concerned.

Washington certainly played its part as thousands of court files confirm. By creating a shield around the defendant, Epstein's attorneys successfully thwarted the prosecution's efforts to seek justice. R. Alex Acosta and Ann Marie Villafaña were no doubt "assaulted" as Acosta points out in his letter, by the money-power relationship that trumps all, and has for so many years worked well in the halls of power. One can even argue that Epstein's money and his attorney's influence gratuitously exposed a corruptible system that led to the longest running human trafficking case in the United States.

An example of how his generous political donations might have worked in his favor, in the 2016 presidential election year, Epstein's case exposed the dangerous challenges confronting campaign finance reform. Epstein's campaign contributions to Democratic candidates from 1990-2012, excluding universities and other organizations with possible ties to a handful of politicians, exceeded hundreds of thousands of dollars.

His contributions between 1990-2012 included upwards of two thousand dollar donations to: Democratic Senatorial Campaign Committee ($34,00), DCSS/Non-Fed Unincorp Association ($25,00), Democratic National Committee ($20,00), Independence Party Federal Committee ($5,000), Liberal Party of New York ($5,000), Utah State Democratic Committee ($5,000), DNC Non-Federal Individual ($5,000), Campaign America Inc. ($4,000), Democratic Party of New Mexico ($1000), Freedom Project ($1,000), Hillary Clinton ($21,000), Chuck Schumer ($22,000), Jeff Bingaman ($8,000), Daniel Robert Glickman ($4,000), John Kerry ($4,000), John Glenn ($3,000), Joe Lieberman ($3,000), Tom McMillan ($3,000), Daniel Patrick Moynihan ($2,000).[12]

* * *

Footnotes

1. http://www.palmbeachdailynews.com/news/news/local/vict ims-ask-to-join-epstein-lawsuit/njfZM/

2. http://www.nytimes.com/2015/12/13/business/alan-dershowitz-on-the-defense-his-own.html?hp&action=click&pgtype= Homepage&clickSource=story-heading&module=second-column-region&region=top-news&WT.nav=top-news

3. http://www.nytimes.com/2015/12/13/business/alan-dershowitz-on-the-defense-his-own.html?smid=pl-share&_r=0&mtrref=www.abajournal.com&gwh=E16379 C04F8DF815A2F3A2E1856E77C0&gwt=pay

4. http://www.abajournal.com/files/DershowitzAffidavit.pdf

5. http://www.nytimes.com/2015/12/13/business/alan-dershowitz-on-the-defense-his-own.html?hp&action=click&pgtype=Homepage&clickSour ce=story-heading&module=second-column-region&region=top-news&WT.nav=top-news

6. http://www.abajournal.com/news/article/dershowitz_and_b oies_spar_in_an_increasingly_virulent_war_over_rape_acc usat

7. http://www.abajournal.com/news/article/dershowitz_and_b oies_spar_in_an_increasingly_virulent_war_over_rape_acc usat

8. http://www.abajournal.com/news/article/dershowitz_and_b oies_spar_in_an_increasingly_virulent_war_over_rape_acc usat

9. http://www.nytimes.com/2015/12/13/business/alan-dershowitz-on-the-defense-his-own.html?hp&action=click&pgtype=Homepage&clickSour ce=story-heading&module=second-column-region&region=top-news&WT.nav=top-news

10. http://www.motherjones.com/politics/2015/01/bill-clinton-jeffrey-epstein-conservative-media

11. http://www.theguardian.com/us-news/2015/feb/10hillary-cinton-foundation-donors-hsbc-swiss-bank

12. http://littlesis.org/person/36043/Jeffrey_Epstein/political

Chapter Twelve

A Procurer or A Madam?

"There is no presumption of innocence in the court of public opinion." Alan Dershowitz

If Virginia Roberts Giuffre story is true, then the pending defamation case filed in New York against Ghislaine Maxwell will become an important legal victory for the victim, other victims of human trafficking awaiting justice and most importantly, at-risk-children.

In the latest twist of events, U.S. District Court Judge Robert Sweet of the Southern District of New York ordered Ghislaine Maxwell to submit her deposition by March 25, 2016. Maxwell, who had been served in September 2009, was able to avoid taking a deposition in reference to the Epstein case.

The hearing took place Thursday, March 17, 2106, at the New York City Court House since both Maxwell and Roberts-Giuffre live in different states, "And the amount in controversy was greater than seventy-five thousand dollars."[1]

The Court was awarded jurisdiction over the case because Virginia Roberts-Giuffre lived in Colorado at the time of the filing and Maxwell lived and maintains a residence in New York City. According to Roberts-Giuffre, Maxwell's defamatory statements were made in New York, and she was sexually abused by Jeffrey Epstein "in the District," which gave the Court additional leverage to claim jurisdiction.

After hearing the motions, Judge Sweet ordered Maxwell to produce all documents and e-mail communications exchanged between Epstein and the "Madam," from 1999 until 2016 concerning the "sex trafficking ring," they allegedly created.

Sigrid McCawley, representing attorney for Virginia Roberts-Giuffre did not respond to my calls or most e-mail communications except to forward the transcript.

Brad Edwards, representing Roberts Giuffre in the Florida case said, "This is going to be along case. Marathon, not a sprint."[2]

The Complaint revealed that, "Between 1999 and 2002, with the assistance and participation of Maxwell, Epstein sexually abused Giuffre at numerous locations including his mansions in West Palm Beach, Florida, and in this District. Between 2001 and 2007, with the assistance of numerous co-conspirators, Epstein abused more than 30 minor underage girls, a fact confirmed by state and federal law enforcement. As part of their sex trafficking efforts, Epstein and Maxwell intimidated Giuffre into remaining silent about what had happened to her."[3]

Maxwell's testimony is significant because, "In September 2007, Epstein entered into a Non-Prosecution Agreement ("NPA") that barred his prosecution for numerous federal sex crimes in the Southern District of Florida. In the NPA, the United States Attorney's Office agreed that it would not introduce any federal criminal charges against any potential co-conspirators of Epstein's." At the time of his arrest the alleged procurers included: Maxwell, Jean Luc Brunel, Haley Robson, Sarah Kellen, Nadia Marcinkova, Adriana Ross, and several others.[4]

The case comes on the heels of Alan Dershowitz's deposition taken October 15, 2015 where he confirmed his legal team negotiated the deal. Several media reports published the story. "As a co-conspirator of Epstein's, Maxwell was consequently granted immunity in the Southern District of Florida through the NPA."[5]

Virginia's attorneys argued that, "Maxwell's fabrications constitute libel since they exposed Giuffre to public contempt, ridicule, aversion, and disgrace, and induced an evil opinion of her in the minds of right-thinking persons."

Maxwell's comments, McCawley argued, "Tended to injure Roberts Giuffre in her professional capacity as the president of a non profit corporation designed to help victims of sex trafficking, and attempted to destroy her credibility and reputation among members of the community that seeks her help and that Virginia seeks to serve."[6]

Maxwell's offensive public statements against Virginia implied that "Giuffre acted with fraud, dishonesty and unfitness for the task," when "Speaking out against sex trafficking," the Complaint explained. In other words, Maxwell insinuated that Virginia "lied about being recruited by Maxwell and sexually abused by Epstein and Maxwell." According to Virginia, "Maxwell lied directly and through agents who, distributed and published Maxwell's statements in 'reckless disregard of the truth and with the malicious intent to destroy Virginia's reputation and credibility."[7]

The Complaint closely followed Virginia's long standing story that, "Maxwell sexually abused Roberts-Giuffre and helped Epstein to sexually abuse Giuffre, and then, in order to avoid having these crimes discovered, Maxwell wantonly and maliciously set out to falsely accuse, defame, and discredit Roberts-Giuffre."[8]

"Virginia now wants punitive and exemplary damages to deter Maxwell and others from wantonly and maliciously use a campaign of lies to discredit her and other victims of sex trafficking."[9]

Maxwell's attorneys, Laura Menninger and Jeffrey Pagliuca told reporters that Giuffre's lawyers were "overly broad," in their demands. "What the heck does communication with the Duke, HRH Prince Andrew Duke of York,, in 2013 have to do with this case? Nothing!" Pagliuca cried out. McCawley, refuted his argument, "Epstein's long standing practice of luring girls-some minors-with cash to have sex with him and his friends was relevant to her client's charges."[10]

In fact Prince Andrew has a great deal to do with this case since he remains a close friend of Maxwell's and she was the person responsible for introducing Epstein and Roberts-Giuffre to the Duke.

Thanks to Maxwell's public relations efforts several photos of a young Giuffre with the Prince can be viewed online when she was apparently coerced and paid for having sex with the Prince. In the past five years, photographs and media reports have also corroborated the close friendship between the Prince and his Brooklyn predator.

As far back as April 2007, during Virginia Roberts' telephone conversation with Edwards and Scarola, the victim described Ghislaine Maxwell's place within the Epstein organization. Her description was quite different than Professor Dershowitz's portrayal of Maxwell in his deposition.

On October 15, 2015 during the taking of his deposition, Professor Dershowitz referred to Maxwell as Epstein's "major domo." Her role, Dershowitz said, was to "arrange travel as well. She would tell you when you could meet with him, when to come over. She would call me at my office… I would say that Ghislaine was the senior person organizing his kind of academic contacts and Sarah Kellen was the junior person. They worked in overlapping roles."[11]

That was an unusual title Professor Dershowitz dispensed given that she's a woman who primarily relies on her social pedigree and family name to open doors and build relationships including the one with former President Clinton who apparently considers her part of his inner circle and supposedly "funded Maxwell's The Terra Mar Project nonprofit according to the Foundation website."[12]

Maxwell's relationship with Epstein and Clinton is close. One report claimed that, "Even after Epstein's prosecution, Maxwell donated to Hillary Clinton's presidential campaign with a maximum personal contribution. Maxwell's contribution may be illegal given that she is not a U.S. citizen and foreign nationals are prohibited under criminal penalty from contributing to any U.S. political campaign."[13]

* * *

Footnotes

1. https://ecf.nysd.uscourts.gov/doc1/127116800606

2. Text message send from Brad Edwards to Conchita Sarnoff on March 18, 2016.

3. https://ecf.nysd.uscourts.gov/doc1/127116800606

4. https://ecf.nysd.uscourts.gov/doc1/127116800606

5. https://ecf.nysd.uscourts.gov/doc1/127116800606

6. https://ecf.nysd.uscourts.gov/doc1/127116800606

7. https://ecf.nysd.uscourts.gov/doc1/127116800606

8. https://ecf.nysd.uscourts.gov/doc1/127116800606

9. Case 1:15-cv-07433-RWS Document 1 Filed 09/21/15 Page 10 of 12

10. http://www.nydailynews.com/new-york/court-hear-jeffrey-epstein-alleged-sex-trafficking-article-1.2568619

11. Case: CACE 15-000072 Seventeenth Judicial Circuit for Broward County, Florida. Bradley Edwards & Paul G. Cassell vs. Alan M. Dershowitz. P.180-333, Friday, October 16, 2015.

12. http://dailycaller.com/2015/03/12/clinton-ties-to-teen-sex-ring-are-still-troubling/#ixzz43q3jFjkc

13. http://dailycaller.com/2015/03/12/clinton-ties-to-teen-sex-ring-are-still-troubling/#ixzz43q9n4skh

Chapter Thirteen

The Prosecution

The back-story is usually as important if not more than the story.

"After an extensive investigation by the Palm Beach police and the FBI, the Justice Department immunized Epstein for multiple alleged offenses involving underage girls in exchange for his guilty pleas to two comparatively minor sex crimes in Florida state court. Epstein's lawyers persuaded the federal government to keep the terms of the agreement secret, according to the court filing by victims' attorneys Bradley Edwards and Paul Cassell, (a former District Federal Judge from 2002-2007 appointed by President George W. Bush now Special Council with Hatch James & Dodge in Salt Lake City)."[1]

In addition to this, apparently, Epstein's counselors also convinced the Department of Justice that his private physician's evaluation was a sufficient indication of his mental health and character. It was not difficult to predict the end result. Epstein's unusual request to have his private physician submit his evaluation was considered exceptional by the Palm Beach Police Chief, Michael Reiter.

Reiter also mentioned that during the investigation both he and Detective, Joe Recarey, were under surveillance for several months, without knowing who ordered it. This exception and several more allowances extended to Epstein over the course of the two year investigation and exposed many layers of the corrupted onion; the power of his defense team; and the level of influence peddling that took place at the highest echelons of government during his prosecution.

Another example of the power of his defense team came by way of Bruce Reinhart, a distinguished former Assistant U.S. Attorney between 1996-2008. His unexpected exit from the United States Attorneys Office was surprising given the timing. According to a number of defense lawyers representing the victims, it seemed Reinhart left USAO midstream while still working on the Epstein case with prosecutors R. Alex Acosta, Villafaña and others. In fact, Reinhart apparently went to work for Epstein and his attorneys for a period of time.

Then there was the case of Cecile de Jongh, wife of United States Virgin Islands (USVI) Governor, John de Jongh, a Democrat and close Epstein friend. It is no secret the USVI is a recognized tax haven for the rich. It seemed very convenient that Epstein hired the Governor's wife to be his 'Office Manager' at Financial Trust Company, his offshore company, while she worked simultaneously as a board member at the Antilles School on St. Thomas.

Apparently, it seems strange if not downright unprincipled that Mrs. De Jongh did not notify the private school and parents in light of the fiduciary and ethical responsibilities. Given her close association with Epstein and the laws governing the proximity between a predator and school aged children, it might have made sense to at least notify the school board of their professional relationship.

As it happens, Mrs. De Jongh was the first wife of a sitting governor in the United States to be employed by a convicted sex offender. In January 2016, Cecile de Jongh, no longer first lady, remains in her employ as Epstein's office manager.[2]

Epstein's company domiciled in the USVI manages his investments and the 72-acre private island, Little St. James, he owns. It has also been his primary residence since he was released from house arrest. According to several sources, Epstein received tax breaks from the Virgin Islands Economic Development Corporation apparently thanks to Cecile de Jongh's efforts and relationships.

A Daily Caller story on April 22, 2012 reported, "The benefits permit recipients to avoid some and in some cases, all of their tax burden if they live in the U.S. for the majority of a year and fulfill certain financial and development obligations to the local economy."[3]

Given Mrs. De Jongh's privileged position as the Governor's wife and Epstein's employee, she was in the position to facilitate many benefits to help her boss including perhaps obtaining tax breaks. A recent report claimed that, "Governor de Jongh and his tax break programs have come under increased scrutiny. When the Daily Caller questioned the Economic Development Corporation concerning the story they declined to answer.

A source at the Justice Department also revealed that, "Governor de Jongh accepted part of a $20 million cash-bribe payout from alleged financial criminals who are under sealed federal indictments, in exchange for favors from his administration."[4]

The same scandal involving The Virgin Islands Economic Development Corporation program was published by The Daily Caller: "The [USVI] Governor, his attorney general and a number of USVI legislators also accepted bribes. The former U.S. Attorney General, Eric Holder, was aware that prosecutors and the elected officials were bribed and compromised but did not hold anyone accountable."[5]

Which brings me back to the Department of Justice and why it was possibly influenced by Epstein's lawyers to allow the testimony of only a few victims even though countless underage girls came forward against him. The court files made available to the public also showed how more than 100 minor girls courageously testified. Of these sworn statements no more than two-dozen or so were allowed by the prosecutor's office to come forward.

U.S. Attorney, R. Alex Acosta's email to Jay Lefkowitz, one of Epstein's principal attorney's helps explain this phenomenon. The email dated December 13, 2007 began like this:

"Dear Jay,

I am writing to respond to your "policy concerns" regarding Mr. Epstein's Non Prosecution Agreement, which will be addressed by the United States Attorney, but the time has come for me to respond to the ever-increasing attacks on my role in the investigation and negotiations.

It is an understatement to say that I am surprised by your allegations regarding my role because I thought that we had worked very well together in resolving this dispute. I also am surprised because I feel that I bent over backwards to keep in mind the effect that the agreement would have on Mr. Epstein and to make sure that you (and he) understood the repercussions of the agreement.

For example, I brought to your attention that one potential plea could result in no gain time for your client; I corrected one of your calculations of the Sentencing Guidelines that would have resulted in Mr. Epstein spending far more time in prison than you projected; I contacted the Bureau of Prisons to see whether Mr. Epstein would be eligible for the prison camp that you desired; and I told you my suspicions about the source of the press "leak" and suggested ways to avoid the press.

Importantly, I continued to work with you in a professional manner even after I learned that you had been proceeding in bad faith for several weeks—thinking that I had incorrectly concluded that solicitation of minors to engage in prostitution was a registrable offense and that you would "fool" our Office into letting Mr. Epstein plead to a non-registrable offense...

Another reason for my surprise about your allegations regarding misconduct related to the Section 2255 litigation in your earlier desire to have me perform the role of "facilitator" to convince the victims that the lawyer representative was selected by the Office to represent their interests alone and that the out of court settlement of their claims was in their best interests.

"You now state that doing the same things that you had asked me to do earlier is improper meddling in civil litigation... You and your co counsel also impressed upon me from the beginning the need to undertake an independent investigation. It seems inappropriate not to complain because our independent investigation uncovered facts that are unfavorable to your client...

You do not want our Office to inform the State Attorney's Office of facts that support the additional charge nor do you want any of the victims of that charge to contact Ms. Belohlavek or the Court.

Ms. Belohlavek's opinion may change if she knows the full scope of your client's actions. You and I spent several weeks trying to identify and put together a plea to federal charges that your client was willing to accept.

Yet your letter now accuses me of "manufacturing" charges of obstruction of justice, making obscene phone calls, and violating child privacy laws. When Mr. Lourie told you that those charges would "embarrass the Office," he meant that the Office was unwilling to bend the facts to satisfy Mr. Epstein's desired prison sentence—a statement with which I agree...

The indictment was postponed for more than five months to allow you and Mr. Epstein's other attorneys to make presentations to the Office to convince the Office not to prosecute. Those presentations were unsuccessful...Since the signing of the Non Prosecution Agreement, the agents and I have vetted the list of victims more than once. In one instance, we decided to remove a name because, although Mr. Epstein touched the minor victim inappropriately, we decided that the link to a payment was insufficient to call it "prostitution." I have always remained open to a challenge to the list, so your suggestion that Mr. Epstein was forced to write a blank check is simply unfounded... None of the victims was informed of the right to sue under Section 2255 prior to the investigation of the claims. Three victims were notified shortly after the signing of the Non Prosecution Agreement of the general terms of that Agreement.

You raised objections to any victim notification, and no further notifications were done... All_documents related to the grand jury investigation have been filed under seal, and the Palm Beach Police Department's probable cause affidavit has never been filed with the Court.

If, in fact, you are referring to the *Ex Parte* Declaration of Joseph Recarey (the police officer working at the Palm Beach Police Department in charge of the Epstein case), that was filed in response to the motion to quash the grand jury subpoena, it was filed both under seal and *ex parte,* so no one should have access to it except the Court and myself...

You also accuse me of "broadening the scope of the investigation without any foundation for doing so by adding charges of money laundering and violations of a money transmitting business to the investigation. Again, I consulted with the Justice Department's Money Laundering Section about my analysis before expanding that scope. The duty attorney agreed with my analysis."[6]

A separate e-mail dated September 16, 2007 was sent by Ann Marie Villafaña, former Assistant U.S. Attorney during the criminal investigation, to one of Epstein's lawyer, Jay Lefkowitz. Strangely, Villafaña sent the note using her personal e-mail account rather than the official DOJ account.

When I realized this, it reminded me of the 2016 Clinton 'E-mail-gate,' currently under investigation. The Clinton e-mail investigation stems from the former Secretary of State, Hillary Clinton's, use of her personal blackberry for State Department business and the potential breach of national security interests. Ms. Villafaña's e-mail read:

"Hi Jay...I talked to Andy and he still doesn't like the factual basis. In his opinion, the plea should only address the crimes that we were addressing, and we were not investigating Mr. Epstein abusing his girlfriend (she is referring to Nadia Marcinkova)."[7]

It was odd USAO did not investigate the Marcinkova case since the girl was apparently 14 years old when she moved in with Epstein from a foreign country. As several court documents confirmed, Marcinkova, had been a victim turned procurer since she was underage when she and Epstein first met.

Marcinkova along with Ross-Muscinka, Maxwell and a handful of alleged foreign-born victims turned procurers were implicated although never charged. Most girls who testified in the Florida case were American. Given the importance of jurisdictional authority in a criminal case such as this, it is curious that other federal agencies beside the FBI and DOJ did not participate in the investigation involving non-nationals like Marcinkova, Maxwell and others. Two that come to mind are: US Citizenship & Immigration (USCIS), and Immigration & Customs Enforcement (ICE).

Another question that troubled me concerned Marcinkova. If indeed she was more a victim than a procurer, given her age at the time she met Epstein, and Epstein's 14 year-old 'girlfriend' when the alleged crimes were committed, why was her visa status not investigated? Why did the United States Attorney's Office abstain from moving forward with an investigation into Marcinkova's case?

Villafaña's e-mail presented an interesting point:

"As to timing, it is my understanding that Mr. Epstein needs to be sentenced in the state after he is sentenced in the federal case, but not that he needs to plead guilty and be sentenced after serving his federal time. Andy recommended that some of the timing issues be addressed only in the state agreement, so that it isn't obvious to the judge that we are trying to create federal jurisdiction for prison purposes. My understanding is that Mr. Epstein should sign a state plea agreement, plead guilty to the federal offenses, plead guilty to the state offenses, be sentenced on the federal offenses, and then be sentenced on the state offenses, and then start serving the federal sentence.

Re the two paragraphs following your paragraph 8: I will mention "co conspirators," but I would prefer not to highlight for the judge all of the other crimes and all of the other persons that we could charge. Also, we do not have the power to bind Immigration and we make it a policy not to try to, however, I can tell you that, as far as I know, there is no plan to try to proceed on any immigration charges against either Mr. Ross (Adriana Ross) or Ms. Marcinkova (Nadia Marcinkova).

Also, on the grand jury subpoenas, I can prepare letters withdrawing them as of the signing of the plea agreement, but I would prefer to take out that language. In my eyes, once we have a plea agreement, the grand jury's investigation has ended and there can be no more use of the grand jury's subpoena power."

An early Plea Agreement draft dated September 14, 200 and e-mailed to attorney Jay Lefkowitz by USAO made the following stipulations:

"1. The defendant agrees to plead guilty to the Information which charges the defendant as follows: Count 1 charges that the defendant intentionally harassed another person, that is Jane Doe #1, in an attempt to delay, prevent, and dissuade Jane Doe #1 from reporting to a law enforcement officer of the United States the commission of a federal offense; in violation of Title 18, United States Code, Sections 1512 9d) (2), and 2: and Count 2 charges that the defendant, while in an airplane over the high seas, did knowingly commit a simple assault on a person who was over the age of 16 years, that is S.K. (Sarah Kellen); in violation of Title 18, United States Code, Section 113 (a) (5)."

Yet another curious e-mail was sent by USAO to Lefkowitz instructing him to talk to his client read:

"...Talk to Mr. Epstein about a young woman named redacted... We have hearsay evidence that she traveled on Mr. Epstein's airplane when she was under 18, in around the 2000 or 2001 time frame. That falls outside the statute of limitations, but perhaps we could construct a 371 conspiracy around that?"

In legal parlance, a 371 conspiracy is defined as a scheme, "when one or more persons conspire to commit an offense against the United States, or any agency thereof or for any purpose, the persons shall be fined under this law and imprisoned for no more than five years or both."[8]

Several police reports confirmed that a number of underage girls who testified were transported across State borders. One victim in particular was instructed to give 'massages' to Epstein's influential friends. That one victim claims she met global leaders such as politicians, aristocrats and businessmen. That story comes later.

It seems that in most criminal cases involving similar charges and a sizeable number of victims, the allegations would have met, at the very least, the federal stipulations for a federal rather than a state prosecution.

The seemingly overwhelming evidence cannot explain why Epstein's case did not qualify for prosecution under the federal law Trafficking Victims Protection Act (TVPA). By any prosecutorial standard a case of this magnitude should have been prosecuted under the federal bill, TVPA, enacted in Florida in 2000.

Over the years I have sought out the opinion of many criminal attorneys, law enforcement officials and immigration lawyers working on this subject. In the final analysis, by perhaps failing to protect the victims under the TVPA, most attorneys agreed the Non Prosecution Agreement did a great disservice to the victims and all future of at-risk girls, including those living in or nearby Epstein's communities.

One of the greatest concern's today is whether Epstein can become a repeat offender? Although it is not an exact science what the rate of recidivism is for convicted pedophiles, some stories indicate that sex offenders are mostly repeat offenders. If this is true, then Epstein's alleged sex crimes might continue to pose a threat to the local communities he frequents such as: Palm Beach, New York, Paris, London, Stanley, New Mexico and the USVI.

By pairing down the criminal charges and withholding prosecution to the full extent of the law and not prosecuting the alleged procurers, many vulnerable underage girls perhaps continue to be in danger of the predator's potential inability to control his sexual urges with underage girls.

If you take this one step further, Epstein was never properly diagnosed for his condition and has not to anyone's knowledge undergone therapy on an inpatient or out patient basis for pedophilia since his release. Pedophilia has recently become such a widespread and disturbing concern that only a few weeks ago, a science magazine announced Swedish clinical trials now testing a medication to control pedophilic impulses. The drug, developed by a Swiss pharmaceutical is currently on the market for a different indication.[9]

The most recent photographs of Epstein, taken by a couple of newspapers in New York City continue to show Epstein in the company with very young girls. One photograph in particular portrayed the predator with his hand hugging the derriere of a young girl while looking into the camera. These photos and other stories recently published perhaps indicate that he continues to frequent the company of very young girls and that he continues to invite some of these young girls on his travels.

After so many photos were published where Epstein was photographed with very young girls, two incidents were brought to my attention in August 2012. Both incidents occurred at Inter Mix a clothing boutique and chain for young women in New York.

According to the salesgirl and manager at the time, who do not wish to be identified, Epstein visited Manhattan's Inter Mix boutique on June 11, 2012. The boutique located on 1003 Madison Avenue between 77th and 78th Streets is just seven blocks from Epstein's triplex on East 71st Street.

At the Manhattan boutique, store number 440002, Epstein purchased over one thousand two hundred dollars worth of clothing for girls clothing. The items included girl's roll-up shorts, high-rise cuffed shorts, linen Tee shirts, and an open back 'Stewart.' All the items were girl's size small. The purchases were handed to the young girls at the shop after Epstein paid the bill.

During his visit, the salesgirl was aware of Epstein's criminal history because of the media reports published by the New York Post and other local dailies that year. According to the girl, Epstein came to the shop with approximately five young girls in tow.

Clearly, it is not a crime for an adult male to escort young girls to a boutique to purchase clothing. It is also not a crime for an adult male to gift adolescent girls clothing except that it becomes a questionable activity when that older man happens to be a convicted pedophile and level 3-registered sex offender. At the very least that activity should have raised eyebrows and an investigation at the Manhattan District Attorney's office.

The girls in question were not relatives or seemed particularly close to Epstein according to the salesgirl. The manager confirmed how Epstein entered the boutique by himself immediately after the young girls entered the store. Except for Epstein no other adult was present during the shopping spree.

The girls and Epstein did not greet each other when he walked in according to those who where there. That seems odd if in fact Epstein bumped into them at the shop. The salesgirl assumed the girls and Epstein were casual friends shopping together. Inter Mix did not have a camera inside the boutique so it did not record the incident. After Epstein paid in cash for the girl's clothing he left the shop by himself. The young girls trailed behind.

The employees described their meeting as friendly and casual. While looking around for clothes the girls and Epstein were huddled together. They were in the shop perhaps half an hour to forty-five minutes before the girl rang up the items. Epstein paid the bill and left. The salesgirl never questioned the girls or asked for identification since that would have been unusual and inappropriate. Epstein was also a regular client according to one of the girl's.

A second incident occurred at the Manhasset Inter Mix boutique, store number 440013. At that shop, on July 29, 2012, Epstein purchased two articles of clothing for $119.40. I do not have the specifics about that incident only the receipt.

Soon after I was informed, I forwarded the information and receipts to attorneys Jack Scarola, Brad Edwards and the Manhattan D.A. Cyrus Vance Jr. As far as I know, there has not been a follow up investigation. On November 26, 2012, I forwarded a second e-mail to the Manhattan D.A. concerning the incident. I copied Mr. Vance's assistant, Marlene Turner. This was the response.

Dear Ms. Sarnoff,

As noted in response to your prior inquiries, our office does not comment on hypotheticals nor provide individualized responses to general questions about NYS law.

Marlene Turner

Given the USAO's golden record, the Epstein prosecution seems like an *in flagrante delicto*. It is a paradox that the United States Attorneys Office could have allowed itself to be influenced by Epstein's defense team, rather than stand by the laws they are meant to enforce in order to protect the most vulnerable.

Three reasons why the Department of Justice should have proceeded more prudently come to mind. One, the outrageously aggressive tactics used by Epstein and the defense team against the victims during the investigation. Two, the outrageously aggressive tactics deployed by Epstein and his defense team against the Palm Beach Police Department specifically the Chief of Police, Michael Reiter; and three, the same outrageously aggressive tactics displayed by Epstein and his defense team against the United States Attorneys Office.

The bizarre e-mail trail between the prosecutor's office and Epstein's attorneys, and the peculiar exchange negotiated in Washington D.C., after the Florida prosecutor, R. Alex Acosta handed down what should have been the final order, should have raised far more eyebrows in Washington.

As a result of the NPA disclosure, the media's response was inflammatory so much so that in 2016, ABC News reported the following news:

> "Prosecutors went to great lengths to keep secret the non-prosecution agreement reached in 2007 with Jeffrey Epstein, attorneys for the victims allege, "because of the strong objection they would have faced from victims of Epstein's abuse, and because of the public criticism that would have resulted from allowing a politically-connected billionaire who had sexually abused more than 30 minor girls to escape ... with only a county court jail sentence...

Throughout the negotiations -- and for nearly a year after the agreement was signed -- the victims were kept in the dark, their attorneys said, strung along as government lawyers promised victims they were still investigating even long after they had cut Epstein an "indulgent" deal...

And as Epstein first faced federal prosecution a few years later, one of his lawyers, Gerald B. Lefcourt, wrote to prosecutors to tout Epstein's pedigree as "part of the original group that conceived of the Clinton Global Initiative," according to a letter attached to Wednesday's court filing...

On the day the deal was signed, an attorney for Epstein sent an email to the federal prosecutor handling the case which read, "Please do whatever you can to keep this from becoming public," according to an email exchange attached to Wednesday's filing."[10]

Hundreds of pages of newly-disclosed correspondence between federal prosecutors and Epstein's defense lawyers, including Jay Lefkowitz, Kenneth Starr, Alan Dershowitz, Roy Black, and Lefcourt, provide an inside look at Epstein's efforts to forestall the federal prosecution and conceal the resulting deal, despite repeated acknowledgements by government lawyers that they were legally required to inform the victims.

"Neither federal agents nor anyone from your Office should contact the [alleged victims] to inform them of the resolution of the case," wrote Lefkowitz in a letter to then-U.S. Attorney R. Alexander Acosta a month after the deal was signed. "Not only would that violate the confidentiality of the agreement, but Mr. Epstein also will have no control over what is communicated to the identified individuals at this most critical stage. We believe it is essential that we participate in crafting mutually acceptable communication to the [alleged victims]."[11]

While the relationship between Epstein's legal team and the U.S. attorneys developed into what Acosta later described as "a yearlong assault on the prosecution and the prosecutors," the early negotiations seemed to possess an accommodating tone that allowed defense lawyers and prosecutors to work together to formulate lesser criminal charges for Epstein. The question is why?

* * *

Footnotes

1. http://abcnews.go.com/US/victims-feds-hid-sweetheart-deal-sex-offender-deep/story?id=36843144

2. http://dailycaller.com/2012/04/22/virgin-islands-governors-wife-employed-by-convicted-sex-offender-billionaire/

3. http://dailycaller.com/2012/04/22/virgin-islands-governors-wife-employed-by-convicted-sex-offender-billionaire/

4. http://dailycaller.com/2012/04/22/virgin-islands-governors-wife-employed-by-convicted-sex-offender-billionaire/

5. http://dailycaller.com/2012/02/01/bribery-compromised-officials-leave-indicted-financial-crime-suspects-free-from-prosecution-under-holders-doj/

6. Exhibit H. Epstein vs. Edwards, et al. Case No 50. 2009 CA 040800XXXXMBAG U.S. Attorney, R. Alex Acosta's Email correspondence to Jay Lefkowitz, dated December 13, 2007.

7. Exhibit H. Epstein vs. Edwards, et al. Case No 50. 2009 CA 040800XXXXMBAG U.S. Attorney, R. Alex Acosta's Email correspondence to Jay Lefkowitz, dated December 13, 2007.

8. Exhibit H. Epstein vs. Edwards, et al. Case No 50. 2009 CA 040800XXXXMBAG U.S. Attorney, R. Alex Acosta's Email correspondence to Jay Lefkowitz, dated December 13, 2007.

9. http://www.sciencemag.org/news/2016/04/swedish-trial-examine-drug-men-pedophilic-impulses

10. http://abcnews.go.com/US/victims-feds-hid-sweetheart-deal-sex-offender-deep/story?id=36843144

11. http://abcnews.go.com/US/victims-feds-hid-sweetheart-deal-sex-offender-deep/story?id=36843144

Chapter Fourteen

The Dershowitz Deposition

The former Harvard University law professor, Alan Dershowitz, agreed to take a video taped deposition on October 15 and 16, 2015 at the offices of Cole Scott & Kissane at 110 Southeast 6th Street, Fort Lauderdale, Florida.

More than any other attorney hired to defend Epstein in the 2005 criminal case, Dershowitz, understood the complexities of the case. His longtime friendship with Epstein, perhaps Maxwell, and other high profile players associated with Epstein played a critical role in constructing Epstein's defense.

Unlike the attorneys hired to defend Epstein, Dershowitz knew who needed the most protection. During his deposition, Professor Dershowitz testified about his relationship with Epstein, Virginia Louise Roberts, Leslie Wexner, Bill Clinton and others implicated in the Epstein story.

Several lawyers were present. Jack Scarola represented his clients, Brad Edwards and former Judge Paul Cassell, former Judge Thomas Scott Emerson Jr. and Steven Safra, represented Professor Dershowitz. Martin Weinberg and Darren Indyke represented Jeffrey Epstein participated via the phone. Sigrid Stone McCawley, a partner at David Boies, Schiller & Flexner represented Boies' client, Virginia Louise Roberts-Giuffre.

The reason for the deposition is rooted in the \ ˍ˥
defamation case filed by Brad Edwards and Paul Ca, ˍ˪˼ against
Professor Dershowitz for character assassination. Cassell and
Edwards sued Dershowitz who counter sued the attorneys.

The case *Bradley Edwards, Paul G Cassell vs. Alan
Dershowit,* # CACE: 15-000072 was filed exposing several
prominent politicians and high profile business leaders because
their client, Virginia Louise Roberts, accused Dershowitz along
with Prince Andrew and other high profile men of having sex with
her when she was a minor. Dershowitz denied the charges and
accused her two lawyers of acting improperly.

In my attempt to simplify the case and not lose the integrity
of the conversation, segments of the deposition were transcribed
exactly as they unfolded. The opening exchange between Scarola
and Dershowitz went like this:

> SCAROLA: In fact, you have been making public
> statements of your intention to seek the disbarment of
> Bradley Edwards and Paul Cassell for approximately ten
> months, correct?

> DERSHOWITZ: That's right. That's correct.

> SCAROLA: You are aware of the ethical obligation that a
> lawyer has when that lawyer has direct knowledge of
> unethical conduct on the part of another member of the
> Bar-

> DERSHOWITZ: That's right.

SCAROLA: To report that unethical conduct, correct?

DERSHOWITZ: Yes.

SCAROLA: Have you done that?

DERSHOWITZ: I have conferred with three leading ethics experts and I have been advised that to file a report while there is ongoing litigation is not the proper approach. But rather to gather the evidence and the information and to make sure that all of the allegations I make are well founded, unlike what your clients did, and then at the appropriate time, when the litigation is concluded, seek the disbarment of Bar Association... I fully intend to seek disbarment... of your clients because I believe they engaged in unprofessional, unethical and disbar- able conduct. And I've continued to do so until as recently as last week.

When Scarola asked Dershowitz who was representing him, the professor identified over two-dozen lawyers. The list was so extensive it covered 17 pages of the deposition, beginning on page 25 through 42 of the October 15, 2015 transcript.

Dershowitz said he was "offered legal advice by his research assistant at Harvard, Carlos Sires— also a partner in the Boise firm —who volunteered to represent me along with one of his partners, but then withdrew from the representation when he discovered that I had a conflict of interest."[1]

Given the dates when the Roberts' Defamation case was filed, September 21, 2015, and the Dershowitz counter suit against Edwards and Cassell was filed, January 4, 2015, the dates seemed at odds. Assuming that Dershowtiz approached Sires to represent him in early January 2015, after Edwards and Cassell first filed the Defamation Complaint, it would put Dershowitz ahead of Virginia Roberts request, to have David Boies represent her in the Maxwell defamation case.

So unless the filing dates were incorrect, why would Sires believe there was a 'conflict of interest,' when Dershowitz first approached him? The time line is important because Roberts' statement, alleging she was forced to have sex with Dershowitz, was published by politico.com on December 31, 2014. In any case, given the actual filing dates, it was David Boies and not Carlos Sires who should have raised 'the conflict of interest,' clause with their potential client.

When I asked Scarola to comment on Dershowitz's claims and dates regarding the conflict, he said, "Dershowitz's conflict claim is not supported by facts or law." I called Carlos Sires. He did not return my call.

During the deposition, Dershowitz identified two new players never before mentioned in the case. A woman named Rebecca and her husband Michael. The family names were 'purposefully omitted to prevent the media from chasing them.'

Dershowitz claimed that Rebecca, "had been told directly by her friend, Virginia Roberts, who stayed with her overnight for a period of time, that she never wanted to mention me in any of the pleadings. And that her two lawyers who filed the pleadings, Cassell and Edwards, pressured her in to including my name and details."[2]

DERSHOWITZ: Virginia Roberts never wanted to mention me, but she was pressured by her lawyer into mentioning me… And that was the truth.

Rebecca then said that I was not the object of this effort. The object of the effort was a billionaire who lives in Columbus, Ohio, (Leslie Wexner), who owns Victoria's Secret and The Limited, too.

DERSHOWITZ: Rebecca told me she did not know the name of that billionaire, but that Virginia and her lawyers hoped to get 1 billion, B-I-L-L-I-O-N, $1 billion or half of his net worth from him by alleging that he had improperly engaged in sexual misconduct with Virginia Roberts.

That money would be divided three ways: A third of it to Virginia Roberts, a third of it to a charity that she and her lawyers were setting up for battered women, and a third of it to the lawyers.

She then told me they were trying to get ABC News to interview Virginia Roberts so as to give her credibility in order to pressure the billionaire from Columbus, Ohio Leslie Wexner into paying a large sum of money. And that I was named as an effort to try to show the billionaire what could happen to somebody if they were accused of sexual misconduct.

And that would encourage him to settle a lawsuit or pay money in exchange for his name not being mentioned or revealed. I had no idea about this. And I didn't -- I didn't ask about this. She just stated this.

And I then corroborated the fact that she was absolutely correct in everything she had said to me.

SCAROLA: You corroborated the fact that she was absolutely correct in everything that she had said to you?

DERSHOWITZ: That's right.

SCAROLA: How?

DERSHOWITZ: Okay. Let me answer that question. I was very -- I wasn't sure, so I called Leslie Wexner. I got his wife on the phone, Abigail Wexner. Obviously I knew that the only billionaire in Columbus, Ohio who owned Limited Too and who owned Victoria's Secret was Leslie Wexner. I had met Leslie Wexner on two occasions, I think, and his wife. I called Abigail on the phone and I said, I think you ought to know that there is an extortion plot being directed against your husband by unscrupulous lawyers in Florida.

And she said, oh, we're aware of that, they've already been in contact with us, which surprised me... I then also -- I can't give you the chronology of that. I then was in touch with ABC and found out she was absolutely correct about her efforts to try to get interviewed on ABC television.

DERSHOWITZ: In fact, I learned that your client, Brad Edwards, had sent a communication to people in the area urging them to watch her interview that was scheduled to be on three Television programs.

If I'm not mistaken, it was Good Day Show, the evening news, and the show Nightline. I then was in communication with ABC and helped to persuade them that they would be putting false information on the air if they allowed Virginia Roberts to tell her false story.

So, I was able to corroborate that. Then also corroborated the fact that she had never mentioned me when her boyfriend appeared on Television and publically stated that she had never mentioned me in any of her description of people who she had sexual contact with.

So, I was then completely satisfied that Rebecca was telling me the complete truth. And that in my view, there was an extortion plot directed against Leslie Wexner, a criminal extortion plot directed against Leslie Wexner, and that your clients were involved in that extortion plot.

SCAROLA: If we were to try to fix the time of this second phone call, one way in which we would fix the time of this second phone call, in addition to getting your telephone records, would be to find out when this ABC interview took place, correct? Since the phone call you're telling us came after the ABC interview, that you convinced ABC not to air?

DERSHOWITZ: No, I didn't state that. Let me be very clear. I found out from her that there was going to be an ABC television interview. I don't think I was aware of the fact that there was going to be a television interview at that point.

I remember then getting a -- either a phone call or e-mail from ABC informing me of that and that corroborated to my mind the fact that she, Rebecca, was telling me the truth about the ABC interview.

She also told me -- and this was corroborated, she also told me that the television interview with ABC had to be postponed because her husband- Virginia Roberts' husband, had beaten her up so badly that she was hospitalized and that she could not appear on television with the bruises because she didn't want to have to explain that her husband had beaten her up.

And I ultimately corroborated that information as well by investigating the fact that she, in fact, filed a complaint against her husband and had been hospitalized. So everything that Rebecca told me has proved to be absolutely true and absolutely corroborated. And, therefore, I believe it and believe that your clients were engaged in what I believe is an extortion plot against Leslie Wexner, conspiracy to commit extortion in which I was a victim, as well as Leslie Wexner, of being a victim.

SCAROLA: Did you speak directly to Leslie Wexner or only to his wife?

DERSHOWITZ: Only to his wife and his lawyers.

SCAROLA: And you spoke by telephone?

DERSHOWITZ: Yes.

SCAROLA: Where were you and where was she?

DERSHOWITZ: I called from, I think, New York and I spoke to her about it. I told her what I said I said. She said what I said she said. And then she said that her lawyers would be in touch with me. And her lawyer then called me and corroborated again that there had been contact and eventually there was greater contact.

SCAROLA: Contact by whom with whom?

DERSHOWITZ: Contact by Virginia Roberts' lawyer, lawyers. I wasn't – it wasn't clear at that point.

SCAROLA: Which lawyer or lawyers?

DERSHOWITZ: I wasn't clear at that point. They didn't indicate to me which lawyer or lawyers –

SCAROLA: Didn't you ask?

DERSHOWITZ: Who were the contacts?

SCAROLA: Didn't you want to know who is–making this request?

DERSHOWITZ: I asked -- whether there was a letter and they wouldn't show me a letter. I asked if there were phone calls. They were a -- they wanted to be discreet about how the contact had occurred. But they told me that the contact had occurred.

SCAROLA: But they wouldn't tell you who?

DERSHOWITZ: They wouldn't show me any letter.

SCAROLA: That's not my question. Did they tell you -- did you ask who contacted Leslie Wexner?

DERSHOWITZ: The first answer was Virginia Roberts' lawyer. I then subsequently learned that among those who contacted Leslie Wexner's lawyers, was David Boies and Sigrid McCawley.

SCAROLA: Not Bradley Edwards, correct?

DERSHOWITZ: I was not given the name Bradley Edwards at that time. But was subsequently told by David Boies that Bradley Edwards and Paul Cassell --

SIGRID McCAWLEY: I'm going to object to the extent this reveals any conversations that happened in the context of settlement discussions.

DERSHOWITZ: That I was ultimately told by David Boies that he had done an extensive investigation of the allegations against Leslie Wexner and had concluded that they were --

McCAWLEY: Again, I'm going to object to this since that happened in the context of settlement --

DERSHOWITZ: False.

McCAWLEY: -- negotiations. I'm going to move for sanctions if information is revealed that happened in the context of settlement discussions.

SCOTT: I don't know whether -- I don't believe there were settlement discussions. But even if they weren't, they would still be admissible.

DERSHOWITZ: Let me continue --

SCOTT: For discovery purposes--

DERSHOWITZ: -- that David Boies had done --

McCAWLEY: I disagree. I think we're going to have to take this to the judge, then, if we're going to reveal settlement conversations in this conversation, then we need, to go to the judge on it.

SCOTT: Whatever you need to do.

DERSHOWITZ: Let me continue the -- what he told me. That David Boies had

McCAWLEY: No, we're --

SIMPSON: No, no, no.

McCAWLEY: -- going to discontinue. We will contact the judge.

SCAROLA: We'll move on to another area and address that issue with the judge as to whether or not a protective order is appropriate.

DERSHOWITZ: Would you like to establish the foundation for why it's not protected?

SWEDER: Alan --

SCOTT: Alan, just let it alone. Let it alone.

DERSHOWITZ: Okay.

SCAROLA: This second conversation you've told us was conducted while you were in New York, correct?

DERSHOWITZ: That's my best recollection.

SCAROLA: The first conversation also conducted while you were in New York?

DERSHOWITZ: That's my best recollection.

SCAROLA: Are you aware that New York is a one-party consent state for purposes of permitting the recording of communications, correct?

SCOTT: Objection. Do you know?

DERSHOWITZ: I'm -- I think that's right, yeah.

SCAROLA: Okay. So you knew that these significant conversations could have been recorded by you had you chosen to record them, correct?

DERSHOWITZ: I don't think I thought about that at the time.

SCAROLA: Are you aware that years before December when the CVRA pleading was filed, that your name had come up repeatedly in connection with Jeffrey Epstein's abuse of minors, correct?

DERSHOWITZ: Let me answer that question. I am aware that never before 2014, end of December, was it ever, ever alleged that I had acted in any way inappropriately with regard to Virginia Roberts, that I ever touched her, that I ever met her, that I had ever been with her. I was completely aware of that.

There had never been any allegation. She claims under oath that she told you that secretly in 2011, but you have produced no notes of any such conversation. You, of course, are a witness to this allegation and will be deposed as a witness to this allegation. I believe it is an entirely false allegation that she told you, in 2011, that she had had any sexual contact with me. I think she's lying through her teeth when she says that.

DERSHOWITZ: And I doubt that your notes will reveal any such information. But if she did tell you that, she would be absolutely, categorically lying.

DERSHOWITZ: So I am completely aware that never, until the lies were put in a legal pleading at the end of December 2014, it was never alleged that I had any sexual contact with Virginia Roberts. I know that it was alleged that I was a witness to Jeffrey Epstein's alleged abuse and that was false. I was never a witness to any of Jeffrey Epstein's sexual abuse.

And I wrote that to you, something that you have falsely denied. And I stand on the record. The record is clear that I have categorically denied I was ever a witness to any abuse, that I ever saw Jeffrey Epstein abusing anybody.

And -- and the very idea that I would stand and talk to Jeffrey Epstein while he was receiving oral sex from Virginia Roberts, which she swore to under oath, is so outrageous, so preposterous, that even David Boies said he couldn't believe it was true.

McCAWLEY: I object. I object. I'm not going to allow you to reveal any conversations that happened in the context of a settlement discussion.

DERSHOWITZ: Does she have standing?

McCAWLEY: I have a standing objection and, I'm objecting again. I'm not going to –

DERSHOWITZ: No, no, no. Does she have standing in this deposition?

DERSHOWITZ: I'm not sure she has standing.

SCAROLA: Are we finished with the speech?

SCAROLA: I'd like him to finish the speech so that we can get to my question and then we can take a break.

DERWSHOWITZ: So the question -- the answer to your question is --

SIMPSON: Wait a minute. Wait a minute. Wait a minute. Please don't disclose something that she has a right to raise that objection if she wants to.

DERSHOWITZ: Okay.

SCOTT: Ask your question.

SWEDER: Maybe you want to read back the last couple of sentences.

SCAROLA: No, how about just reading back the last question and maybe we can get an answer to the question.

SCOTT: Again, I move to strike your comments, Counsel, because it's inappropriate and you're too good a lawyer to know that that's not true --

SCAROLA: Nothing inappropriate about my insisting upon an answer to the question that I asked instead of a speech.

SCOTT: Well, you know, he's trying to answer your question to the best of his ability. Counsel objected to it. I wanted to take a break to make sure that we explained to him the position so that we didn't have a problem, and

I was trying to protect everybody in this room.

SCOTT: But if you want to proceed, we can do it.

SCAROLA: Well, if we simply answer the questions that are asked, there won't be a problem.

SCOTT: Well, I guess everybody -- you can characterize it one-way, I can characterize it another, that he's doing the best he can to answer your questions.

SCAROLA: And ultimately Judge Lynch will make that determination.

SCOTT: Absolutely. So be it.

SCAROLA: So read back the last question, if you would, please. We'll get a--hopefully get an answer to that and then we can take a break.

COURT REPORTER: "Are you aware that 12 years before December of 2014, when the CVRA pleading was filed, that your name had come up repeatedly in connection with Jeffrey Epstein's abuse of minors, correct?"

SCOTT: Objection, asked and answered

DERSHOWITZ: And then -- we discussed the charity. And I think it was called VR, which is her initials, Virginia Roberts, and also it stood for something, I don't know, Victims Rights or something like that.

And she said that the lawyers had contributed $80,000 of their own money to start the charity. She didn't indicate which lawyers.

DERSHOWITZ: But the lawyers had contributed $80,000 of their own money to start the charity and that they were going to fund the charity by contributions from Leslie -- from the man from Columbus who owned Victoria's Secret and they expected a very substantial contribution. They also said that --

SCAROLA: I'm sorry, but "they" is not helpful to me.

DERSHOWITZ: She -- when I say "they" -- when I talk about the substance, I'm always talking about her Abigail. I never had any conversations about the substance with him Wexner. She said that they were hoping to fund the charity by substantial contribution from Leslie Wexner and that they thought that by getting on television, they would increase the chances of raising this money from Leslie Wexner.

And that she thought they had already made contact with Wexner and that they had already made -- with the man from Columbus Wexner, and they had already made contact with ABC. But I don't think she knew at that point whether the actual interviews did or did not occur.

SCAROLA: So it has been ten months since you allegedly became aware of that suborning of perjury and some eight months since your allegedly having become aware of the extortion plot, but you have filed no criminal complaints against anyone, correct?

DERSHOWITZ: To answer that question requires me to disclose conversations I had with David Boies. I would love to answer that question.

SCAROLA: No, sir, it does not.

DERSHOWITZ: Yes, it does.

SCOTT: Whoa, you can't -- how can you.

SCAROLA: Whether you filed a criminal complaint or not?

DERSHOWITZ: Yes, it does.

SCOTT: Please, Jack, he can't say that.

DERSHOWITZ: It does involve conversation I had with David Boies.

SCAROLA: Well, in that case, in light of the fact that that is a matter that will be addressed by the Court, we'll save that question for another time.

DERSHOWITZ: I'm anxious to answer it.

SCAROLA: And I'm anxious to get an answer.

DERSHOWTIZ: Well, I hope we can agree I should be able to answer it.

SCAROLA: Have we exhausted, You know that Virginia Roberts is not the only person who has sworn under oath that you were present at Jeffrey Epstein's Palm Beach home with young girls, right?

DERSHOWITZ: No.

SCAROLA: You don't know that?

DERSHOWITZ: No. I know that —

SCAROLA: Well, that's fine. You've answered my question. That's not something you know?

DERSHOWITZ: I was not present in Jeffrey Epstein's home with any underage young women, period. Never, ever under any circumstances. I am not aware that anyone has sworn under oath that I was there during the relevant periods of time, which is a three-year period between the summer of 1999 and the summer of 2002. Because I was never -- as far as I know, I was never in Jeffrey Epstein's home during that period of time, period.

SCAROLA: I want to go back to the Ashes, if I could. Joanne Ashe is not a lawyer, is she?

DERSHOWITZ: Joanne Ashe is not a lawyer, no.

SCAROLA: And is Alexi Ashe a lawyer?

DERSHOWITZ: Yes.

SCAROLA: Has Alexi Ashe ever been your lawyer?

DERSHOWITZ: I have discussed the case with Alexi Ashe. She is a full-time sex trafficking prosecutor whose whole career has been going after sex traffickers in the Brooklyn District Attorney's office and I have discussed my case with her.

SCAROLA: Has Alexi Ashe ever been your lawyer?

DERSHOWITZ: I would say not, no.

SCAROLA: Beginning approximately January 3 or 4 2015, you began a mass media campaign battle against Bradley Edwards and Professor Paul Cassell alleging that they were sleazy, unethical lawyers who fabricated false charges against you, correct?

DERSHOWITZ: That's a false --

DERSHOWITZ: That's a false statement. I did not begin. It was your clients who began it. Your clients began it by filing false statements in a federal court, which the judge struck and sanctioned them for as being irrelevant and pertinent and he used other language.

They began it. It is my belief that they began it in order to get massive press attention to it. And my -- my responses were when the press called me, the press called me immediately and asked me for my reaction.

I was totally shocked that any lawyer would make these kinds of outrageous career-destroying allegations without even calling me and asking me if I would deny it or have any evidence to provide for them. And when I was called by the media I did what you would do, Mr. Scarola, or what your clients would do, I defended myself. What any American would do under the First Amendment, I categorically denied career-destroying false statements and I told the truth, which is what the United States Constitution is all about and why we fought for liberty. Yes, I told the truth to the media.

SCAROLA: You engaged in a mass media campaign to convince the world that Bradley Edwards and Professor Paul Cassell were unethical lawyers who had fabricated false charges against you, correct?

DERSHOWITZ: No, that's not correct. I responded to press inquiries by telling the truth. My goal was to let the world know that Virginia Roberts' allegations against me were totally false.

DERSHOWITZ: These stories appeared, as far as I can tell, in every single newspaper in the world and on every media, which was part of their plot and the plan of your clients, which is why they absurdly mentioned Prince Andrew, claiming in the most absurd way --that they mentioned him because he was trying to lobby prosecutors to get a reduced sentence for Jeffrey Epstein.

They obviously put Prince Andrew in there in order to get massive publicity around the world. And every media in the world practically called me from the BBC, to CBS, to ABC, to CNN and I responded to lies with the truth.

SCAROLA: And the truth that you attempted to convey was that Bradley Edwards and Professor Paul Cassell were unethical lawyers who fabricated false charges against you, right?

DERSHOWITZ: The truth --The truth that I intended to convey was that the charges against me were false and fabricated, that I never had any sexual contact --

SCAROLA: Fabricated by whom, sir?

DERSHOWITZ: Please don't interrupt me.

SCOTT: Objection, interrupting.

SCAROLA: Please answer the question.

DERSHOWITZ: Please don't interrupt --

SCOTT: He's answering them. You may not like the answer, but he's answering them.

DERSHOWITZ: Now you've -- you've made me lose my train of thought, so –

SCOTT: Can you read the question back and the -- read the question back and his answers, please.

COURT REPORTER: The question was: "And the truth that you attempted to convey was that Bradley Edwards and Professor Paul Cassell were unethical lawyers who fabricated false charges against you, right?"

COURT REPORTER: And the answer was: "The truth that I intended to convey was that the charges against me were false and fabricated, that I never had any sexual contact" -- and then the question was -- the answer was interrupted.

DERSHOWTIZ: Okay. Let me continue. That I never had any sexual contact with Virginia Roberts because Professor Cassell insisted on conveying to the public that he was a former judge and that he was a

Professor, and that he was using, improperly in my view, the stationery and name of his university to add credibility to his claims, I felt that it was imperative for me to indicate that he was engaging in improper and unethical conduct.

It would have been improper for me to have allowed his use of his credibility as a former federal judge, as a professor who uses, misuses his University imprimatur, it was very important for me to attack the credibility of the messengers of the false information.

And it was important for me to also remind the public that Bradley Edwards was a partner of Rothstein, a man who is spending 50 years in jail for fraudulently creating a Ponzi scheme to sell Jeffrey Epstein cases that didn't exist. Yes, it was very important for me to indicate the back --

DERSHOWITZ: the real backgrounds of these lawyers and to make sure that the public didn't believe that because they were credible, their story must be credible.

In fact, one of the first questions that I was asked repeatedly by the media is: Why would a former federal judge level a false charge against you? Why would a distinguished personal injury lawyer level a false charge against you?

And it was important for me to indicate why they would, that they were trying to do it for crass financial reasons, they were trying to do it to open up a non-prosecution agreement, they were trying to do it for reasons that were improper.

So, yes, I did -- you know, Mr. Edwards, your client, is shaking his head, but when he's deposed under oath, he's not going to be able to simply shake his head. He's going to have to answer specific and direct questions.

SCAROLA: Let me try my question. Did you charge Bradley Edwards and Professor Paul Cassell in your mass media appearances with fabricating false charges against you?

DERSHOWITZ My media appearances were largely in response to media requests of me. I did not conduct a media campaign. The object of my speaking to the media was to respond to their questions. Their questions were, number 1, did you ever have any sexual contact with Virginia Roberts? And I unequivocally stated no.

DERSHOWITZ: I stated that I knew there were no videos or photographs because the event didn't occur. I stated that I would submit a sworn affidavit, which in effect waived the statute of limitations. I stated unequivocally that I was innocent of those false charges. I was then asked by the media, well, why would somebody who is a former federal judge and professor at a law school make these false charges?

I responded to those questions. Why would somebody like a distinguished personal injury lawyer make those false charges? And I responded to those questions. And everything I said was the truth, as I believed it to be at the time.

SCAROLA: Do you remember the question that was asked of you?

DERSHOWTIZ: Yes, I've answered it.

SCAROLA: What was the question?

DERSHOWITZ: As part of massive media campaign, I did charge your clients with deliberately falsifying a charge against me, and my answer satisfies that question.

SCAROLA: No, I don't think it does. Can you tell us whether that's what you did, did you charge --

DERSHOWITZ: I just did.

SCAROLA: Them with having intentionally fabricated false charges against you?

DERSHOWITZ: I believe that they intentionally fabricated false evidence against me. I believe that they pressured their client into fabricating false evidence against me. I believe that they helped to draft a perjurious affidavit that was filed in Court after they knew that I said I could prove that I couldn't have been there four of the five places that the alleged acts could have occurred.

DERSHOWITZ: I believe that when they recently sought to submit an additional claim repeating these charges into the federal court, that they did it knowing full well that these charges were false. That's my belief, yes.

SCAROLA: Are you aware that your lawyers filed a pleading on your behalf in this case with the title Defendant Alan M. Dershowitz's Answer to the Complaint and Counterclaim?

DERSHOWITZ: I'm not aware of that.

SCAROLA: Pardon me?

DERSHOWITZ: I'm not aware of the title of any legal pleadings.

SCAROLA: Do you know that an answer has been filed to the defamation action that has been brought against you?

DERSHOWITZ: Of course I mean I'm sure there's been a legal answer prepared. Of course, that's what lawyers do.

SCAROLA: Are you aware that there's also a counterclaim that has been filed on your behalf?

DERSHOWITZ: Yes, I authorized the counterclaim to be filed because I believe that your clients defamed me and that Mr. Cassell wrote a letter to ABC, which not even plausibly is within the claim of privilege, which asserts that I had -- asserts falsely and in a defamatory way that I had had sexual contact with Virginia Roberts, yes.

SCAROLA: Did you read the answer to the complaint and counterclaim --

DERSHOWITZ: I'm sure I did.

SCAROLA: before it was filed?

DERSHOWITZ: I'm sure I did.

SCAROL: And I assume that you approved of it, correct?

DERSHOWITZ: I assume I did, yes.

SCAROLA: Okay.

SCOTT: I object to anything as far as using pleadings like this, but go ahead and do it.

SCAROLA: As a law professor, would it be fair for us to assume that you know the difference between simple negligence and recklessness?

DERSHOWITZ: That's something that you could spend an entire semester teaching the difference between simple negligence and recklessness.

DERSHOWITZ: That's very much a matter of degree and the courts are – are split very much on what the meaning of "recklessness" is, particularly in the context of defamation. It's a very complicated subject.

SCAROLA: Do you personally recognize that there is a difference between simple negligence and recklessness?

DERSHOWITZ: At the extremes, yes, simple negligence is failure to perform a duty and recklessness is failure to perform a duty knowing that there -- knowing or should know that there is a likelihood of some harm being committed. That's just what I remember from first year torts.

SCAROLA: And you do also recognize that there is a distinction between simple negligence and recklessness on one hand and intentional wrongdoing on the other, correct?

DERSHOWITZ: Again, I've argued cases about this issue. And it's a continuum. Sometimes courts say "that should have known" is the equivalent of "knowing." So it's a continuum. There's not an absolute straight line between those two, yeah. Moving forward...

SCAROLA: Were there any other entourage members that traveled with Jeffrey Epstein when he came to your home?

DERSHOWITZ: I have no recollection of any of them ever coming to my home. I don't remember but if that's whom he traveled with. Sometimes he would travel -- he almost always had a regular girlfriend.

DERSHOWITZ: And I remember a few of them. One of them was a student at the business school who's -- I may be merging two of them. One of them was a student at the business school. Another, maybe the same one, was a wealthy woman whose father owned banks in Great Britain.

Another was a woman from either the Czech Republic or Slovakia who was probably between 20 and 25, he is referring to Nadia Marcinkova who was 14 years old when Epstein brought her to the United States. Probably closer to 25. And he would travel with a posse, basically, an entourage of -- of people. But I never met some of the people who are in the entourage. They were just there.

SCAROLA: They were there at the same time that you were there and Jeffrey Epstein was there?

DERSHOWITZ: Well, they were –

SCOTT: Wait a minute. That's vague.

DERSHOWITZ: I mean, there in the house, there in Massachusetts?

SCAROLA: There, wherever. When you were in Jeffrey Epstein's presence, Jeffrey Epstein usually had what you have described as some regular girlfriend.

DERSHOWITZ: That's right.

SCAROLA: And you have described a variety of different regular girlfriends who were with him, correct?

DERSHOWITZ: Yes.

SCAROLA: Usually in the age range, you would estimate, between 20 and 25; is that correct?

DERSHOWITZ: I would say--

SCOTT: Objection. That's not it.

DERSHOWITZ: I would say between 22 and 25 would be a closer -- closer estimate. But 23, in that range. There were none that I ever believed were in any way teenagers. And they all performed tasks. They were taking notes or they were arranging, serving coffee or doing various things. And that's the way Jeffrey would travel when he went to academic meetings. And these people were seen not only by me. They were seen by Larry Summers, they were seen by Church, they were seen by Marvin Minsky, they were seen by some of the most eminent academics and scholars in the world. There was no hint or suggestion of anything sexual or improper in the presence of these people.

SCAROLA: Describe the motor vehicle that Jeffrey Epstein used to travel from the airport to your home on those occasions when you observed --

DERSHOWITZ: I have no recollection. They were rented cars.

SCAROLA: Limousines?

DERSHOWITZ: Limousines, yeah, yeah.

SCAROLA: And did you ever travel from your home with Jeffrey Epstein in a limousine?

DERSHOWITZ: Not during the relevant time period, no, no.

SCAROLA: So, you can state with certainty, that at no time between 1999 and 2002 did you ever travel from your home in a limousine with Jeffrey Epstein?

DERSHOWITZ: I can't imagine any reason why I would have. I did not fly in his plane during that period of time, my records establish. And I would see no reason why I would have. I don't have any recollection whether I specifically drove with him during that period of time. But I think I did not because I did not have any reason. Normally if I drove with him, it would be to go to the airport to get on his plane. That was the only reason that I would have ever to go in a limousine that I know of.

SCAROLA: What records establish that you were not on Jeffrey Epstein's plane during what you have described as the relevant time period?

DERSHOWITZ: No, you've described it as the relevant time period. You said 2009 to 2000- --

SCAROLA: No, sir. In the answer you just --

DERSHOWITZ: -- 1999 --

SCAROLA: -- gave, you used the phrase "relevant time frame," time period.

DERSHOWITZ: Yeah, I was picking up on your terms between 1999 and 2002. So can we agree that's the relevant time period?

SCAROLA: You can tell me what -- what your response is based on that you never traveled on Jeffrey Epstein's airplane during the relevant time period, whatever you consider that to be.

DERSHOWITZ: Okay. Number 1 my own calendars, which have been provided to you. Number 2, my cell phone records. Number 3 my wife's calendars. Number 4 my teaching and other schedule. Number 5 my own recollection.

DERSHOWITZ: And number 6, as far as we know, the airplane manifests do not have me on any airplanes during that time period.

Scarola asked Dershowitz if he understood that, "More than 30 underage women have come forward to report that your friend, Jeffrey Epstein, paid them for sex and that he pled guilty to procuring underage girls for prostitution, and that he paid very large sums of money to settle their civil claims against him."

SCAROLA: Do you still insist that he had not engaged in sex or erotic massages with any minors?

Martin Weinberg, Epstein's attorney, immediately interrupted and instructed Dershowitz not to answer the question. Thomas Scott, Dershowitz's attorney, also instructed him not to answer.

In spite of their recommendations and knowing that he was Epstein's attorney, Dershowitz responded:

DERSHOWITZ: Marty, you're the lawyer for my client. Do you -- do you order me to answer the question or not? I am going to follow the instruction. I have no choice. He's my client.

SCAROLA: You know that he pled guilty to sexual abuse of minors, correct?

DERSHOWITZ: Could you tell me exactly what he pleaded guilty to so I can answer that question?

SCAROLA: Well, do you know? You represented him during the period of time that he was under – that he was -- that he was under criminal charges, didn't you?

SCOTT: So you're withdrawing the prior question; you're now asking this question? Okay.

SCAROLA: That's correct, I'm asking –this question

DERSHOWITZ: So I represented him -- I represented him first in Palm Beach County, and at that point, he had been prepared to plead guilty to, I think, one count --

WEINBERG: Alan, I'm sorry. This is again, going right into the work that you did for him as his lawyer and I instruct you not to answer.

SCOTT: That's it, then follow his -- as your attorney, I'm telling you to follow the lawyer's advice.

DERSHOWITZ: Uh-huh.

SCAROLA: Do you agree, Mr. Dershowitz that deciding the issues in this case will depend on evaluating not only Virginia Roberts' credibility but your credibility as well?

SCOTT: Objection, legal conclusion, not relevant here.

DERSHOWITZ: I think that I can prove my complete innocence and the fact that -- Virginia Roberts made up the story out of whole cloth without my credibility being at issue, but I'm perfectly happy to put my credibility at issue because I am telling the blue absolute truth about everything regarding Virginia Roberts.

SCAROLA: One way to evaluate credibility is to compare an individual's statements with available documentary evidence, correct?

DERSHOWITZ: That's too broad a question. Depending on what the documentary evidence could be. Documentary could be lies. Documents contain lies and oral statements contain truth. So, no, I don't think that's a particularly good way. It depends on the nature of the document. For example, videotape would be very good. If you had an videotape that in some way supported Virginia Roberts' statements and it undercut what I said, that would be fine. That's why from day one I've asked to have if there is any videotape shown or any photographs because I know what happened.

DERSHOWTIZ: I know that I never had any contact, any sexual contact, any, improper contact with Virginia Roberts. And I know, therefore, that there cannot be any evidence that contradicts that because you can't simply make up facts. So I am telling you the absolute truth.

SCAROLA: You also know that all of the videotapes that were taken through surveillance cameras throughout Jeffrey Epstein's home were destroyed don't you?

DERSHOWITZ: Of course I don't know that.

SCAROLA: You don't know?

DERSHOWITZ: Of course not.

SCAROLA: So you didn't read the police reports then?

SCOTT: Objection. Mr. Epstein, do you want him to answer that question?

SIMPSON: Mr. Weinberg.

SCOTT: Mr. Weinberg?

WEINBERG: It's the same objection.

DERSHOWITZ: Oh, so there's no question.

SCAROLA: You have stated publicly repeatedly that the airplane manifests will exonerate you, correct?

DERSHOWITZ: I have stated publicly that the airplane manifest, the one that I have seen, do not show me on any of Jeffrey Epstein's airplanes in the 7 relevant period of time, which I define as the summer of 1999 through the summer of 2002, number one. Number two, that none of the airplane manifests will show me on the same plane with Virginia Roberts. And three, that none of the manifests will show me on an airplane with Jeffrey Epstein and any underage girls that were at least visible in the passenger part of the airplane.

SCAROLA: Well, that raises an interesting point, Mr. Dershowitz. Tell us about the interior – of that plane.

DERSHOWITZ: Why is it interesting? My recollection is the plane was a 160 Gulfstream IV. That it had a cabin that seated approximately one, two, three, four -- maybe ten -- ten people. It had mostly seats -- I used to sit in

the seat facing backward, that's the way I prefer to fly. And in the back of the plane there was a toilet, a place to serve food. And a couch that served as a seat with seat belts for maybe two or three additional people. But I never saw the plane -- the only time I ever saw the plane filled to capacity was when I went down to watch a launch of a satellite --

SCAROLA: Does that have -- anything to do with the configuration of the interior of the plane?

DERSHOWITZ: To outer space, yes. Yes, I'm telling you that I've mostly seen it only with four or five people. The only time I've seen the couch -

SCAROLA: Did I ask you how many people –

SCOTT: Well, you're interrupting –

SCAROLA: Were in the plane, at the time I asked you, what the configuration of the cabin was, Mr. Dershowitz?

DERSHOWITZ: I'm explaining

SCAROLA: Is that part of the question that I asked --

DERSHOWITZ: I'm explaining the couch.

SCAROLA: or is that your effort to make speeches in an effort to consume the limited amount of time that we have?

SCOTT: I would object to that characterization.

DERSHOWITZ: I wanted to start at -- I wanted to start at 12:00 -- at 1:30 today.

SCOTT: And the speech.

SIMPSON: Alan, Alan.

DERSHOWITZ: All the delays have been caused by you not me. And I'm ready to go to 5:30, but you're quitting at 5 -- or 4:30.

SCAROLA: Yes, sir, I have -- a commitment -- I have a commitment to chair an -- Easter Seals fundraiser.

DERSHOWITZ: So don't blame any delays on me, sir. Don't we all. We all have commitments.

SCAROLA: You've known –did you see a bed in the plane?

DERSHOWITZ: I never saw a bed in the plane. As far as I know, there was no bed in the plane. And that's what I was trying to explain. That the only time I've seen that couch used is when two or three people were sitting in it when we went down to watch the launch of the satellite because that was the only time I saw the plane filled.

Other than that, it was a plain, ordinary couch that was never used by anybody during the flights. We were all sitting in our seats. I do not know for a fact that that couch becomes a bed. I never saw it as a bed. And the answer is categorically no.

SCAROLA: Well, the question was: Is there a bed on the plane? The answer to that question is not a categorical no; the answer to that question is you don't know; is that right?

DERSHOWITZ: The answer to that question is there is a couch on the plane like it is on all -- as far as I know, all Gulfstream IVs. I have no idea whether or not that couch becomes a bed.

SCAROLA: You told the American lawyer on January 15, 2015 a statement that you have repeated on multiple occasions: "I've been married to the same woman for 28 years. She goes with me everywhere." Do you acknowledge making that statement?

DERSHOWITZ: Yes. My wife goes with me everywhere today. These days, now that our daughter is grown, 18 up and went to high school and college, she travels with me everywhere. It's a rare, rare occasion when my wife doesn't travel with me. In fact, I have a condition of my speaking engagements that the speaking engagements have to pay for my wife to come with me.

I hate traveling alone. I almost never do it unless there is an absolutely essential reason for Carolyn to be somewhere else, such as taking care of her 96-year-old mother. But it is true I travel with my wife.

SCAROLA: In fact, the airplane manifests that have been produced reflect your having traveled on Jeffrey Epstein's airplane on ten separate occasions and on none of those occasions --

DERSHOWITZ: Is that testimony, Sir?

SCAROLA: On none of those occasions – is your wife reflected as having been a passenger at the same time that you are were on Jeffrey Epstein's airplane, right?

SCOTT: Object to the form. There's no timeframe or anything of that nature. If you can answer --

SCAROLA: All of the manifests that have been produced in this litigation, the ones that you say corroborate your testimony and exonerate you, demonstrate that you never flew on Jeffrey Epstein's plane in the company of your wife, correct?

DERSHOWITZ: No. That's not true. I flew in the company of my wife and my daughter from Charleston, South Carolina to Guadalupe --

SCAROLA: I'm asking about what the manifests show, Sir.

DERSHOWITZ: I'm telling you what –

SCAROLA: the ones that you say exonerate you.

DERSHOWITZ: Well, I said that --

SCAROLA: Is there a manifest that shows that you and your wife were on Jeffrey Epstein's plane at the same time together?

SCOTT: Let me object to the -

DERSHOWITZ: I don't know that.

SCOTT: -- argumentative nature and compound nature. He's trying to answer you questions.

DERSHOWITZ: Let me go through each of the times

DERSHOWITZ: Okay. Okay.

SCAROLA: Is there a manifest that shows that your wife ever accompanied you on a flight on Jeffrey Epstein's private airplane?

SCOTT: Let me object again. There's no reference to the timeframe or the relevant timeframe --

SCAROLA: Any time ever.

DERSHOWITZ: My wife accompanied me on two occasions, my nephew SCAROLA: Is there a manifest --

SCOTT: You're cutting him off, Counsel.

DERSHOWITZ: Let me finish.

SCAROLA: He's not answering my question.

SCOTT: Yes, he is answering your question.

DERSHOWITZ: My nephew accompanied me on one occasion. My research assistant, Mitch Webber, accompanied me on one occasion.

My son or grandson, I'm not sure which, accompanied me on one occasion. And the occasions that I flew on Jeffrey Epstein's plane were almost always business occasions during a time when my daughter, Ella, was in elementary school, if we're talking about the relevant period of time. And during that period of time, on occasion my wife did not fly with me.

SCAROLA: Is there --

DERSHOWITZ: But let me emphasize -- let me emphasize that the manifests that do exculp me, do not show me flying with Virginia Roberts, they do not show me flying with any young women.

They know that on every trip I took, there was a business reason for it, there were other people on the plane, and it is inconceivable that during any of those periods of time, the lies that Virginia Roberts told about me could have been true.

SCAROLA: So it's your contention that no manifests show you traveling outside the company of your wife is that correct? -- No manifest shows you traveling outside the company of your wife?

DERSHOWITZ: I'm confused. That's a double, triple negative.

SCOTT: Do you understand the question?

DERSHOWITZ: I don't, no.

SCOTT: Rephrase it.

SCAROLA: There is not a single manifest of the ten that shows you as a passenger on Jeffrey Epstein's plane that shows your wife there at the same time, correct?

DERSHOWITZ: I am not aware that there are ten manifests. I would be happy to look at the manifests. I have explained -- Unfortunately --

SCAROLA: -- each of the times -- we won't have time to do that this afternoon --but we will have time to do that eventually.

DERSHOWITZ: We will -- I welcome that time, because I can give complete context to every single trip I took. And if you're trying to convey the impression that there was any occasion on which I had any improper conduct while I was on that airplane that is a categorical lie.

SCAROLA: What I am trying to do, Sir is to test the veracity of your public assertions that you have never traveled outside the presence of your wife.

DERSHOWITZ: That is a lie.

SCAROLA: That is what I'm trying to do.

DERSHOWITZ: That is a lie, Sir, a categorical lie. I challenge you to find any statement where I said I have never traveled outside the presence of my wife.

SCAROLA: Well, how about this --

DERSHOWITZ: Sir, find me that statement.

SCAROLA: -- do you -- do you remember having -- stated publicly on multiple occasions that you never received a massage – from Jeffrey Epstein?

DERSHOWITZ: No.

SCOTT: Unless you can show and characterize them by date and time, you just can't say here -- it's improper impeachment -- that you've done this ten times. It's just improper completely.

SCAROLA: Can you answer the question --

SCOTT: And it's overly broad.

SCAROLA: do you have any recollection of saying that you never received a massage?

DERSHOWITZ: I did receive a massage.

SCAROLA: Do you have any recollection --

DERSHOWITZ: A. I have no recollection --

SCAROLA: --of making that public statement that you never received a massage?

DERSHOWITZ: I can't imagine me saying that. If I said it I was mistaken. I had one massage, to my recollection.

SCAROLA: Okay. Tell us about where that occurred.

DERSHOWITZ: That occurred in my bedroom of Jeffrey Epstein's home in Palm Beach. I was asked whether Palm Beach. I was asked whether I wanted a massage. I had been asked repeatedly whether I wanted a massage and I had said no.

DERSHOWITZ: Then I was told that they had a masseuse coming from Miami who was a specialist of some kind, she was very good, she was Russian, and she worked, I think, in the Russian baths or something like that, and I agreed to have a massage.

I regretted it. She massaged me in a very tough and rough way. And she wanted to put her knees on my shoulder and I said no.

I immediately called my wife when the massage was over and I told her about the bad experience I had. And I said to her, see, I really don't like massages. But my wife likes massages. And she has had -- she has massages frequently.

SCAROLA: This massage occurred in your bedroom in Jeffrey Epstein's house; is that correct?

DERSHOWITZ: Not in my bedroom, in the bedroom that I had been assigned, which was a guest bedroom. The door was open. The -- a massage table was brought in. I kept my undergarments on. And I was massaged maybe for 20 minutes or 25 minutes. And then -- and

then she left and I had an unpleasant experience and I called my wife and I told her about it.

SCAROLA: Was the bedroom to which you were assigned, which you previously referred to as your bedroom --

DERSHOWITZ: No, no. I said "my bedroom" in the sense that I was in it.

SCAROLA: Was the bedroom to which you were assigned in the private section of the residence?

SCOTT: Do you understand the question?

DERSHOWITZ: Yeah, let me explain exactly. This requires a long answer.

There -- when you walk into Jeffrey Epstein's house, there are two areas. If you walk up the left side of the stairway, there are guest bedrooms, three or four guest bedrooms.

Those were assigned to people like Senator George Mitchell, Ehud Barak, prominent guests who would stay in his house. Each one had its own bathroom and its own bed.

I stayed there with my wife for a period of time. But then there was another area of the house, which I have never been in, ever, and which nobody was allowed basically into, which was Jeffrey Epstein's part of the house, which contained his bedroom and whatever other rooms. I've read about them, but I've never seen them. So it was in the guest area of the house over the kitchen.

SCAROLA: Who told you no one was allowed in that area of the house?

DERSHOWITZ: I was told by the people that that was off -- off limits, that that was Jeffrey's --

SCAROLA: Which people?

DERSHOWITZ: Ghislaine Maxwell, Sarah Kellen, that was Jeffrey's area of the house and the guests were limited to the public areas of the house and the -- and I think that's common in many houses when you go and stay at somebody's house, you don't go into their bathrooms and their bedrooms.

SCAROLA: Jeffrey Epstein's art consisted of photographs of young naked girls all over the house, right?

DERSHOWITZ: Are you testifying? That's false. I never saw any such thing. Ever. Never saw a picture, with one exception, of a nude. The one exception was a sepia print of Rodin's model that appeared on one of his desks. But in all the times I was at Jeffrey Epstein's house in Palm Beach, the one time I was in his house in -- on the island, certainly the one time in -- in the ranch because there was nothing there, it was just a construction site, I never saw a picture -- or in his house in New York, I never saw a picture of a naked woman, ever.

In late December 2015, I asked an attorney close to the case what he thought about the Dershowitz deposition. The attorney who asked to remain anonymous said, "The court is recognizing that many of the statements made by Dershowitz are not accurate. The courts in the course of the Defamation litigation are finally examining the exaggerations he made and the strategic silence of Virginia Louise Roberts in the face of various untruths. This is just one of several rulings in that case."

To date, the attorney explained, "Boies has not filed any case against Dershowitz. Professor Dershowitz simply lied about what he and Boies discussed in the course of settlement discussions, which are privileged. There is nothing unusual about counsel and their clients having settlement discussions."

The same source explained that, "If Dershowitz or any other defendant and counsel want to discuss a potential settlement, lawyers have a duty to find out what the other party has in mind. That is what happened in this case. Evidently, there was no settlement arising out of those discussions. Angry about that, Dershowitz, apparently violated the privilege and claimed Boies said various things that Boies actually did not say."

"Whatever the circumstances involving Dershowitz, whether he will be prosecuted for making false claims or not, that's up to the prosecutors," the attorney said. The attorney pointed out that, "No prosecutor has expressed any opinion about whether Dershowitz is being investigated or will be prosecuted," he explained.

It seems Dershowitz perhaps had a premonition. In January 2015, Dershowitz told The Boston Globe, "Someone will be disbarred. Either it will be me, or the two lawyers. In the end, someone's reputation is going to be destroyed, either mine or theirs."[3]

As it happened, none of the attorneys were disbarred. The case was settled on Friday, April 8, 2016 when Edwards and Cassell issued a notice of withdrawal for partial summary judgment and they reached a settlement agreement.

In "The Confidential Settlement Agreement, Ms. Giuffre reaffirmed her allegations, and the withdrawal of the referenced filings is not intended to be, and should not be construed as being, an acknowledgement by Edwards and Cassell that the allegations made by Roberts Giuffre were mistaken."

"Edwards and Cassell acknowledged that the public filing in the Crime Victims' Rights Act case against Dershowitz became a major distraction from the merits of the well-founded CVRA case by causing delay and, as a consequence, turned out to have been a tactical mistake. For that reason, Edwards and Cassell have chosen to withdraw the referenced filing as a condition of settlement."[4]

On April 9, 2016, I e-mailed Professor Dershowitz asking for a statement. He did not respond. When I asked Edwards and Cassell, Edwards said, "We did not withdraw a complaint. We settled the defamation action and as part of the settlement certain pleadings that were filed by Jack Scarola as well as Alan's Dershowitz attorney were withdrawn."

On April 11, 2016, Vivia Chen at The American Lawyer, reported, "I got what I always wanted. They withdrew everything!" Dershowitz told her. He also said that, "He spent over $1 million on legal fees (insurance covered a chunk of it), he won't disclose if the settlement entails any monetary rewards, citing a confidentiality clause. But he says he's not suffering financially because of the ordeal, "I continue to be sought after; people call me every day for legal work...Part of me," he said, "Wanted to have a trial and have evidence come out."[5]

"If Dershowitz was looking for total vindication," Chen reported, "I'm not sure this cuts it. But he was satisfied with the wording in the settlement... As a legal matter, Giuffre's lawyers couldn't admit she was wrong to accuse him." Dershowitz explained," They can't take back the claims because that could be used against her on a perjury indictment. That would mean throwing her under the bus." Ultimately, they'll have to make a claim that it was a case of mistaken identity, that it was done in good faith."[6] The settlement was reached with prejudice, which means that was the end of the case.

* * *

Footnotes

1. Alan Dershowitz Deposition: October 15, 2015, Transcript #1 pages, 1-178

2. Alan Dershowitz Deposition: October 16, 2015, Transcript #2 pages 179

3. https://www.bostonglobe.com/metro/2015/01/06/sued-for-defamation-dershowitz-thrilled-chance-question-lawyers-sex-crime-accuser/21QibSrwNC343eKMadWNeL/story.html

4. http://m.americanlawyer.com/#/article/1202754581393/2/Dershowitz%20Settles%20Sex%20Case,%20But%20Is%20He%20Vindicated

5. http://m.americanlawyer.com/#/article/1202754581393/2/Dershowitz%20Settles%20Sex%20Case,%20But%20Is%20He%20Vindicated

6. http://m.americanlawyer.com/#/article/1202754581393/2/Dershowitz%20Settles%20Sex%20Case,%20But%20Is%20He%20Vindicated

Chapter Fifteen

Something Other Than the Truth

Dershowitz's testimony was important for several reasons, not the least of which was to tell the truth, set the record straight, and explain the details of his relationship, if any, with Virginia Louise Roberts, Jeffrey Epstein, Ghislaine Maxwell and former president Bill Clinton.

If past is prologue, given the calendar year, Dershowitz's statement about his insights into the relationship between former president Clinton and some underage girls is invaluable on two fronts. The year 2015-2016 is a presidential election year. Epstein's case and the allegations of impropriety implicating Clinton and two underage girls, plus the donations gifted to them by Epstein prior to and after his indictment could potentially derail his wife's presidential bid in November 2016.

Given Bill Clinton's history of sexual misconduct and his impeachment for perjury in 1998; talks of the Lewinsky scandal and "bimbo eruptions" as the Secretary's staffers refer to the women who accused her husband of sexual misconduct; and Kathleen Wiley's 2015 open testimony concerning former president Clinton, all point to a history of bad behavior of a President while holding public office.

As a result of the president's friendship with Epstein, even though their relationship was in the past, the history could have negative implications for the Secretary's presidential campaign. Professor Dershowitz' transcript shed some light.

SCAROLA: Did you state during the same interview, the CNN Don Lemon interview: "She, Virginia Louise Roberts, has said that Bill Clinton was with her at an orgy on Jeffrey's island"?

DERSHOWITZ: I did state that, yes.

SCAROLA: Was that statement intended as fact, opinion, or was it intended as rhetorical hyperbole?

DERSHOWITZ: It was a statement based on what I believed were the facts at the time I said them...Various newspapers and blogs had placed Bill Clinton on, quote, "orgy island" on -- in the presence of Jeffrey Epstein when there were orgies...And at the time I made that statement, I had a belief that she had accused Bill Clinton of participating or being -- as being a part of or an observer or -- or a witness or a participant in orgies on what was called Jeffrey Epstein's orgy island. That was my state of belief, honest belief at the time I made that statement.

SCAROLA: Yes, sir. And what I want to know is what the source of that honest belief was? Identify any source that attributed to Virginia Roberts the statement that Bill Clinton was with her at an orgy on Jeffrey's island.

DERSHOWITZ: We can provide you about, I think, 20 newspaper articles and blogs, which certainly raise the implication that Bill Clinton had improperly participated in sexual activities on the island either as an observer or as a participant...The issue was raised on Sean Hannity's program. The headlines in various British media had suggested that...

It's my belief that Virginia Roberts intended to convey that impression when she was trying to sell her story to various media, which she successfully sold her story in Britain, that she wanted to keep that open as a possibility... And then when I firmly declared, based on my research, that Bill Clinton had almost certainly never been on that island, she then made a firm statement that she -- which was a -- perjurious statement, a firm, perjurious statement, saying that although Bill Clinton had been with her on the island and had had dinner with her. The perjurious statement was that Bill Clinton had been on the island with her...

The lie was that she described in great detail a dinner with Bill Clinton and two under aged Russian women who were offered to Bill Clinton for sex but that Bill Clinton turned down... So she then put in her affidavit that although -- perjuriously, although she had seen Bill Clinton on that island, she then stated that she had not had sex with Bill Clinton... To my knowledge that was -- to my knowledge at least, that was the first time she stated that -- that she not had sex with Bill Clinton...

DERSHOWITZ: She had certainly implied, or at least some of the media had inferred from her statements that she may, very well have observed Bill Clinton in a sexually compromising position... So, when I made that statement to Don Lemon, I had a firm belief, based on reading newspaper accounts and blogs, that it was true.

SCAROLA: Can you identify a single newspaper that attributed to Virginia Roberts the statement that Bill Clinton was with her at an orgy on Jeffrey's island?

DERSHOWITZ: I think there -- I don't have them in my head right now. But I do recall reading headlines that talked about things like, sex slave places, Clinton on 'Orgy Island', things of that kind. I would be happy to provide them for you. I don't have them on the top of my head.

SCAROLA: There's a big difference between saying that Bill Clinton was on Jeffrey's island and saying that Bill Clinton was at an orgy on Jeffrey's island, isn't there?

SCOTT: Objection

SCAROLA: Do you recognize a distinction between those statements?

SCOTT: Form.

DERSHOWITZ: I don't think that distinction was clearly drawn by the media.

SCAROLA: I'm asking whether you recognize the distinction?

DERSHOWITZ: Oh, I -- I certainly recognize a distinction.

SCAROLA: Oh, so-

DERSHOWITZ: Let me finish. I certainly recognize a distinction between Bill Clinton being on the island, which I believe she perjuriously put in her affidavit, and Bill Clinton participating actively in an orgy. I also think it's a continuum...And there is the possibility, which I don't personally believe to be true, that he was on the island...There was the possibility, which I don't believe to be true, that he was on the island when orgies were taking place...

There was the possibility that he was on the island and observed an orgy, and there was the possibility that he was on the island and participated in an orgy.

Newspapers picked up those stories. I'll give you an example of a newspaper that actually said that she had placed or that I was on the island and -- that I participated in an orgy along with Stephen Hawkings, the famous physicist from Cambridge University, that was a newspaper published in the Virgin Islands, which falsely claimed that I was at an orgy with Stephen Hawkings.

DERSHOWITZ: So, many newspapers were suggesting, implying, and I inferred from reading those newspapers that that's what she had said to the media...

If I was wrong about that based on subsequent information, I apologize. But I certainly, at the time I said it, believed it and made the statement in good faith in the belief that it was an honest statement.

SCAROLA: Okay. So you now are withdrawing the statement that you made that Virginia Roberts said that Bill Clinton was with her at an orgy on Jeffrey's island; that was wrong?

DERSHOWITZ: I don't know whether she ever said that...I would not repeat that statement and have not repeated that statement based on her denial. As soon as she denied it, I never again made that statement and would not again make that statement.

SCAROLA: Having reviewed the available airplane flight logs, you are aware that Bill Clinton flew on at least 15 occasions with Jeffrey Epstein on his private plane, correct?

According to my pilot logs, President Clinton traveled on Epstein's jet seventeen (17) times.

DERSHOWITZ: Yes.

SCAROLA: Have you ever attempted to get flight log information with regard to former President Clinton's other private airplane travel?

DERSHOWITZ: No.

SCAROLA: Never made a public records request --

DERSHOWITZ: Yes.

SCAROLA: Under the Freedom of Information Act with regard to those records?

DERSHOWITZ: Well, we have made a Freedom of Information request. My -- my attorney in New York, Louis Freeh, the former head of the FBI, (appointed by President Bill Clinton who also worked on the Epstein criminal investigating team), has made a FOIA request for all information that would conclusively prove that Bill Clinton was never on Jeffrey Epstein's island, yes.

SCAROLA: And you were denied those records, correct?

DERSHOWITZ: No, no, no.

SCAROLA: Oh, you got them?

SCOTT: Well, wait a minute. Let's take it slow. Ask a question.

DERSHOWITZ: As any lawyer knows, FOIA requests take a long, long period of time. So they were neither denied nor were they given to us. They are very much in process.

MINUTES LATER:

SCAROLA: Mr. Dershowitz, what is rhetorical hyperbole?

DERSHOWITZ: Rhetorical means verbal and hyperbole means exaggeration.

SCAROLA: Something other than the truth, correct?

DERSHOWTIZ: Truth --Truth has many, many meanings and is a continuum. The Supreme Court has held that rhetorical hyperbole cannot be the basis, for example, of perjury prosecutions or generally of a Defamation prosecution. So it depends on the context. You might just look at the dictionary and probably get a variety of definitions for it.

SCAROLA: Well, what I'm concerned about, Mr. Dershowitz is not a dictionary definition. I want to know what your understanding of rhetorical hyperbole is. And do you agree that pursuant to your understanding of rhetorical hyperbole, it is an exaggeration beyond the facts?
SCOTT: Objection, argumentative and compound, three questions.

DERSHOWITZ: No --

SCOTT: You can answer.

DERSHOWITZ: I would not agree with that definition.

SCAROLA: Okay. Then define it for us, if you would, please.

DERSHOWITZ: I think I have already.

SCAROLA: … I didn't understand it, so I would like you to try to give us a direct response to that question if you're able to.

DERSHOWITZ: I will repeat exactly what I said. A rhetorical means verbal and hyperbole means some exaggeration of the facts for political or other reasons, but generally it is truthful in a literal sense but perhaps -- it all depends on context...And if you tell me the context in which I used it, I will be happy to describe what I meant in that context. But I don't think you can really answer a question about what two words put together mean without understanding the context.

SCAROLA: Okay. Well, we're going to talk about some context. Do you recall having been interviewed on 'CNN Tonight' on January 5, 2015?

DERSHOWITZ: I have no current recollection of – Well I have no memory of what specifically I said.

SCAROLA: Do you recall having been interviewed on CNN Tonight by Don Lemon in early January of 2015, where you spoke about matters that have become the subject of this litigation?

DERSHOWITZ: Yes, I do.

SCAROLA: Did you make the following statement during the course of that interview: "As to the airplanes, there are manifests that will prove beyond any doubt that I was never on a private airplane with this woman or any other underage girl"?

DERSHOWITZ: That is a truthful statement. I would repeat it right now. I've reviewed the manifests. First, I know I was never on the airplane with any underage woman. I know that for a fact. I have absolutely no doubt in my mind about that. And the records that I have reviewed confirm that.

They have Virginia Roberts on a number of airplane flights with Jeffrey Epstein. They have me on a number of flights, none -- let me emphasize, none within the relevant time period, none within the relevant time period.

That is, there are no manifests that have me on Jeffrey Epstein's airplane during the time that Virginia Roberts claims to have -- falsely claims to have had sex with me. So, yes, not only do I recall making that statement, but I repeat it here today. And it is absolutely true. And it just confirms what I know, and that is that Virginia Roberts made up the entire story.

It is a well-known fact that pilot logs and pilot manifestos have not always included names, ages and relevant information of every passenger on all their scheduled flights. This was the case in the logs identifying the passengers who were traveling on Epstein's jet. On many occasions, only the initials or gender of the passenger were included.

SCAROLA: Your statement was that you were never on a private airplane with this woman, which I assume was a reference to Virginia Roberts, correct?

DERSHOWITZ: It is, yes.

SCAROLA: Or any other underage girl?

DERSHOWITZ: That's right.

However, on April 16, 1999, Alan Dershowitz appears on the pilot log alongside Emmy Tayler's (an underage girl at the time and friend of Ghislaine Maxwell), Epstein and one unidentified male. David Rogers signed the pilot's signature line.

SCAROLA: All right. How many times --

DERSHOWITZ: Well, let me be very clear. I have no idea who was in the front cabin of the airplane with the two pilots. Obviously what I intended to say and what I say here now is I never saw an under aged person on an airplane. Now, when I -- when I flew with Jeffrey Epstein to the launch, my recollection is that there may have been a couple on the plane with their child who was going to see the launch.

According to the pilot logs, Dershowitz flew several times on Epstein's jet unaccompanied by his wife, daughter, or son as he declared in an earlier statement. His family's names do not appear on the logs. The earliest log available to me, dates back to 1997.

Dershowitz traveled on his jet beginning February 9, 1997 with one unidentified female, Emmy Taylor, Epstein, Maxwell, Joel Pashcow, C. Hazel, and Mandy (family name illegible). On October 21, 1998, he traveled alone with Epstein from Bedford to Teterboro. Again on April 16, 1999 he traveled with Epstein, Emmy Taylor and one unidentified male.

On February 5, 2004, he flew with Epstein, his assistant and alleged procurer, Sarah Kellen. On November 17, 2005 Dershowitz traveled on a multi leg flight originating in Bedford, New York, to CYUL (Pierre Trudeau in Montreal) back to Bedford with a final stop in Teterboro (TEB). He traveled with two unidentified females identified as AM and Tatiana.

DERSHOWITZ: But that was certainly not the context in which I made the statement. I never saw any underage, young person who would be the subject or object of any improper sexual activities. Had I seen Jeffrey Epstein ever in the presence of an underage woman in a context that suggested sexuality, I would have, a, left the scene; b, reported it; and, c, never had any further contact with Jeffrey Epstein.

SCAROLA: You have also made the statement that you were never on a private airplane with any underage women or any young women, correct?

DERSHOWITZ: The context was underage women in a sexual context. If it was a -- you know, a four-year-old child being carried by her mother, that would not be included in what I intended to say.

SCAROLA: Your sworn testimony yesterday, according to the transcription, the official transcription of that testimony, was that, quote:

"Let me emphasize that the manifests that do exculpate me do not show me flying with Virginia Roberts, they do not show me flying with any young women." That was the testimony you gave under oath. Do you stand by that testimony today?

DERSHOWITZ: The manifests that I saw corroborate my own memory -- my own memory is as clear as could be -- that I never saw any inappropriately aged, under aged women on any airplane to my knowledge that were visible to me at any time that I flew. That is my testimony, yes.

SCAROLA: Well, that's not a response to the question that I asked. Is it your testimony today that you never flew on a private airplane with, quote, "any young women"?

DERSHOWITZ: By young women, I obviously meant in that context underage women. And underage women in the context of sexuality and, yes, I -- I stand by that statement.

SCAROLA: All right. So your -- your clarification of your earlier testimony is that you never saw any young women in a sexual context?

DERSHOWITZ: That's not clarification. I think that's what I initially said. That's what I initially intended. And that's the way any reasonable – any reasonable person would interpret what my original testimony was. So I don't believe my original testimony required any clarification.

SCAROLA: So what you meant to convey by the statement that you made when you said you never flew with any underage girl or any young women was you never flew with any underage girl or young women in a sexual context?

DERSHOWITZ: Let me simply repeat the fact and that is, to my knowledge, I never flew on an airplane or was ever in the presence on an airplane with any underage woman who would be somebody who might be in a sexual context. I say that only to eliminate the possibility that some four-year-old was on the lap of a mother or somebody was on the airplane with family members.

But, no, I do not recall -- and I'm very firm about this -- being on an airplane with anybody who I believed could be the subject of Jeffrey Epstein or anyone else's improper sexual activities.
Scarola presented Dershowitz with a photograph of a young woman.

SCAROLA: Do you recognize that young woman, Mr. Dershowitz?

DERSHOWITZ: No.

SCAROLA: Never saw her?

DERSHOWITZ: Not that I know of.

SCAROLA: Never flew on a private airplane with her?

DERSHOWITZ: Not that I know of.

SCAROLA: Do you recognize the name Tatiana?

DERSHOWITZ: I do recall that Jeffrey Epstein had a friend named Tatiana.

SCAROLA: That you flew with?

DERSHOWITZ: I don't remember that I flew with her or not. I may have. But I don't recall necessarily. But I did meet -- I remember meeting a woman named Tatiana. This does not look like Tatiana, like the woman I met.

SCAROLA: Okay. So that's a -- that's a different Tatiana?

DERSHOWITZ: No, I don't know. I have no idea. I do not recognize this woman. She's not familiar to me at all. I can tell you this: Without any doubt, I never met anybody dressed like this on any airplane or in the presence of Jeffrey Epstein or in any context –related to this case.

SCAROLA: Did she have -- more clothes on, or less, clothes on when you met her? When you met the woman that you're referencing, did she have more clothes on or less clothes on than that woman?

DERSHOWITZ: Every woman that I met in the presence of Jeffrey Epstein was properly dressed, usually in suits and dresses and -- and appropriately covered up. I never met any women in the context of Jeffrey Epstein who were dressed anything like this.

SCAROLA: Would you agree that that is a young woman in that photograph?

DERSHOWITZ: I have no idea what her age is.

SCAROLA: So you don't know whether she was underage, 12, or overage, or a young woman, or not a young woman?

DERSHOWITZ: I don't --know this woman, so I have no idea how old a woman in a picture is. She could be – 17 she could be 30. She could be 25. I have no idea.

SCAROLA: Or she could be 15 or 16?

DERSHOWITZ: I don't think so.

SCAROLA: But you don't know?

DERSHOWITZ: This doesn't -- well, I don't know how old you are. This does not strike me --

SCAROLA: Old enough to know that –

Approximately ten minutes later, after much back and forth between Scarola, Dershowitz and Scott, the attorneys decided to appoint a Special Master for the proceedings to help Scarola obtain some answers. Seconds later, Dershowitz answered the question:

SCAROLA: Is the last name on the photograph spelled exactly the same way as the last name on the flight log?

DERSHOWITZ: If you're talking about a flight log that I was not on that flight, the answer is yes.

SCAROLA: All right. Thank you very much, Sir. Now, that flight log also shows you flying repeatedly in the company of a woman named Tatiana, correct?

DERSHOWITZ: I've only seen one reference to Tatiana on November 17. If you want to show me any other references, I'd be happy to look at them.

Scarola shows Dershowitz Exhibit 5.

SCAROLA: Do you see the name of the woman in the photographs I have handed to you is Tatiana K-O-V-Y-L-I-N-A, a Victoria's Secret model. The photographs identify the woman as Tatiana Kovylina, correct?

DERSHOWITZ: Yes, but.

After much bantering back and forth over the spelling of the girl's name. Scarola resumed his questions.

SCAROLA: All right, would you describe for us, please, the Tatiana that you flew with Jeffrey Epstein on November 17, 2005.

DERSHOWITZ: First, I want to emphasize that that's three years later than any of the issues involved in this case. I have no recollection of flying with this woman. I saw the name Tatiana on a manifest. And my recollection of Tatiana—I have no recollection of flying with her, but my recollection of Tatiana is that she was a serious, mid 20s woman, friend of Jeffrey Epstein, who I may have met on one or two occasions when he was with her in-perhaps Harvard University where he was meeting with academics and scholars, or perhaps—I think that is probably the context where-where she might have been.

SCAROLA: But you never flew with her?

DERSHOWITZ: I have no recollection of flying with her.

SCAROLA: OK, Well let's see if this helps to refresh your recollection, Mr. Dershowitz.

Scarola presented Dershowitz with photographs of the woman in question and again Professor Dershowitz argued over the spelling of the last name. Apparently, it showed the woman's name on a return flight.

DERSHOWITZ: ...I have nothing on the record that suggests that it's a return flight. And it has different people on it. So I have no reason to believe it's a return flight.

SCAROLA: Is the last –the question that I asked you, Mr. Dershowitz, is: Is the last name spelled exactly the same as the last name is spelled in the two photographs I have shown you?

DERSHOWITZ: Let me look. So, on the 20th of November

SCAROLA: Is the last name---

SCOTT: Whoa, whoa!

SCAROLA: Spelled the same way on both the flight log and the two photographs I have shown you?

DERSHOWITZ: On-you mean on a flight lot I was not on the flight? Is that right? You're talking about a flight log that I was not on the flight, right?

SCAROLA: That flight log shows you on multiple flights, does it not?

DERSHOWITZ: It shows me not on that flight. It shows me on a number of flights, but not on that flight.

SCOTT: What's the date of the flights?

DERSHOWITZ: The date of that flight is---looks like November 20, 2005. More than three years after Virginia Roberts left for—

After a great deal more bantering back and forth between the three attorneys Scarola asked the same question again.

SCAROLA: Is the last name on the photograph spelled exactly the same way as the last name on the flight log?

DERSHOWITZ: If you're talking about a flight log that I was not on that I was not on that flight, yes.

SCAROLA: All right. Thank you very much. Sir. Now, that flight log also shows you flying repeatedly in the company of a woman named Tatiana, correct?

DERSHOWITZ: I've only seen one reference to Tatiana on November 17th, if you want to show me any other references, I'd be happy to look at them.

SCAROLA: All right, Sir. Thank you.

* * *

Chapter Sixteen

Virginia L. Roberts-Giuffre vs. Ghislaine Maxwell

Among other things, another reason the Dershowitz deposition was important was to shed light on the relationship between Virginia Louise Roberts and Ghislaine Maxwell. A relationship so contentious, that on September 21, 2015, Virginia L. Roberts Giuffre filed a defamation suit against Ghislaine Maxwell in New York.

It occurred to me that given the cities where the plaintiff and defendant lived, it was an interesting twist of fate or perhaps a mere coincidence that Roberts-Giuffre who lives in Colorado is represented by a Manhattan firm, Boies, Schiller & Flexner, and Maxwell who resides in New York part-time, is represented by the Colorado firm, Haddon Morgan Foreman.

Sigrid McCawley, a partner at Boies Schiller & Flexner law firm represents Roberts Giuffre Laura Menninger and Jeffrey Pagliuca represent Maxwell. The presiding District Judge, the Honorable Robert W. Sweet, for the Southern District of New York, a renowned jurist and senior United States Federal Judge was appointed by President Jimmy Carter.

Coincidentally, one of his law clerks was Eliot Spitzer former Governor of New York recently accused, in February 2016, of assaulting a twenty-year-old woman allegedly his girlfriend in a hotel room at The Plaza Hotel in New York City. Luckily for the former Governor, the woman recently fled the country and no longer wishes to press charges against him.[1]

At the very beginning of the case, Judge Sweet ruled New York was the appropriate jurisdiction because Maxwell was a resident of New York City. The defamation case was filed under *Virginia Giuffre vs. Ghislaine Maxwell*, 1:15-cv-07433.

After several hearings and many motions including Maxwell's request to dismiss the victim's suit, Judge Sweet ruled on February 29, 2016, that Roberts-Giuffre had the right to pursue a defamation suit against Maxwell for describing her allegations as lies. Maxwell's attorneys argued their client was defending herself from Roberts.

Judge Sweet disagreed and said, "That to suggest Roberts Giuffre lied about being sexually assaulted as a minor, points to something deeply disturbing about the character of an individual willing to be publically dishonest about such a reprehensible crime." Maxwell and Roberts-Giuffre's lawyers have not responded.[2]

The Manhattan lawsuit filed against the 53-year-old Maxwell did not mention Prince Andrew by name. Instead, it described how Roberts, who assumed her married name, Giuffre, in the legal filings, was exploited by Epstein and became a victim of his sex trafficking ring after being recruited by Maxwell.

The Complaint stated that, "Between 2001 and 2007, with the assistance of numerous co-conspirators, Epstein abused more than thirty (30) minor girls, a fact confirmed by state and federal law enforcement. As part of their sex trafficking efforts, Epstein and Maxwell intimidated Roberts Giuffre into remaining silent about what had happened to her. After Epstein approved the Non Prosecution Agreement (NPA) that barred his prosecution for numerous federal sex crimes in Florida, DOJ, agreed that it would not institute any federal criminal charges against any potential co conspirators. As a co conspirator of Epstein, Maxwell was consequently granted immunity in Florida through the NPA."[3]

It also said that, "With Maxwell's assistance, Epstein was able to recruit and sexually abuse Roberts- Giuffre for years until the girl turned 19 when she escaped to Thailand." Roberts said Epstein sent her to Thailand to bring back a 12-year-old girl, where Roberts Giuffre met a *Muai Thai* fighter, fell in love and in seven days they married. She rang Epstein to tell her she "was in love" and he said, "have a good life and hung up the phone." That was the last she heard of Epstein until the FBI called her during the criminal investigation.[4]

During the criminal investigation, Roberts claimed that, "As part of their sex trafficking efforts, Epstein and Maxwell, intimidated her to remain silent about what had transpired."[5]

The twelve -page filing explained how after Roberts went public Maxwell began a "concerted and malicious media campaign to discredit Roberts Giuffre…and ensure her claims would not be credible."[6]

Presumably, Maxwell influenced the "attack on Roberts Giuffre's honesty and truthfulness." In other words, Maxwell accused Roberts Giuffre of lying and "made a deliberate effort to 'maliciously discredit Giuffre and silence her efforts to expose the global sex crimes committed by her, Epstein and other powerful persons. Maxwell made the statements knowing full well they were false," wrote the Daily Mail.[7]

By January 14, 2016 attorneys for Maxwell and Roberts-Giuffre were in front of Judge Robert Sweet. Laura Menninger, an eminent trial lawyer, argued that her client had the right to refute the allegations and it was the reason why the defamation case should be dismissed. Sigrid McCawley, equally illustrious, disagreed, "It's the 'old story' of wrongly portraying sex abused victims as liars." "This may sound hard to believe," she said, "but it happened."[8]

So far, Maxwell "has refused to speak to the news media about her involvement with Epstein, the criminal and civil cases and has denied any and all involvement in Epstein's sex trafficking operation." While Roberts Giuffre argued that, "With the assistance of Maxwell, Epstein was able to sexually abuse her for years until she eventually escaped."[9]

Given the ongoing developments, other events may perhaps emerge that can one day open the doors for victim's rights attorneys in the Epstein case to introduce new cases against the perpetrators. In light of the barrage of media coverage, it would not surprise me if a new victim steps forward and new charges are filed. Perhaps then, law enforcement officials in New York, New Mexico, Florida, USVI, England and France, or wherever else it is that Epstein and Maxwell frequent, can conduct an investigation.

As of publication and unlike the Maxwell case that is in the beginning stages, there are two pending cases in Florida. The Maxwell case is important because it "contains the first public allegations made by Roberts Giuffre against Maxwell."[10]

If the Judge rules in favor of the victim, he will establish once that, "Roberts Giuffre was a victim of sexual trafficking and abuse while she was a minor child. Defendant Maxwell not only facilitated that sexual abuse but, most recently, wrongfully subjected Giuffre to public ridicule, contempt and disgrace by, among other things, calling Giuffre a liar in published statements with the malicious intent of discrediting and further damaging Giuffre worldwide."[11]

Roberts vs. Maxwell dates back to 1998 when the two women first met. Maxwell like several other procurers was never charged in the criminal case, which infuriated the victims, including Virginia, and their attorneys. During 2008-2009, "As the civil litigation against Epstein moved forward, on behalf of Giuffre and many other victims, Maxwell's testimony was sought concerning her personal knowledge and role in Epstein's abuse of Giuffre and others."[12]

Possibly to avoid taking the 2010 deposition, Maxwell claimed that her mother was deathly ill and left the United States for London, the day prior to the scheduled deposition, with no plans of ever returning. According to several sources, the elder Mrs. Maxwell, was not ill at the time of her daughter's deposition.

The 2007 telephone conversation between Roberts, Scarola and Edwards,' became the springboard for Roberts' 2015 defamation case because Virginia described her relationship with Maxwell, established in great detail Maxwell and Epstein's pattern of behavior and repeated the alleged crimes committed by Maxwell and Epstein.

The most recent depositions established that as far back as 2011, "Two FBI agents who found Roberts Giuffre in Australia— where she had been hiding from Epstein for several years— arranged to meet with her at the U.S. Consulate in Sidney. Since that meeting, Roberts Giuffre continues to provide information to the FBI about Epstein and Maxwell's apparent abusive behavior."[13]

All evidence to the contrary, Maxwell claimed Roberts was a liar. That story, wrote John Riley in Newsday, "became the latest in a long running legal battle involving the convicted pedophile and his alleged procurer, Maxwell."[14]

According to the Complaint, Roberts Guiffre was allegedly recruited by Maxwell when she was 14-years-old, in June of 1998 at Mar-A-Lago in Palm Beach, Florida. Roberts Giuffre, born August 9, 1983, was just shy of her fifteenth birthday when she met them. A year or two later, while 'working' for Epstein, the girl was introduced to HRH Prince Andrew to perform sexual activities on three occasions. According to the filing Roberts also took part in an orgy on the financier's private Caribbean island where the Prince attended.

In a hearing transcript sent to me by McCawley, dated March 17, 2016, a couple of unresolved issues stood out during the hearing. Among them was Maxwell's delayed tactics to avoid taking the deposition. It seemed this was the second time Maxwell challenged attorneys in an attempt to avoid service. Like Edwards before her, McCawley, was having a difficult time obtaining Maxwell's statement.

Based on the transcript, Boies Schiller requested Maxwell's deposition in October 2015. At publication, the deposition has not been taken.

The notes published in the reports revealed that, "Jeffrey would send me out, just like in the US to go talk to pretty girls, the younger the better. I would offer them money to come meet my gentleman friend and tell them I'd show them how to massage."[15]

According to Roberts, Maxwell and Epstein, allegedly "Fooled her parents into believing she was training with them to become a professional masseuse." Instead, they, "Helped their underage plaything get a passport for a vacation." On her first overseas trip to Europe, Roberts' first stop was Paris, France. Once there, Roberts' claims that her daily list of chores included, "Massages, sex and even dressing Epstein."[16]

After she left Paris, Roberts was taken to Spain, Morocco and England. The first night in London, Roberts stayed with Maxwell who Virginia identified as "her Madame, Maxwell" "The next morning," Roberts' said, " Ghislaine, chirpy, came into my room. She sat down next to me, as I was just starting to uncover the sheets and told me excitedly we were going shopping because I needed a new dress I could wear to dance with a prince. 'Wow, what?' were the first words that popped into my head, not knowing that meant using my body as entertainment for another rich pedophile, or worst, being convinced it was exciting."[17]

Roberts' claims that Maxwell, "didn't seem to care about anything except pleasing Epstein and Prince Andrew. She accompanied Roberts to buy everything from expensive dresses and embroidered jeans to makeup and perfume."[18]

The tragedy of it all was how Roberts' perceived her situation. During the Radar Online interview she confessed, "The way these men adored me, and many others like me, kind of made us feel like we weren't so awkward after all. That was the nice side to these predators, the other side was learning to accept money to degrade ourselves morally and end up another lost girl down a chain of…victims."[19]

Several more issues were raised at the March 2016 hearing. One was Menninger's refusal to abide by the extensive time period of emails requested by McCawley and the second was the "over breath" of emails requested by McCawley.

As McCawley explained the long-standing history of the case revealed that Epstein's, "Flight logs show Maxwell 360 times with Jeffrey Epstein, 20 of which were with her client when she was underage." In addition, "We have the Palm Beach police report, which shows over 30 minors who reported that during that time period, up until 2006, they being abused in that circumstance in Palm Beach. Then we have the arrest that happens of Jeffrey Epstein in 2006."[20]

"In 2008, Virginia received from the US government a victim notification letter. In 2009, Maxwell's deposition was sought in underlying civil cases. She fled the country, did not take the deposition and said her mother was ill in England, and could not be deposed. She showed up in New York weeks later and, (on July 31, 2010), attended Chelsea Clinton's wedding. So clearly, she was around, she was able to do something, but she avoided that deposition. Her testimony was never taken in that case," McCawley said.[21]

In 2011, "Maxwell started issuing different statements to the press. She issued a statement in 2015, which is the statement that we are here about in this case. So I contend, you Honor, that all of those years have relevant information in them with respect to my client."[22]

A separate issue along with obtaining the e-mails communication, was the desire by both attorneys to issue a protective order so that Maxwell's transcript i.e. deposition could be kept confidential and not made available to the press as most transcripts usually are.

According to the court file, Laura Menninger wanted McCawley to hand over her client's diary or journal between 1996-2002 that was published by Radar Online. Earlier, on January 13, 2015, Radar Online published a handwritten note by Virginia given to them for publication. Maxwell's attorney, Menninger, argued the notes constituted a 'journal, or diary.'

McCawley disagreed and said that her client did not keep a journal and that Radar Online's reporting was based on Virginia's hand written notes not on a diary per se. McCawley also pointed out that her client "was sent to Thailand by Mr. Epstein and Ms. Maxwell for training and to pick up another."[23]

McCawley also seemed annoyed that she had forwarded three thousand documents of Virginia's testimony to Maxwell's attorneys, while Haddon had sent her only two emails and two emails in response. She was very concerned because July 2016 would mark the last month that Maxwell's deposition could be filed since the discovery phase would close that month.

McCawley told the Judge, "The underlying issue in this case is whether or not Ms. Maxwell lied when she said my client was not subject to the abuse that she said she was subject to. In order to prove that," she said, "for defamation with malice, we have to prove that my client was abused by these individuals, that these individuals did take advantage of her in the way that she expressed…That is why one of the requests are the documents relating to communications of Jeffrey Epstein."[24]

"What is relevant to that is the sexual trafficking ring," McCawley said. "If after my client left they are also trafficking other under aged girls repetitively, that is relevant to prove the truth of my client's allegations as well. We are entitled to that discovery, Your Honor."[25]

At the outset, Menninger objected to McCawley's request because she believed they were requesting, "All documents relating to communications with Jeffrey Epstein from 1990 to present... Not specifically concerning trafficking, or under aged girls, which makes it all documents relating to... which could be anything in the universe."[26]

Seemingly upset, Menninger asked, "All documents relating to communications with Andrew Albert Christian Edward, Duke of York, from 1990 to present. You know, what the heck does a communication with the Duke in 2013, any old communication, have to do with anything in this case? Nothing, if you ask me."[27]

The other side of that argument was what McCawley was trying to prove. That by restricting the time period of the relevant emails and giving them a "very short window," Menninger narrows the possibility of a successful discovery. At play is an e-mail sent by Maxwell where she is, "Emailing Jeffrey Epstein about the girls she's going to send over to him in 2004, before he is arrested," and that was "relevant to her client's claim...So we shouldn't be told that we're not entitled to these documents or that we're only entitled to 2 emails out of all of our requests," McCawley responded.[28]

McCawley explained that Boies Schiller asked two "people" involved in the case, for documents and communications with Sarah Kellen and Nadia Marcinkova. In their depositions pertaining to Maxwell's charges involving sexually trafficking underage girls, "both individuals took the Fifth." Beside those documents, Boies Schiller wanted all e-mail communication between Maxwell and Kellen that included those issues at any time period from 1990 to present. "And while they say that day-to-day communications with Epstein wouldn't be relevant, they would. If they're communicating on a daily basis, that's relevant."[29]

In spite of her claims, Roberts, now 32, was told last year by Judge Kenneth Marra in Florida that she could not join the legal action brought by two other victims, Jane Doe #1 and Jane Doe #2, who were also under age when they Epstein allegedly abused them. So it seems the only two cases that might help vindicate Roberts-Giuffre's and perhaps other victims' are the defamation case filed against her alleged procurer, Ghislaine Maxwell in New York and the Crime Victims' Rights Act (CVRA) case filed in Florida on behalf of Jane Doe #1 and Jane Doe #2.

As it stands, Maxwell, 54, must comply with Judge Sweet's order instructing her to disclose "documents and records of conversations (e-mails) she had with Epstein and others related to the sex trafficking operation between 1999 and 2016," if Roberts-Giuffre is specific in her pretrial discovery questions and identifies the individuals who communicated with Maxwell about the alleged sex trafficking of girls.[30]

As of April 11, 2016 the case is pending and Maxwell has yet to be deposed.

* * *

Footnotes

1. http://www.usatoday.com/story/news/nation/2016/02/15/new-york-ex-gov-eliot-spitzer-accused-assault/80396398/

2. http://www.reuters.com/article/us-maxwell-defamation-lawsuit-idUSKCN0W34ZN

3. http://www.nydailynews.com/life-style/real-estate/alleged-madam-50k-month-ues-townhouse-article-1.2316572

4. Case 1:15-cv-07433-RWS Filed 09/21/15 P. 5

5. https://ecf.nysd.uscourts.gov/doc1/127116800606

6. http://images.politico.com/global/2014/12/31/epsteinjanedoe102complaint.pdf

7. http://www.dailymail.co.uk/news/article-3245036/Virginia-Roberts-claimed-sex-Prince-Andrew-sues-British-socialite-Ghislaine-Maxwell-denying-claims-recruited-sex-slave.html

8. http://www.newsday.com/news/new-york/virginia-giuffre-files-defamation-suit-against-british-publishing-magnate-ghislaine-maxwell-1.10874152

9. http://www.dailymail.co.uk/news/article-3245036/Virginia-Roberts-claimed-sex-Prince-Andrew-sues-British-socialite-Ghislaine-Maxwell-denying-claims-recruited-sex-slave.html

10. Email communication on April 7, 2016. Conchita Sarnoff and Brad Edwards.

11. Case 1:15-cv-07433-RWS

12. Case 1:15-cv-07433-RWS Filed 9/21/15

13. Case 1:15-cv-07433-RWS Filed 9/21/15

14. http://radaronline.com/exclusives/2015/01/jeffrey-epstein-sex-slave-virginia-roberts-writes-sex-prince-andrew/

15. http://radaronline.com/exclusives/2015/01/jeffrey-epstein-sex-slave-virginia-roberts-writes-sex-prince-andrew/

16. http://radaronline.com/exclusives/2015/01/jeffrey-epstein-sex-slave-virginia-roberts-writes-sex-prince-andrew/

17. http://radaronline.com/exclusives/2015/01/jeffrey-epstein-sex-slave-virginia-roberts-writes-sex-prince-andrew/

18. http://radaronline.com/exclusives/2015/01/jeffrey-epstein-sex-slave-virginia-roberts-writes-sex-prince-andrew/

19. http://www.nydailynews.com/news/world/socialite-defamation-lawsuit-sex-slave-tossed-article-1.2497773

20. Transcript Giuffre vs. Maxwell, 15cv7433, United States District Court, Southern District of New York, March 17, 2016. 2:18 PM

21. Transcript Giuffre vs. Maxwell, 15cv7433, United States District Court, Southern District of New York, March 17, 2016. 2:18 PM

22. Transcript Giuffre vs. Maxwell, 15cv7433, United States District Court, Southern District of New York, March 17, 2016. 2:18 PM

23. Transcript Giuffre vs. Maxwell, 15cv7433, United States District Court, Southern District of New York, March 17, 2016. 2:18 PM

24. Transcript Giuffre vs. Maxwell, 15cv7433, United States District Court, Southern District of New York, March 17, 2016. 2:18 PM

25. Transcript Giuffre vs. Maxwell, 15cv7433, United States District Court, Southern District of New York, March 17, 2016. 2:18 PM

26. Transcript Giuffre vs. Maxwell, 15cv7433, United States District Court, Southern District of New York, March 17, 2016. 2:18 PM

27. Transcript Giuffre vs. Maxwell, 15cv7433, United States District Court, Southern District of New York, March 17, 2016. 2:18 PM

28. Transcript Giuffre vs. Maxwell, 15cv7433, United States District Court, Southern District of New York, March 17, 2016. 2:18 PM

29. Transcript Giuffre vs. Maxwell, 15cv7433, United States District Court, Southern District of New York, March 17, 2016. 2:18 PM

30. Transcript Giuffre vs. Maxwell, 15cv7433, United States District Court, Southern District of New York, March 17, 2016. 2:18 PM

Chapter Seventeen

The Valley of Kidron

By March 2011, The Daily Beast had posted five Epstein stories. A few more stories followed on the Huffington Post and then suddenly the media went 'dark.' I didn't understand what had happened until of course I knew who was really pulling the strings.

Given the restrictive media environment, I decided to finish the book although more information was needed to understand the challenges besieging abolitionists and law enforcement officials especially when fighting similar cases. For about two years, I worked hard trying to convince my editor to publish the book. A million excuses followed and the book was never published.

Before I accidentally stumbled into the Epstein case, I was in Mexico investigating another sex trafficking case. That case was the basis of the story for the Random House Mexico book deal signed in July 2009,"Sex Slaves in America."

The book was to publish in Spanish in Mexico and Spanish speaking Latin America. It featured a monstrous human trafficking case that extended from Mexico to the United States.

The victims in the Mexican case were sourced in Mexico, mostly in San Miguel de Tenancingo, smuggled into Texas, transported across the country and sold over and over again in New York and other cities. Some victims ended up in West Palm Beach. Unbeknownst to me in 2009, the two shared common ground. But that is another story.

After extensive fieldwork and research during which time my safety was compromised, I gained great insight into the issue of human trafficking and the networks that control it. I learned a great deal more about how the victims are sourced, recruited and transported.

Around the same time, the Court of Public Opinion remained blissfully unaware about human trafficking and the information available. Most of it was obsolete and scarce. It was time to change direction and build a platform in which to educate, raise awareness and rescue victims of trafficking. The Alliance To Rescue Victims of Trafficking was born in mid October 2013.

The years between 2011 and 2015 were somewhat troubling. Unable to publish my book for reasons beyond my control, I focused on building a platform to raise awareness of the issue and subsequently came up with the organization, Alliance to Rescue Victims of Trafficking. Then on January 1, 2015 it all started again. The media was a buzz with new and scandalous developments in the Epstein case.

Wasn't everyone on holiday or at least resting? Apparently not. My cell phone began to ring very early that morning and did not stop all day. At first I did not answer. There were too many calls. I listened to the messages. The media had finally caught on.

The first message I received was a reporter at The Guardian, a UK daily. The calls came in from quite a number of journals from different countries. I received a call from MSNBC in New York, ABC network, the BBC in London, another from a reporter in Toronto working with the Canadian Broadcast Corporation (CBC) and yet another from an Australian television station that rang several times. Requests from other networks followed.

The press was in an uproar and wanted the backstory. Specifically they wanted to know what I knew about Epstein and his special relationship with Professor Dershowitz. They wanted to know about Virginia Louise Roberts. Was she really forced to have sex with the professor and if so, did they? The other question everyone was asking was how could a renowned Harvard law professor allow himself to be implicated in a child sex trafficking scandal of this magnitude involving a registered level-3 sex offender? Were the predator and professor friends?

Most reporters requested radio or on-air interviews. Others asked for information to help them expand their stories. The phone calls and emails continued round the clock for several days.

The incident that propelled the frenzy began December 31, 2014, when Josh Gerstein, an astute and courageous reporter at Politico.com, blogged about a Complaint filed by Brad Edwards and Paul Cassell on behalf of their client, Virginia Louise Roberts.

New Year's Eve has usually been a quiet day for the media, which made the decision to publish on that day thought provoking. The politico.com strategy evidently worked. By mid afternoon on January 1, 2015, the story had caused such an international scandal and a media frenzy that Professor Dershowitz's legacy was at stake.

I declined to give interviews for two reasons. I could not reach Professor Dershowitz for comment, he did not return my call, and my book had not been published. It was not the right time to share my opinions and I knew there was a lot more to come. Evidently, what politico.com had published was simply the tip of the iceberg.

Instead, I published one more story. The report was an on-camera interview of the first victim who came forward to expose Epstein and his sex trafficking operation. The victim was Jane Doe #1 a.k.a. Rosemary. I had met Rosemary, in 2010, and interviewed her early on. I asked permission to print her interview. On January 25, 2015, the Daily Beast posted the story.[1]

It must have been an *annus horribilis* for Epstein, Maxwell and Alan Dershowitz. After Gerstein's story broke, Epstein's case commanded front-page coverage during the first quarter of the year. Dershowitz went on a media guerrilla blitz defending his virtue, innocence, and legacy. Maxwell remained silent and Epstein was unable to escape the media's radar. Dershowitz and Maxwell were caught in the crossfire.

The history behind the 2014 Politico.com report explains a gripping case. In 2008, Brad Edwards and Paul Cassell filed a Complaint on behalf of Jane Doe #1 (not the same Rosemary as above who first came forward and I interviewed) and Jane Doe #2. The case: *Jane Doe #1 and Jane Doe #2 vs. United States Government.*[2]

Unlike Virginia Louise Roberts and Rosemary a.k.a. Jane Doe #1, this other victim, Jane Doe #1 currently suing the Government with Jane Doe #2 is in a court-ordered rehabilitation center in Tampa, Florida without the ability to leave the facility. Jane Doe #1 has not been one of the lucky few to make a U turn yet, possibly as a result of her history with sexual abuse.

According to a telephone conference call dated March 1, 2016, between Florida Judge Kenneth Marra, U.S. Attorneys Ann Marie Villafaña and Dexter Lee (representing the Government), Brad Edwards and Paul Cassell representing the victims, the attorneys agreed they would try to settle the case and send the matter to mediation.

Before the case could go to mediation, Villafaña and Edwards required Jane Doe #1 to participate in the mediation. Given her confinement, the attorneys asked Judge Marra to issue an order requesting the Tampa Court to release Jane Doe #1 for one day from the facility and seek out a magistrate judge in the Middle District in Tampa.

Ann Marie Villafaña and Edwards agreed that Judge Marra's order in combination with the Court that confined her, would allow Jane Doe's release and the opportunity to attend the mediation. Judge Marra agreed to "make some inquiries since two of my law school classmates are district judges in Tampa."[3]

The real story however, began in June 2007, when the FBI mailed Jane Doe #1, "a victim-notification letter explaining that Epstein's case was still 'under investigation.' " The FBI, "Notified Jane Doe #1 of her rights under the Crime Victims' Rights Act "CVRA" and in August 2007, Jane Doe #2 received a similar letter."[4]

Three months later, on September 2007, Epstein and the U.S. Attorney's Office (USAO) began to negotiate a deal. Those negotiations led to an agreement under which Epstein would plead guilty to two state felony offenses for solicitation of prostitution and procurement of minors for prostitution if the U.S. Attorney's Office would agree not to prosecute him for federal offenses." On September 24, 2007, a Non Prosecution Agreement was signed under those terms."[5]

On January 10, 2008, "The FBI sent letters to the victims advising them that their, "Case was under investigation," but did not disclose the existence of the NPA. Later in January 2008, Jane Doe #1 met with FBI agents and the attorneys from the U.S. Attorney's Office to discuss her case. Again the government did not reveal the existence of the NPA."[6]

The attorneys for the victims argued that the U.S. Attorney's Office did not consult with them regarding the plea discussions and deliberately kept secret the negotiations and the Non Prosecution Agreement (NPA). In fact, the victims believed that beginning on September 24, 2007 through June 2008, USAO hid the existence of the NPA even though the attorneys representing the victims had spoken to the U.S. Attorney's Office and the FBI on multiple occasions throughout that period.[7]

Sometime in mid-June 2008, Brad Edwards "contacted the Assistant United States Attorney ("AUSA") to discuss the status of Epstein's investigation. The Assistant U.S. Attorney again did not reveal the NPA." Finally, "on June 27, 2008, AUSA notified Edwards that Epstein was scheduled to plead guilty in state court on June 30, 2008."[8]

The reason the attorneys, Edwards and Cassell, believed their clients had a valid case is evident in emails exchanged between Epstein's attorneys and DOJ during the NPA negotiations. Florida Judge Kenneth Marra confirmed this when he awarded the victims the right to see all correspondence and communication between Epstein's attorneys and the U.S. Attorney's Office.

In those exchanges, the US Attorney's Office does not disclose the existence of the NPA nor the relationship between Epstein's state plea and the U.S. Attorney's Office's agreement to waive federal charges.

The following month, on July 3, 2008, Brad Edwards sent another letter to the U.S. Attorney's Office confirming Jane Doe #1's intentions to bring federal charges against Epstein; and on July 7, 2008, Jane Doe #1 filed a Complaint in Court to enforce her rights under the Crime Victims Rights Act."[9]

Like most victims of sex crimes, Jane Doe #1 and her attorney, Edwards, trusted that, "discussions between the Government and Epstein were under way. They also expected to be notified of all developments during the investigation. By failing to notify the victim, Jane Doe #1 claimed that USAO, 'violated her rights under CVRA."[10]

The United States Government responded on July 9, 2008. "The Government argued that a federal indictment had never been issued against Epstein and therefore the CVRA did not apply." The Government insisted, "They had used their best efforts to comply with the CVRA."[11]

During a court hearing on July 11, 2008, Jane Doe #2 was added on as a petitioner to the case. By August of the same year, the Court ordered USAO to turn over the NPA to all identified victims, including Jane Doe #1 and Jane Doe #2, and work out the terms of a protective order governing the NPA's disclosure."[12]

For about a year and a half, they attempted to negotiate settlement agreements and resolve the CVRA dispute. Three years later, on March 18, 2011, "After settlement efforts failed, the victims filed a series of motions along with Epstein's attorney and former USAO officer, Bruce Reinhart's, Motion to intervene." Reinhart's Motion was denied.[13]

The Crime Victims Rights Act CVRA was intended to, "Protect victims' rights and ensure their involvement in the criminal justice process. It was created to give the victims the right to be reasonably protected from the accused, the right to reasonable, accurate and timely notice of any public court proceeding, or any parole proceeding, involving the crime, or of any release or escape of the accused; And the right not to be excluded from any public court proceeding, unless the Court determines that testimony by the victim would be materially altered if the victim heard other testimony at the proceeding."[14]

In relation to Epstein's case, the attorneys for Jane Doe #1 and Jane Doe #2 claimed that CVRA gave the victims the right to "be reasonably heard at any public proceeding in the district court involving release, plea, sentencing, or any parole proceeding; and the right to fully and timely restitution and the right to hold proceedings free from unreasonable delay. Most significantly, it gives victims the right to be treated with fairness and with respect for their dignity and privacy."[15]

Looking back at December 2014, at what was going on politically in relation to the case it makes sense that Politico.com took an interest in the story. Add to that Judge Kenneth Marra's rejection of Jane Doe #3's and Jane Doe #4's petition to join Jane Doe #1 and Jane Doe #2 CVRA case, and you have an even greater reason why this is a precedent setting case.[16]

In effect, rejection of Edwards' and Cassell's Motion to include Jane Doe #3 a.k.a. Virginia Louise Roberts Giuffre and Jane Doe #4, to join the original petitioners, Jane Doe #1 and Jane Doe #2 in the ongoing 2008 Crime Victims Rights Act case, might set a dangerous precedent for future human trafficking cases.

Perhaps, Judge Marra rejected the intervention because Jane Doe #3 (Roberts Giuffre), described how for sexual purposes she was sold "to many other powerful men, including numerous prominent American politicians, powerful business executives, foreign presidents, a well known prime minister and other world leaders." Perhaps the Judge has other reasons. I contacted Judge Marra's Chambers on April 7, 2016. He assistant Irene said the Judge could not comment on the case."[17]

One thing is certain, in the end the truth shall be revealed. The Jeffrey Epstein case, when it is all said and done, might become the model for what The Department of Justice ought not to do when prosecuting a human trafficking case involving so many victims, high profile personalities, a very rich sex offender, and so many extraordinary attorneys working both sides of the aisle.

* * *

Footnotes

1. http://www.thedailybeast.com/articles/2015/01/25/epstein-s-first-accuser-tells-her-story.html

2. http://online.wsj.com/public/resources/documents/2015_0105_epstein2011order.pdf

3. Doe vs. USA -08-80736 CIV-KAM March 1, 2016, p. 3

4. http://online.wsj.com/public/resources/documents/2015_0105_epstein2011order.pdf

5. http://online.wsj.com/public/resources/documents/2015_0105_epstein2011order.pdf

6. http://online.wsj.com/public/resources/documents/2015_0105_epstein2011order.pdf

7. http://online.wsj.com/public/resources/documents/2015_0105_epstein2011order.pdf

8. http://online.wsj.com/public/resources/documents/2015_0105_epstein2011order.pdf

9. http://online.wsj.com/public/resources/documents/2015_0105_epstein2011order.pdf

10. http://online.wsj.com/public/resources/documents/2015_0105_epstein2011order.pdf

11. http://online.wsj.com/public/resources/documents/2015_0105_epstein2011order.pdf

12. http://online.wsj.com/public/resources/documents/2015_0105_epstein2011order.pdf

13. http://online.wsj.com/public/resources/documents/2015_0105
_epstein2011order.pdf

14. http://online.wsj.com/public/resources/documents/2015_0105
_epstein2011order.pdf

15. http://online.wsj.com/public/resources/documents/2015_0105
_epstein2011order.pdf

16. http://www.plainsite.org/dockets/ijlyjpqc/florida-southern-
district-court/doe-v-united-states-of-america/

17. http://www.palmbeachdailynews.com/news/news/local/victims
-ask-to-join-epstein-lawsuit/njfZM/

Chapter Eighteen

What Lies Beneath

On Thursday, April 7, 2016, I rang the Honorable Judge Marra. His assistant, Irene, said he could not comment since several cases remained open. Recently however, the Judge spoke to The Sun Sentinel, a Fort Lauderdale, Florida daily and said, "He hoped the case will finally be decided within the next few months, possibly after a non-jury trial in federal court in West Palm Beach." He was referring to *Jane Doe #1 and Jane Doe #2 vs. United States Government.*[1]

There are two ways the judge can rule in the case of *Jane Doe #1 and Jane Doe #2 vs. United States Government.* Either Judge Marra will rule in favor of the Department of Justice and the U.S. Attorney's Office and agree with their assertion: That the victims were consulted to the extent required by law and therefore not entitled to a greater level of consultation, or, he could rule in favor of the victims and agree the federal prosecutors did not adequately consult with them.

Whatever decision the Judge makes, it is unlikely the victims will receive further monetary compensation from the government and that Epstein's sentence will be changed, since he already served time, however insufficient that time might seem. It is also unlikely that Epstein will be indicted on other criminal charges related to the same case.

Jack Goldberger, Virginia's primary attorney in 2005, and a member of Epstein's defense team recently spoke to the Sun Sentinel. We spoke several times between 2009 and 2010 but have not since. He told them "If Judge Marra rules the U.S. government violated the Crime Victims' Rights Act, his decision will have no effect on prosecuting Jeffrey Epstein. Due process and double jeopardy would require the agreement, that was reached by the state and federal government, be honored."[2]

Goldberger explained that, "Victims have no right to dictate how the case is resolved." In other words, the same victims cannot prosecute Epstein in the future for the same crimes. "No, it simply can't happen," Goldberger, explained.[3]

Since 2008, when the case was filed, *Jane Doe #1 and Jane Doe #2 vs. U.S. Government* turned into a legal tsunami. In December 2014, a stipulation filed by Edwards and Casell, claimed that Professor Dershowitz sexually abused Jane Doe #3, i.e. Virginia Louise Roberts Giuffre, on six occasions that Epstein arranged for her including in Epstein's USVI island home. Professor Dershowitz vehemently denied the claim and hired former FBI Director, Louis Freeh, to conduct an investigation.

On Friday, April 8, 2016, the day after I rang Judge Marra's Chambers, Edwards, Cassell and Dershowitz filed another stipulation late that afternoon. It made the eight o'clock online news hour. Josh Gerstein, a courageous staff reporter at politico.com drove the headlines once again.[4]

The politico.com report said that Edwards and Cassell withdrew their allegation, which they called a "tactical mistake" according to the statement issued Friday. The reason was because, "They now have access to evidence that refutes Roberts' claims, which they suggested could involve a case of mistaken identity. However, Edwards and Cassell maintain they performed the required due diligence on her allegations before they were filed in court."[5]

Politico claimed that, "The scope of the concession appeared limited by a court filing…in which the attorneys Edwards and Cassell maintained their client Roberts Giuffre stands by her claim." What that basically means is that although Virginia agreed to allow the attorneys to withdraw their claims, Virginia did not agree to retract the sexual abuse accusations against Dershowitz.[6]

The following Saturday, April 9, 2016, I wrote Edwards and Cassell an e-mail asking for comments. Edwards responded, "We did not withdraw a complaint. We settled the defamation action and as part of the settlement certain pleadings that were filed by Jack (Scarola) as well as Alan's (Dershowitz) attorney were withdrawn." I also sent an email to Professor Dershowitz for comment. He did not respond.

I asked Edwards why he had not allowed me to speak with Virginia during the course of that investigation. His response was, "Everything is fine and it's going to turn out well. There is no need to fear or worry." 'Fear or worry' were not exactly what was on my mind. His response was sent via a text message around noontime on Saturday April 9, 2016.

Something didn't sound right. I went back to Edwards and asked about their compensation? Cassell and Edwards did not respond. By the way, the legal settlement was settled "with prejudice," which means the case is over and done with. As part of the agreement, Dershowitz consented to withdraw his claims blaming, "Edwards and former federal judge Cassell, of acting unethically back in December 2014," Edwards said.

If you recall, in the 2014 pleadings, as a result of the governments' failure to respect the CVRA rights of Jane Doe #1 and Jane Doe #2 during the 2007 investigation, Edwards and Cassell sued the government. As Epstein's friend and *consigliore,* Professor Dershowitz led the legal team. Together with Ken Starr and Jay Lefkowitz, who came into the negotiations later, managed to secure a Non Prosecution Agreement (NPA) in Washington D.C. essentially overriding the Florida prosecutor's, USAO's, original Order.

It was that agreement, the NPA that became the basis for Edwards and Cassell's case: *Jane Doe #1 and Jane Doe #2 vs United States Government.* Their intention was to have the Non Prosecution Agreement overturned. That case is pending. The reason that all hell broke loose on January 1, 2015 however, was over a statement made in the 2014 filing that identified Dershowitz as one of Epstein's associates who sexually molested Roberts Giuffre six times in different places.

As a result of the settlement agreement a fresh new media cycle began. On Tuesday, April 11, 2016, Vivia Chen, an incredibly witty reporter for The American Lawyer wrote, "It's not over!"

Part two of her report was even more fascinating because it gave context to this all too bizarre agreement. It was so alarming that Chen's words best describes it.

"If you thought the settlement that Alan Dershowitz reached on Friday with the lawyers representing Virginia Roberts Giuffre puts the controversy to bed, you're naive. Possibly delusional... Giuffre alleged that she was coerced into having sex with Dershowitz and others when she was a minor.

The latest bombshell: Jack Scarola, counsel for Giuffre's lawyers Paul Cassell and Bradley Edwards, emailed me this: "If Mr. Dershowitz were to request a waiver of the confidentiality provisions, we would agree to the request."

Talk about throwing down the gauntlet! That would mean spilling the terms of the settlement—about who had to shell out what to make this messy lawsuit go away. I assumed Cassell and Edwards paid Dershowitz and wanted confidentiality, since they admitted in the settlement to making "mistakes" in alleging that Dershowitz had sex with Giuffre.

But David Boies, who represents Giuffre in a related matter, tells me I'm off target. In a phone conversation on Sunday, Boies dangled this tidbit of information before me: "I don't know the terms of the settlement, but I know that it was proposed that (Edwards and Cassell) be paid hundreds of thousands of dollars (by Alan Dershowitz) to drop the case."

My eyes widened. Go on, Mr. Boies, I said. He continued: "Ask Alan Dershowitz who paid whom. I know Dershowitz asked for confidentiality, and Edwards and Cassell will waive it . . . And if Dershowitz won't waive confidentiality, that should tell you if there's something incriminating."

So I rushed to ask Cassell and Edwards about waiving confidentiality, and got the response from Scarola that they'd essentially do it in a New York minute. Scarola also emailed me a post settlement statement that says this:

What is true is that Mr. Edwards and Professor Cassell entered into a monetary settlement that resolved the defamation claims they filed against Mr. Dershowitz, but they are precluded from revealing the economic terms of the settlement, as the agreement requires the monetary specifics to remain confidential.

Though Dershowitz, citing the confidentiality agreement, wouldn't comment about compensation when I asked him about the settlement, Edwards and Cassell's statement makes it clear that money exchanged hands. But how much? And what about the implication that Dershowitz was the one who paid big bucks for the settlement that supposedly establishes his innocence?

I went back to Dershowitz to get some clarity. Clearly miffed, he took umbrage at Boies' comment: "David Boies doesn't know terms of the agreement because it's subject by confidentiality agreement. My lawyer has advised me that my discussion of the terms would breach the agreement, but I assure you there's nothing incriminating."

So how about waiving the confidentiality agreement to make everything transparent? Dershowitz's answer: No. "I'm sticking with the agreement . . . My lawyers tell me I can't change the settlement, which is multi-faceted and complex."

Later, he adds, however: 'I'd be prepared to enter negotiations to unseal confidential information and other matters if (Edwards, Cassell and Boies) are prepared to enter negotiations to unseal Virgina Giuffre's deposition and my affidavit regarding Boies, which Boies Schiller has demanded be sealed.' The point is, he says, is that 'it has to be mutual.'[7]

A source close to the case that does not wish to be identified said, "So much of this revolves around the integrity of Virginia Louise Roberts. What will be missing though is who she is and what she is all about. To that, we will never know who has given her what advice and if she has always taken it. I hope at some point she can talk about things from her personal experience."

The source added, "For a young woman she has had a very complicated life and she might be able to help others but way down the road. It would probably be in her best interest to come forward unconstrained and unveil the truth about her history with Epstein, Dershowitz, Clinton *et al.*, otherwise, no one will really ever know whether she is being manipulated or if she is the manipulator."

"It seems improbable", the source said, "That a young teenager can "mistake" identifying someone who sexually molested her more than once," in Virginia's case, allegedly it was six times. "So who is Virginia Roberts? It's an ugly story that the players seem to be trying very hard to wrap up," the source whispered

* * *

Footnotes

1. http://www.sun-sentinel.com/news/fl-jeffrey-epstein-victims-civil-20151230-story.html

2. http://www.sun-sentinel.com/news/fl-jeffrey-epstein-victims-civil-20151230-story.html

3. http://www.sun-sentinel.com/news/fl-jeffrey-epstein-victims-civil-20151230-story.html

4. http://www.politico.com/blogs/under-the-radar/2016/04/lawyers-underage-sex-claims-against-dershowitz-a-mistake-221751

5. http://www.politico.com/blogs/under-the-radar/2016/04/lawyers-underage-sex-claims-against-dershowitz-a-mistake-221751

6. http://www.politico.com/blogs/under-the-radar/2016/04/lawyers-underage-sex-claims-against-dershowitz-a-mistake-221751#ixzz45TIa7Itb

7. http://www.americanlawyer.com/the-careerist/id=1202754666961/Did-Dershowitz-Pay-Big-Bucks-to-Settle-Sex-Case-?mcode=1202616610377&curindex=4

Vivia Chen's information came from the online reports:

http://www.americanlawyer.com/the-careerist/id=1202754581393/Dershowitz-Settles-Sex-Case-But-Is-He-Vindicated?mcode=1202616610377&curindex=5

http://www.americanlawyer.com/the-careerist/id=1202755043865/Whats-Everyone-Hiding-in-the-Dershowitz-Case?mcode=1202616610377&curindex=3

Chapter Nineteen

Loose Ends

Then God said, "Let there be light," and there was light.
Genesis 1:3

A bizarre development, stranger perhaps than the settlement agreement, took place during a routine status check. The government made known that two victims who filed the lawsuit, Jane Doe #1 and Jane Doe #2, were not victims after all because they procured other girls for Epstein and received monetary compensation from him.[1]

Edwards was outraged, "Today, is the first we've heard that the victims were complicit and this disqualifies them. This is an additional issue, which will lead to other issues. It is an outrage not to mention to have waited eight years to create another contemptible alibi," Edwards said.[2]

Representing the government was Assistant U.S. Attorney Dexter Lee who told the court, "If someone is complicit in the offenses, they can't be considered victims under the federal Crime Victims' Rights Act... A Crime Victims' Rights Act action is part of a criminal proceeding normally, but there's nothing normal about this case," Lee said. In effect, Lee's statement disqualified the victims from moving forward with their lawsuit.[3]

Edwards' expects to have other victims, he had represented earlier, come and testify. If the agreement is overturned Epstein might face jail time again, although for now that seems highly unlikely. Perhaps if it gets to that point, he will decide to talk his way out of the conviction and agree to bring down the 'bigger fish.'

As Ken Starr explained in the *Justice, Integrity Project Report*, "The Epstein saga raises serious questions about favoritism if not corruption in the courts even if plaintiffs' allegations are overblown. The immunity agreement for alleged co conspirators is so irregular that it reeks of a cover-up."[4]

Given the pending cases and various loose ends could be another the reason some politicians are nervous. In retrospect, it would have been wiser for the defense attorneys and the United States Attorneys Office to allow justice to run its course.

One thing is certain, The Trafficking Victims Protection Act (TVPA: H.R. 972 and later H.R. 7311) first passed into law in 2000 by President Bill Clinton, reauthorized under President George W. Bush in 2003, and again, reauthorized by President Barack Obama, in 2008, is a federal law created to prosecute traffickers and protect victims. It was enacted in Florida, in 2000, five years prior to Epstein's arrest.

The minimum mandatory under TVPA is twenty years for a convicted sex trafficker. The law also gives law enforcement the ability to prosecute traffickers domestically and worldwide. Had justice prevailed, perhaps the victims would have felt some sort of vindication; and the defense attorneys, prosecutors, political leaders and others who have been dragged through the mud for the past eleven years would have saved themselves a great deal of public humiliation. More importantly, the young girls who have been recently photographed in Epstein's company might have saved themselves from potential danger.

"The value of giving lies not simply in the amount given but in the sacrifice it requires and the love that prompts it. To a large extent, living well entails giving well—a giving of some portion of your time, or talent, or money, or all three." (5)

The Epstein story is not about a billionaire's generous contributions to society, quite the contrary. It is a story of how one man attempted to destroy the very essence of humanity by violating human rights. Perhaps part two will have a different ending.

* * *

Footnotes

1. http://www.palmbeachdailynews.com/news/news/local/epstein-victims-complicit-so-not-truly-victims-gov/npTXT/

2. http://www.palmbeachdailynews.com/news/news/local/epstein-victims-complicit-so-not-truly-victims-gov/npTXT/

3. http://www.palmbeachdailynews.com/news/news/local/epstein-victims-complicit-so-not-truly-victims-gov/npTXT/

4. http://www.justice-integrity.org/about-jip2

5. The Moral Compass, William J. Bennett. Simon & Schuster. New York, 1995. Page 716